Duncan Hallas:
Indomitable Revolutionary

Duncan Hallas
Indomitable Revolutionary

Alex Callinicos, Sheila McGregor,
Jack Robertson, John Rudge
and Dave Sherry
with an introduction by Laura Miles

Duncan Hallas: Indomitable Revolutionary
Alex Callinicos, Sheila McGregor,
Jack Robertson, John Rudge
and Dave Sherry
with an introduction by Laura Miles

First edition published by Bookmarks in 2023
© Bookmarks Publications Ltd
c/o 1 Bloomsbury Street, London WC1B 3QE
www.bookmarksbookshop.co.uk

ISBN 978-1-914143-72-4 paperback
ISBN 978-1-914143-73-1 Kindle
ISBN 978-1-914143-74-8 epub
ISBN 978-1-914143-75-5 pdf

Typeset by Colm Bryce for Bookmarks Publications
Cover design by Simon Assaf
Printed by Halstan & Co, Amersham, England

About the authors

Alex Callinicos is Emeritus Professor of European Studies at King's College London. He writes a column for *Socialist Worker*. His books include *The Revolutionary Ideas of Karl Marx*, *Imperialism and Global Political Economy*, *Deciphering Capital*, and *The New Age of Catastrophe*.

Sheila McGregor was one of the first local organisers in the International Socialists/SWP, the first women's organiser, industrial organiser during the miners' strike 1984-5 and is a regular contributor to the *International Socialism* journal.

Laura Miles was the first trans person to be elected to the National Executive Committee of the University and College Union (UCU) and is the author of *Transgender Resistance, Socialism and the Fight for Trans Liberation*. She is a member of the Socialist Workers Party in Wakefield.

Jack Robertson is a former engineering worker and journalist. He wrote a weekly column for *Socialist Worker* under the penname "Birdy" and a monthly column for *Socialist Review* as "The Walrus". More recently he has translated works by Pushkin and Larissa Reisner.

John Rudge is a retired project manager. He is active in Unite and now spends much of his spare time researching obscure corners of IS Tradition history.

Dave Sherry is a retired housing worker and is active in the Unite trade union in Glasgow. He is the author of *John Maclean: Red Clydesider; Occupy! A Short History of Workers' Occupations; Empire and Revolution: A Socialist History of the First World War;* and co-author/co-editor of *Breaking up the British State: Scotland, Independence and Socialism.* He is a long-standing member of the Socialist Workers Party.

Contents

Acknowledgements

During his long period of activity in the revolutionary socialist movement, Duncan touched the lives and influenced literally thousands of people. Equally, many of these people touched and influenced Duncan. Each and every one of them deserves to be acknowledged as playing a part in Duncan's life and Duncan's achievement. It is invidious therefore to name names so the various authors involved in this book are happy to limit their acknowledgement to the following people who helped directly or indirectly in turning the idea of the book into a reality. Apologies to those who have been missed.

Our thanks go out to *Simon Assaf; Ian Birchall; Lindsey Boyle; Geoff Brown; Colm Bryce; Danny Budzak; Phil Evans* (deceased); *Roger Green; Dave Harvey; Richard Kuper; Stewart Maclennan; John Molyneux* (deceased); *Stan Newens* (deceased); *Jim Nichol; John Palmer; John Plant; Bernard Regan; Camilla Royle; Sandra Shepherd; Keith Sinclair; Carol Williams; Carol Withers.* Also, the staff at *Centre for Research Collections, Edinburgh University Library, Pluto Press,* London and the *Working Class Museum Library*, Manchester.

It goes without saying that the various authors benefited greatly from each other's feedback and inspiration.

Introduction
Laura Miles

This book, published a little over twenty years since his death, is a tribute to Duncan Hallas's remarkable life. Many of those new to revolutionary socialist politics might not be aware of him or might only be vaguely aware through his pamphlets or books. Yet for several decades he played a central role in the leadership of the Socialist Workers Party (SWP) and its predecessors the International Socialists (IS) and the Socialist Review Group (SRG), and in the International Socialist Tendency, of which the SWP is part. Duncan was in fact one of the most significant revolutionary Marxists of the second half of the twentieth century and his life and political contributions deserve to be drawn to the attention of new generations of revolutionaries.

Consequently, in *Indomitable Revolutionary* the reader will find essays by John Rudge, Jack Robertson, Dave Sherry, Alex Callinicos and Sheila McGregor that explore wide areas of Duncan's work and influence. There are also a number of key articles from his prodigious written output. Together these offer a sense of the breadth and depth of Duncan's knowledge, not only of trade union and socialist history, but of an enormous range of topics, from science and technology, social science, economics, archaeology and anthropology, and history. With reminiscences of Duncan by some of those who knew him best and worked with him, the whole constitutes an invaluable record of the contribution made over sixty years of activity by a key Marxist activist, writer, educator and thinker.

Unlike most of the contributors in this volume I can't claim to have known Duncan very well. My personal contact was limited to the couple of times he stayed at our house in the 1980s when he came to speak at public meetings of Leeds Socialist Workers Party. The one vivid memory I do have is an image of Duncan slouched in an armchair in our living room after we came back from a meeting, followed by a few pints, with one of our cats perched on his stomach purring loudly. While we got on with preparing a snack, Duncan contentedly stroked the cat muttering quietly to her.

To be in an audience for a Duncan Hallas meeting was always a treat, whether at a local SWP branch meeting or at the bigger events like the Marxism festivals each summer or the Easter events at the Skegness Miners Holiday Camp organised by the SWP. As a young(ish) new member of the International Socialists in the 1970s, having these opportunities to listen to him, or to Tony Cliff and Paul Foot, was undoubtedly a central element of my political development and that of thousands of others over the years.

True, the styles of those three were radically different—Paul Foot the polished orator, Tony Cliff's talks full of quirky similes and asides ("my good god", "I tell you a secret", "you wouldn't believe it") delivered in his heavy accent—but Duncan was incredibly impressive in the way he would build an argument, demolish counter arguments, deploy telling examples and draw it all together into an unassailable logical conclusion. He could win an audience's full attention in the first sentence and hold them hanging on every word to the very end.

His talks, always articulate, deeply knowledgeable and delivered from the skimpiest of notes, generally involved a wildly oscillating volume delivered in his strong Mancunian accent, and they invariably left a deep impression. It was not for nothing that the SWP would often put Duncan forward as a spokesperson to debate with other tendencies on the left. It's well worth the reader looking out the recordings of his debates, for example, with left Labour MPs such as Tony Benn or Eric Heffer at some of the annual Marxism festivals.

Duncan was not just a memorable speaker. He was a lead writer for the weekly *Socialist Worker* over many years and editor of the IS/SWP theoretical journal *International Socialism*. He was a member of the Central Committee and a full-time worker for the SWP and its forerunner the International Socialists for decades from the late 1960s until his retirement through ill health in 1995.

Those who did know Duncan well, as several mention here in their contributions, emphasise that he was a modest man who tended to downplay his own significance and abilities and rarely spoke about his early years. He left virtually nothing by way of autobiographical material. Much of what we do know of his early life and influences has been pulled together in this volume comprehensively by John Rudge and Jack Robertson.

Duncan had come to revolutionary politics in perhaps its darkest period just after Trotsky's assassination by a Stalinist agent in 1940. He joined the tiny Trotskyist group the Workers International League, helping to build a thriving branch in Manchester, selling its paper and being fully involved in the grinding but necessary day to day activity.

Conscripted into the army a little later Duncan landed up in northern France in 1944, suffered a bullet wound in the fighting there, and at the end of the war took part in a mutiny in Egypt demanding that the soldiers be demobbed and sent home.

Having returned to civilian life for several years in the late 1940s and early 1950s, he was part of the British Trotskyist movement, first as a member of the main Trotskyist organisation at that time, the Revolutionary Communist Party, and then in the Socialist Review Group (SRG).

The SRG were supporters of Tony Cliff's theoretical position that Russia was bureaucratic state capitalist in nature, founded after the "state caps" were expelled from the "orthodox" Fourth International organisation. The majority of Trotskyists continued to hold the view that Russia was a degenerated workers' state. The essays in this book by John Rudge, Jack Robertson and Dave Sherry recount the history of this period and explain why these debates and clarifications were so important in terms of holding true to the essence of Marx's historical materialism and the classical Marxist understanding of the state. In short, the issue is not the property form, whether industry is nationalised or not, but whether a ruling class controls the means of production in order to continue to derive profit from workers' labour power. Stalin's regime in Russia had become such a ruling class by the 1930s.

Cliff's theoretical insistence from the late 1940s about the nature of Russia was crucial. Duncan supported Cliff's theory, helping to promote and indeed, develop it. This, combined with Mike Kidron's development of the theory of the Permanent Arms Economy to explain capitalism's ability to recover from wartime devastation and sustain a long period of economic growth, was crucial in orienting the organisation as a revolutionary Marxist current struggling to root itself in the international working-class movement under quite difficult circumstances. Nevertheless, one of the hallmarks of the IS Tendency has always been an orientation on real movements and not the sectarianism of much of the far left, as Alex Callinicos points out in his chapter.

The tiny group of thirty or so around Tony Cliff in the early 1950s developed into an international revolutionary Marxist current that today has thousands of members of the Socialist Workers Party in Britain plus a number of linked revolutionary parties and groups around the world.

This has been a major achievement. The SRG had to address the overwhelming dominance of the main reformist organisation, the Labour Party, which had around a million members. Revolutionaries working in the labour movement also had to cope with the hostility of the Communist Party, which at that time was still a sizeable organisation with considerable influence in many workplaces and on left trade union leaders, as Dave Sherry describes in his essay. CP members were often extremely hostile to the Trotskyists.

In his 1985 book *The Comintern*[1] Duncan brilliantly describes the degeneration of the communist parties from revolutionary organisations formed in the period after the 1914-18 war and the 1917 Russian Revolution, coming together in the Comintern (also known at various times as the Third International or the Communist International) to becoming tools of Stalin's foreign policy by the 1930s.

Duncan didn't stay active in the SRG. John Rudge describes how in 1953 he moved to Scotland to work for the National Council of Labour Colleges. He was not *actively* involved in membership of revolutionary organisations until he re-emerged in 1968 and joined the International Socialists, having moved to London as a schoolteacher. During that fifteen year hiatus he had completed a science degree as a mature student, graduating in 1962.

The crises and social upheavals of the 1960s—against the Vietnam war, against racism, for women's liberation, for gay liberation—sparked new opportunities for the growth of revolutionary socialist organisations. By the late 1960s the IS, with Duncan as part of the leadership, was growing and developing from a mainly student-based propaganda group to an interventionist organisation with an increasing proportion of workers in its membership. Duncan proved to be a steady hand on the tiller. His written output and tireless travelling to local branches and districts on speaking tours were crucial to developing and solidifying the organisation's cadre and recruiting new forces. His wise counsel, based on long experience and intimate knowledge of the labour movement, invariably assisted in tempering many of the "get rich quick" schemes or shortcuts proposed by other sections of the leadership. Duncan's politics were rooted in honest accounting and looking reality in the face.

The Comintern is one of only two books he published, the first, *Trotsky's Marxism*,[2] in 1979 was an important tool in this process of recruitment and consolidation. By examining Trotsky's vital legacy, warts and all, it sought to rescue Trotsky from both Stalinist calumny and the personality cults that blighted "orthodox" Trotskyism. *Trotsky's Marxism* is a succinct tour de force, highlighting his key role in the Russian revolution itself, literally airbrushed from existence by the Stalinists. Duncan spells out how important Trotsky's analysis of fascism is, and how this and his advocacy of the united front tactic remain so relevant for today's anti-fascists and socialist revolutionaries.

Indomitable Revolutionary is published as the objective political situation has become far more favourable for revolutionaries. Decades-high inflation rates, eye-watering increases in the costs of energy, rising food prices and falling wages are sharply posing the question of who will pay? And increasingly this is being answered by workers—not us!

Duncan would have been bubbling with enthusiasm for the strikes that kicked off in early summer 2022 by postal workers, rail and bus workers, BT engineers, dockers and even barristers. He would be revelling in the resurgence of class struggle, but he would also have pointed to the lessons of history to guide how revolutionaries need to engage with this.

Alex Callinicos points out in his contribution that Duncan always rejected any notion of Marxism as a deterministic theory of history. We are, within the constraints of the historical situation, the agents of our own destiny. Over and over in his articles and talks Duncan stressed that effective intervention in the class struggle by revolutionaries had to be based on sound theoretical understanding, and sound theory had to be informed by the experience of the struggle itself.

This raises a second question: can the working class develop sufficient rank and file organisation and confidence to block the inevitable attempts by trade union officials to keep control of the strikes and settle for less than could be achieved? Fine fighting words by trade union leaders are welcome, but as Duncan would often say, they have to be judged by what they do, not what they say. And what they do, in the end, is compromise with capitalism.

The matter of how revolutionaries work both *with* and *against* the reformist trade union officials is likely to be more and more sharply posed. Trade union officials see the limits of their role being to negotiate with the bosses, not to overthrow them, and so they constitute an inherently conservative layer in capitalist society. Many of Duncan's talks and articles focused on this reality and his clarity on these issues remains sharp and relevant. His articles and talks on the united front deserve revisiting today.

He summed up the importance of the united front tactic in one of his shortest and most condensed pieces, "On the United Front tactic: some preliminary notes", in 1976:

> But the yearning for unity among the radicalised minority of workers is real enough, will inevitably grow and is, at bottom, a healthy yearning. The left *must* achieve a degree of unity *in action* if disastrous defeats for the working class are to be avoided. In this situation the united front tactic is of central importance.[3]

The capitalist system is in severe systemic crisis. We're living in a time of increasing political polarisation, with the right ramping up racism, attacking civil liberties and workers' rights, attacking women's rights, LGBT+ rights and waging war on trans people. Those promoting Palestinian rights are vilified as antisemites. Yet interest in Marxism, socialist revolution and system change has been growing, especially among young people. Many of them have been radicalised by the dynamic social movements we've seen in recent years such as #MeToo, Black Lives Matter, Extinction Rebellion and the school climate strikes.

This is one reason why the inclusion of Sheila McGregor's chapter on "Darwin, Women and Human Nature" in this volume is so welcome. Some of Duncan's most perceptive and memorable talks and articles were on the nature of pre-class societies, the roots of oppression and women's status in different class societies and modes of production. He would, I'm sure, be proud of the way the Party has continued in recent years to develop its understanding of oppression and its commitment to fighting racism, sexism, homophobia and transphobia. Sheila's chapter draws out the relevance of these discussions for today.

Duncan died shortly before the US/UK invasion of Iraq, before the historic anti-war march in 2003 organised by Stop the War that the SWP helped to initiate. He would have railed against the bloodletting that followed, the hundreds of thousands of deaths and the wanton destruction driven by imperialist and sub-imperialist interests. No doubt he would have welcomed the defeat of the US and UK in Afghanistan and Iraq almost two decades later and their ignominious withdrawal from those ravaged countries, and he would have been clear about the fundamentally inter-imperialist nature of the current war in Ukraine.

Duncan was part of the leadership of the SWP when the Anti-Nazi League and Rock Against Racism were initiated by the Party and others, defeating and marginalising the National Front. He would have been proud to see the leading role that the Party has played in successfully fighting to marginalise the fascists of the British National Party and the EDL, and our commitment to taking on racism, antisemitism and Islamophobia through Stand Up To Racism and Unite Against Fascism. The SWP can be proud of its role in marginalising the far right. The proof of the pudding is in the eating—one only needs to compare the relatively marginal position of the fascists in Britain with the situation in France or Italy, where the left has failed to build the necessary united fronts of resistance and fascist organisations have become part of the political mainstream.

Millions of people can see that the crises facing humanity have reached existential proportions—global warming out of control, unprecedented wildfires and droughts, recurring pandemics, catastrophic floods, rising sea levels, a plethora of imperialist and sub-imperialist wars over control of resources and markets. We're in an intensely political period. In his 1902 pamphlet *What Is To Be Done?*[4] Lenin proposed the role for a revolutionary party, insisting that it must be "the tribune of the oppressed" and not merely consist of "trade union secretaries". In other words, it must be engaged in addressing the totality of the oppressive social relations in capitalism in order to win the confidence and support of all the oppressed and exploited. In doing so, revolutionaries must always keep their eyes on the prize—the revolutionary overthrow of capitalism and the building of socialist societies.

Duncan Hallas's life was dedicated to that end and this book has a valuable role to play as part of the memory of the working class and its best fighters in helping to educate, guide and inform a new generation of revolutionary Marxists who share the goal of liberation from capitalism.

Notes

1   Duncan Hallas, *The Comintern* (London: Bookmarks, 1985).

2   Duncan Hallas, *Trotsky's Marxism* (London: Pluto Press, 1979).

3   Duncan Hallas, "On the United Front Tactic: Some preliminary notes", *International Socialism*, 1: 85 (January 1976) www.marxists.org/archive/hallas/works/1976/01/unitedfront.htm

4   VI Lenin, *What Is To Be Done? Burning Questions of Our Movement* (1902), www.marxists.org/archive/lenin/works/1901/witbd/

Duncan speaking at a rally in Hyde Park in 1973.

Duncan Hallas:
A Life on the Front Line[1]
John Rudge

Duncan Frederick Hallas was born on 23 December 1925 at 59 Avon Street, Ardwick, Manchester. He was the eldest child of John and Edith (*née* Cretney) Hallas. His only sibling, a younger sister Margaret, was born in January 1932. His father, John, was a paver with Manchester Corporation Highways Department and his mother, Edith, "had been a winder in a weaving shed... then she got a poxy little job in a factory, working in the kitchen. Then she discovered they were taking people on in aviation in Stockport, so she became a riveter".[2]

Duncan's father had followed his grandfather, Agrippa, who had also been employed in the Manchester Corporation's Highways Department.

Ardwick, just south of Manchester city centre, was part of Chorlton-upon-Medlock, named after a stream, which was described in an 1894 report by the sanitation department as "nothing more than an open ditch". At the end of the Second World War, the area was condemned as a slum and large parts of it were cleared, including Avon Street. Today, the nearest marker is the Ardwick Mosque, close to the junction of Thompson Street, Wilson Street and Lauderdale Crescent. All in all it was a solid working class family background in a solidly working class area.

Sometime in Duncan's early years the family moved away from the "down at heel" area of Ardwick to Northernden, near Wythenshawe—18 Rackhouse Road was the Hallas family home for well over 30 years. It would have been quite a step up when his parents moved there. Ardwick and Wythenshawe were two entirely different environments—Wythenshawe, championed by followers of the "garden city" movement, was quite a respectable suburban sprawl designed to re-house people away from some of the worst housing in Manchester.

Duncan's education was not atypical for a working-class child of the time. He attended elementary schools in Ardwick and Wythenshawe followed by Chorlton High School. Whatever his schooling lacked in years, it can be safely assumed that it benefited from the lifelong thirst for knowledge that all who knew him recall. As Nigel Harris recounted, "his self-education had already begun and was to continue for the rest of his life".[3] There must also have been some political discussion in the family. During a speaking tour in Australia for the SWP Duncan is quoted in a newspaper report as saying, "my father was a die-hard Labourite bricklayer".[4]

Duncan's mother Edith died in June 1939 from a pulmonary embolism during an operation for bowel cancer at Manchester Royal Infirmary. She was only 44 years old. Duncan, of course, was only 13 and was traumatised by the event—Nigel Harris describes it thus:

> ...years later, in his cups, he would weep for the mother who faced such hardships to bring up Duncan and his sister, Margaret. This was perhaps the first great emotional crisis in his life. In later years, he rarely mentioned his family, apart from his great attachment to his mother.[5]

The worlds of work and politics open

In January 1940, at the age of 14, Duncan started an engineering apprenticeship in the turbine machine shop at Metro-Vickers on Trafford Park. The pay was poor—the princely sum of 14 shillings and sixpence a week. Known to all in Manchester as "The Big House", the plant was at the heart of the government's re-armament programme from 1936, and by 1938 the workforce was 16,000. At its peak there were over 30,000 employees. It was here that Duncan got his first taste of the battle against the bosses.

The apprentices' strikes of 1941 were among a series of actions by apprentices over a 30-year period. The rash of disputes of 1941 concerned a wage increase of three pence an hour. Negotiations had dragged on for six months when, in March, the Clyde apprentices took action and it spread. Duncan later said that:

> What precipitated the dispute in Manchester was the fact that the employers decided to abolish the Shrove Tuesday half day holiday, which had existed since before the industrial revolution. That was the last straw. So, we raw youth were instructed in the art of picketing and had the first scab bicycled into a ditch. Of course, we loved it. The dispute lasted about a week. The management caved in, not because we could beat them—our parents would have forced us back—but because of the owners' general assessment of the situation in the factories. They didn't want the dispute to spread because a lot of disputes were simmering.[6]

The reality may have been a bit more complex—six of the leaders of the apprentices in Manchester received summonses to appear on a charge of "unlawfully taking part in a strike... not reported to the Minister of Labour under Regulation 58A of the Defence (General) Regulation 1939" and Order 1305—legislation brought in that enabled right-wing Labourite Minister of Labour Ernest Bevin to prevent industrial stoppages. The socialist barrister John Platt Mills, KC, was called in to defend the six.

Members of the Young Communist League (YCL) were at the forefront of the apprentices' disputes both on the Clyde and in Manchester. The young Duncan was presumably impressed as this was still the period before the ending of the Hitler-Stalin pact when the Communist Party was in support of industrial action to defend workers. He joined a YCL that said:

> ...young workers everywhere should band together, organise in factory committees, trade unions and the YCL, and...get together for higher wages—shorter hours—no night work for girls or young lads—for proper trade training... *Youth can make a fine contribution, by fighting for our immediate demands and winning more and more youth to the idea of ending the war.*[7]

Of course, on 22 June 1941, Hitler invaded the Soviet Union and the policy of the Communist Party did an about-face. As Duncan put it in 1985: "The war which on 21 June 1941 was an imperialist war in Britain and France became a war for democracy on the 22nd".[8]

Now the YCL was telling its members:

> ...the most important way in which a young worker (or an older one for that matter) can contribute to the defeat of fascism is by increasing production and in particular by getting together with his mates and forming a Shock Brigade. A Shock Brigade is a group of workers (whether youth or adult) who are eager to increase output by the example they set, by their own efforts. They agree in the main to two principles: 1. To be always on time and not to be absent from work: 2. To work conscientiously

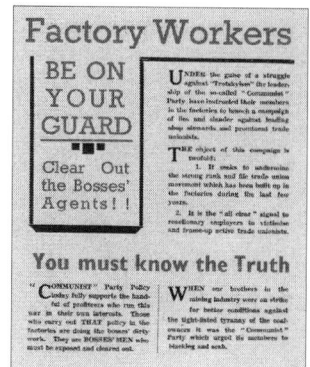

CP Attacks the Workers
International League (1942).
    WIL Fights Back.

at their job and by the example of their individual and collective effort aim to increase output.[9]

Duncan left the YCL in 1942 having never joined the Communist Party, notwithstanding that the CP Factory Branch at Metro-Vickers had around 100 members at the time. As Duncan said much later: "I wasn't happy when Japan entered the war, as it was so manifestly an imperialist war. The CP by this time had a pro-war line".[10]

In the spring of 1943 Duncan bought his first Trotskyist paper, *Socialist Appeal*, the agitational publication of the Workers International League (WIL). At that time there was no functioning branch of the WIL in Manchester but Jimmy Deane, a prominent and extremely able member, came over from Liverpool and recruited him.

Towards the end of 1943 Rachel Ryan, already an experienced Trotskyist, arrived in Manchester to work at Metro-Vickers. She quickly took on the task of organising the WIL's meagre forces. Her regular letters reporting progress to Deane during this period give an inkling of the graft and routine work required. Duncan took on the task of Literature Secretary and Rachel and Duncan sold papers together at Salford Docks.

Duncan was conscripted to the army in the autumn of 1943, by which time the small WIL group in Manchester had about five members. When Duncan was interviewed about his wartime experiences and was asked about the attitude the WIL took to the war, he summarised the position as follows:

> The Trotskyists in the Workers International League said it's an imperialist war, but we're not pacifists, we're against Hitler. Therefore, we cannot refuse military service—you go with your class. We argued for no confidence in the ruling class's so called anti-fascism. The other 40 or so Trotskyists (the official Trotskyists) said this was basically a defensive position of supporting imperialism.
>
> The WIL said protect the working class—we need proper air raid precautions and deep shelters—in general, carry on the class struggle. They denounced profits and took up working class demands. We did not preach abstractly against the war. We preached against imperialism, saying it is an imperialist war. We said we want to get rid of Hitler, but those rich bastards do not—they supported Franco. I still think this was the correct position. You wanted to influence people to do certain things.[11]

You're in the army now!

Duncan was conscripted to the infantry, the First South Lancashire Regiment, and he recalls:

> After we'd finished the 14-week training period they sent us to a holding battalion. We stayed there until we were sent as replacements to Normandy, in July 1944. We were wet behind the ears and we had four weeks of quite heavy fighting around Caen. Casualties were fairly heavy. Then the German army was in retreat.[12]

Danny Budzak once shared a property with Duncan and recalls him saying how:

> I became a sergeant through dead man's shoes. I started carrying the ammunition. But first the machine gun bloke was killed, then the bloke who fed the bullets into the gun. I went up the ranks simply through a process of elimination.[13]

Duncan was wounded in the fighting and longstanding IS/SWP member and full-timer Jim Nichol recounts:

> Duncan, as we know, was quite a private person. He used to come to our house for dinner and supper from time to time but it was always difficult to get him to talk although there was one occasion when he dropped his trousers to show us where he was shot when in Normandy. The bullet went through the inside of his upper thigh just missing his privates. So, to sum that up, he was a private person, shot near the privates, when he was a private.[14]

After the fighting around Caen, Duncan's battalion never saw any serious action and at the end of the war everybody expected to be sent home. That was not to be the case—the Labour government still thought there was an empire to defend and troops were diverted in all directions.

In the spring of 1946 Duncan's battalion was in Egypt. Unsurprisingly, the main thought of the ordinary conscript was "we just want to go home" and so started a series of mutinies—in the RAF and the army—in Ceylon, India, Malaysia, Egypt and beyond.

Duncan was a sergeant at this time and when he and many of his fellow Non-Commissioned Officers (NCOs) refused to carry out orders the upper ranks were powerless:

We were in a place near Ismaliya in the canal zone of Egypt. We heard that they'd mutinied in Ismaliya. It wasn't highly sophisticated politically, but was around the demand that, "We want out!" So initially we refused to do guard parade and other duties. Within a short time, the authorities were in real trouble. The RAF and other forces had gone, and the officers were isolated. The officers worked through NCOs. It was like the film *Carry on Sergeant*—when the officer doesn't know what to do, he says "Carry on Sergeant"! When the NCOs won't do what they're supposed to, they're buggered. Most of the NCOs, including the majority of senior NCOs in our battalion, refused to carry out orders. Therefore, the whole thing collapsed. The mutiny lasted about three and a half weeks.[15]

Duncan was imprisoned for a short period but neither charged nor court martialled.[16]

Duncan tells us that he did not personally encounter other Trotskyists in the British Army in Egypt—but they were there. Some even managed to contact Egyptian Trotskyists and, in turn, those Egyptian Trotskyists were in touch with the movement in Britain.[17] Perhaps even more strangely, Duncan's fellow WIL member and future comrade and close friend in IS and the SWP, Frank Henderson was close by. Frank writes in his autobiography:

Duncan Hallas was just down the road. He was in the canal zone at the same time as I was and in one of the interviews with him in *Socialist Review* he told how he enjoyed swimming in the great lakes every day. I was there, a bit farther up the road, enjoying a swim in the same lakes every day. As far as I know, I never bumped into him. The annoying thing was they sent him home for demob and they sent me to bloody Palestine.[18]

Socialist Appeal supports the protests in Egypt.

Back in Manchester

Returning to Manchester in 1947 Duncan started again at Metro-Vickers and picked up with his comrades. By this time the main Trotskyist forces in Britain, miniscule as they still were, had fused to become the Revolutionary Communist Party (RCP). The marriage was not always a match made in heaven but on his return, Duncan found an RCP branch of between 12 and 15 members. It was not many but after Duncan had left for the army Rachel Ryan had also moved away and the organisation had been built afresh. This was done in a carefully planned manner utilising local knowledge from nearby Liverpool comrades, and by bringing in cadre from recently de-mobilised comrades. By the start of 1947 eight such comrades had arrived in Manchester, six of whom were in the one factory that had been chosen as the centre of their organisation—the Barton Works of Platt Brothers—an ex-Ford Motors factory that now manufactured machinery for the textile industry. RCP members Harry Ratner, Alan Christianson, Don Ellis and Alec Miles were among the six. At its high point following a strike Christianson relates that:

> ...in the coming months the Trotskyist comrades estab-
> lished complete domination of the Shop Stewards
> Committee and through this the workers' side of the
> Works Committee.[19]

There were some other successes. In April 1947 Jock Haston, General Secretary of the RCP, spoke to an audience of 60-70 at the Queen's Park Parliament, a workers' debating society on "What is Trotskyism?". In the same year the branch was commended for an increase of 300 percent in the sales of *Socialist Appeal*—the best performance in the country. A report in October 1947 shows they sold 200 *Socialist Appeal* anti-fascist supplements at a large National Council of Labour Colleges (NCLC) "Ban the Fascists" meeting—and they also sold 21 copies of Tony Cliff's *Middle East at the Crossroads* pamphlet at the same meeting. In the same week they sold another 70 supplements at their own open-air meeting in Platt Fields, where the attendance varied between 50 and 200. In November Alan Christianson also spoke at the Queen's Park Parliament, this time to 60 people on "Marxism and the Crisis". In January 1948 Christianson spoke to a smaller meeting of 20 on "Europe in Revolt".

However, the RCP was in a precarious situation, split between a "Majority" who favoured continuation of the organisation as an open party and a "Minority" that favoured entry into the Labour Party. The open party group was led by the existing leadership of Jock Haston, Ted Grant, Jimmy Deane and others. The entrists

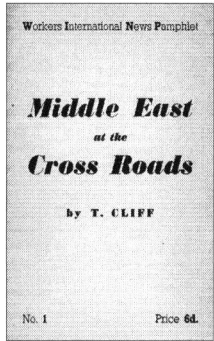

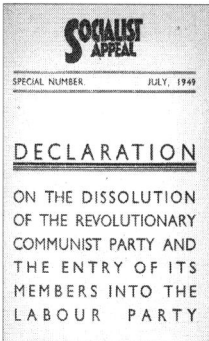

RCP Pamphlet by Tony Cliff.   Goodbye to the RCP.

were led by Gerry Healy. In Manchester, the Minority faction only had four members. Duncan was a member of the Majority.

In October 1947 the International Executive Committee of the Fourth International supported what amounted to splitting the RCP by allowing the Minority to enter the Labour Party with its own organisation. According to Christianson this led to the ridiculous situation where the Minority comrades left the branch and organised their own group, meeting at the other end of Manchester. The Majority soldiered on until June 1949, when a Special National Conference of the RCP voted by a substantial majority to dissolve the organisation and call upon the members to enter the Labour Party. Those that did not depart Trotskyism completely were therefore left to enter the Labour Party, where they were to experience the tender embrace of Gerry Healy and his group of deep entrists who traded under the name of "The Club".

On 6 August 1952 Duncan wrote a letter to Edward Grant, a fellow member of the Socialist Review Group, which gives this interesting summation of some of the issues:

> ...it is essential to recognise the limits of develop-
> ment, given the best organisation, with a given political

line. Let me illustrate this concretely. I joined the WIL in 1943; at that time, it was growing rapidly. In spite of a not very efficient machine we were within sight of putting Trotskyism on the map as a serious political tendency. We had only four comrades in Manchester, three of them very young and very raw, yet we were able to exert considerable influence, sufficient to alarm the local Stalinist hacks. Simply because we had a favourable situation and the right programme and emphasis. In the later years (1946-1948) we had far more members (about 20), a far better organisation, good sales of the paper (about 400 a fortnight), control of a key factory (Fords at Barton) and were much more experienced. Nevertheless, we declined and finally disintegrated. We had our old slogans and orientation, which no longer suited the situation. Haston and Co. were unable to readjust themselves and we lost the best cadre British Trotskyism ever had.[20]

Membership of The Club under the leadership of Healy was to prove to the best of the remaining ex-RCP Trotskyists just what they feared it would be. Two groupings formed amongst these new entrants—a State Capitalist group around the ideas of Tony Cliff and a second group around Ted Grant and Jimmy Deane. Both groups were to feel the full force of Healy's big stick. Raymond Challinor and Duncan Hallas both got the news of their expulsion from Harry Ratner,[21] although Ratner himself in his autobiography only refers rather cosily to "the split with that faction" without reference to his own role.[22] Most of the other "state caps" also got their marching orders in the run up to The Club's 1950 Conference.

One area where The Club was active was in the Labour Party's youth organisation the Labour League of Youth (LLOY). This had been formed by the Labour Party in 1945 and in 1948 the upper age limit for membership was raised to 25 years, meaning that Duncan was eligible to join.

The main campaign that the left was pursuing within the LLOY was for a set of demands that would give the organisation appropriate status within the party—an annual conference empowered to elect its own executive, for resolutions and a League delegation to the Labour Party Conference, for a representative on the NEC and for the League's own executive to control its own publications. The campaign to achieve these goals was given the name the National Status Movement, and Duncan was on its committee for the Manchester area alongside his comrades Trevor Park and Ted Morris.

A LLOY event attended by Duncan that had significance for him in more ways than one was the week-long Filey Rally organised by the Labour Party as a holiday camp and summer school in September 1949. The rally was attended by about 2,000 young people and whilst they could go "dancing to Mantovani and his Orchestra and Charles Amer and his Butlin Boys in the Viennese and Regency Ballrooms",[23] it was also a hotbed of politics where the National Status Movement got a big kickstart.

Duncan met Irene Alice Gosling at Filey. They were both active in Salford Labour Party and they married on 28 August 1950 at Manchester Registry Office. At this time, Duncan was 24 and was no longer at Metro-Vickers—he was a technician at a medical laboratory. Irene was 22 and a typist for a film company.

In the wider scheme of Duncan's life, another life-changing event was to occur just one month later—the foundation of the Socialist Review Group—later to become the International Socialists and then, in 1977, the Socialist Workers Party.

The Socialist Review Group

By September 1947 Tony Cliff had been expelled from Britain and was living in Ireland. His wife Chanie Rosenberg was allowed to remain and Cliff was able to visit for a period each year. Cliff made an extended visit to the country between June and October 1950, using the opportunity to talk at meetings with what remained of the country's Trotskyist forces and to elicit their support. He seems to have been far more active than Ted Grant and one of Grant's supporters, Sam Levy, wrote on 7 September 1950:

> The "State Capitalists" claim 30 members, seven in London proper, six in Thames Valley and the rest in the provinces... It seems he [Cliff] just went into the provinces to pick up people for the asking. He claims to have the six Sheffield comrades who dropped from the party, he also claims five or six in Birmingham, including Bill Ainsworth.[24]

The Foundation Conference of the Socialist Review Group (SRG) was duly held in London on the weekend of 30 September to 1 October 1950. Levy's information proved to be fairly accurate in that the minutes of the founding meeting show that the group had a total of 33 members. The one location not mentioned by Levy that had the semblance of organisation was Manchester where, in addition to Duncan (Don) Hallas, Ted Morris, John Smethurst, Bill Donnelly and Trevor Park were fellow founding members. The first key decision of the Foundation Conference was that the new organisation needed to work in the LLOY and have a youth publication. This was an obvious decision as, of the 33 founding members, 19 were members of the LLOY. Another decision was the need for a theoretical publication and the name *Socialist Review* was chosen. Don (he was not known as Duncan in those days) Hallas was to be actively involved in both areas.

At the first National Committee of the new organisation in December 1950 Hallas reported on the latest developments with the youth paper *Rally* which at that time was controlled by the Grant-Deane Tendency. It was agreed that the SRG should open negotiations with them for it to become a joint venture subject to several conditions, the main one being both organisations to have the same number on the Editorial Board (EB). Don was given the job of negotiating, which he undertook with Jimmy

Deane. An agreement was reached between them but when it was presented to the SRG Secretariat and the National Youth Fraction, they rejected it on the basis that whilst both organisations would have the same number on the EB, it was also proposed that two independents sit on it. Don and two fellow Manchester members, Ted Morris and Bill Donnelly, wrote a document (the style is undoubtedly of Hallas) in protest. It was simply titled *To All Members* and dated 28 February 1951. The document is noteworthy as an extremely early example of Don's political maturity and knowledge.

The document contains this important lesson for revolutionary work within larger organisations:

> Some comrades seem to imagine that we can "control" the developing left wing by means of majorities on committees, boards, etc. This idea is completely false and derives from centrist conceptions. The only possible "control" we can exert in any serious leftward movement is the ideological "control" due to the power of our ideas. In general, the bigger and more serious the leftward movement the smaller will be our organisational influence; but the greater if we pursue correct tactics our ideological influence. It is from this fact that the tactic of entry was first developed. If we had sufficient forces to control organisationally a big leftward tendency, entry would be unnecessary.[25]

The SRG and its successors have generally learned this lesson well. Whilst the Communist Party scurried to capture trade union positions through Broad Lefts and other less savoury methods, groups of Trotskyists burrowed to conceal themselves in the Labour Party in acts of deep entry. Duncan, both in 1951 and throughout his political life, stood for an honest political accounting. An emergency meeting of the SRG had to be called to resolve the youth publication issue. Hallas and his supporters (who included Raymond Challinor) lost

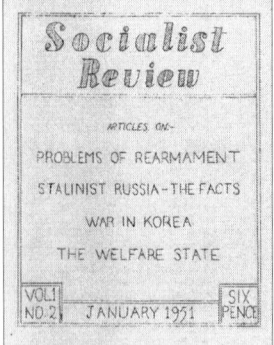

Socialist Review
January 1951.

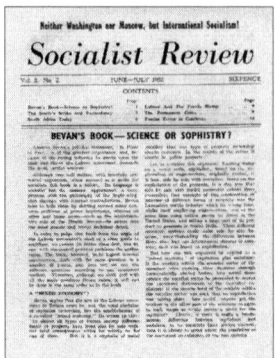

Socialist Review
June-July 1952.

the argument and the SRG started its own youth paper *Young Chartist*.

Turning to the publication front, the first issue of *Socialist Review* appeared in November 1950, but, in its earliest years, with Cliff in Ireland and not being overly productive, and a membership numbering in the tens, getting quality, original articles was difficult. Don Hallas produced three of the best that have each, in their own way, stood the test of time.

The earliest of these, "Problems of Rearmament", appeared in the second issue in January 1951.[26] For the purposes of this short tour, it pays to consider this one alongside his third article, "The Permanent Crisis" from June-July 1952.[27] They both deal with the same pressing political issue, and Gonzalo Pozo described them as:

> ...two articles for *Socialist Review* which, in quite general but incendiary terms, expressed the group's concern with the connections between rearmament and the notion of waste, the booming post-war economy and imperialism.[28]

They both bear re-reading today and, of course, their themes were to become integral parts of IS Tradition theory through the later works of Tony Cliff, Mike Kidron and Chris Harman.

The third important article produced by Hallas in this period was "The Significance of Nationalisation" which appeared in May 1951.[29] I know that this article was highly regarded by Chris Harman, and that is a good recommendation indeed. It was written in the context of the nationalisation undertaken by the previous Labour government and its introduction makes clear its purpose:

> Within the Labour Party itself, questions of the purpose, methods, and extent of nationalisation are a frequent source of discussion—and of dispute! This article is an attempt to analyse, from a Marxist viewpoint, the significance of those measures, and to suggest what steps socialist militants in the Labour Party should now propose.[30]

Hallas then takes us through a condensed but interesting Marxist tour of capital, the state and the changing role of both that lead to the development of state capitalism. He draws the conclusion:

> The evolution of state property forms takes place in each individual country as the result of a complex of the politico-economic needs of the ruling class and the exigencies of the class struggle. Whilst in each case there are unique features, there are also common ones—and the decisive common feature is, that every measure of statification is necessary to the economy, and, therefore, also to the ruling class. But at the same time, every measure of statification weakens the direct economic, and therefore, political power of that same ruling class. The capitalist state becomes increasingly

independent of the capitalist class, a trend which, *so long as the working class movement exists*, renders the continued existence of capitalist class rule increasingly precarious... The more the state takes over production, the more it involves itself, the less it is able to pose as an "impartial" arbitrator in the class struggle...

We support nationalisation measures as a means of weakening the power of the ruling class, of increasing the conflicts within it, and, above all, of bringing the workers into conflict with the state. Against "left" sectarians we insist upon the progressive character of nationalisation, against reformists of all shades we insist upon the capitalist character of this type of statified production, combat the illusion that it can, of itself, solve any of the problems of society, and argue the vital necessity of destroying the imperialist state machine. Today, more than ever before, it is all or nothing: either the working class will destroy state capitalism and establish that consistent democracy that is socialism, the classless society, or state capitalism will destroy the workers' movement and impose a totalitarian servitude that may last for centuries. In the long run there is no third alternative.[31]

The article is a relatively forgotten early part of the IS Tradition's canon on state capitalism. In fact, it was originally scheduled to be even more ambitious: "The second part of this article, which deals with the specific problems raised by the nationalisation measures of the past five years in Britain, will appear in our next issue". Unfortunately, the second part was never written.

This lapse in completing the article is symptomatic of an aspect of Duncan's political activity—his sometimes disorganised and tardy approach to tasks. Instances are legion. The September 1951 meeting of the SRG National Committee: "agreed that the Secretariat write to Manchester instructing them to hold regular meetings"; at the November 1951 meeting

Socialist Review
May 1951.

Manchester had to ask for their debts to be written off; at the February 1952 meeting Cliff moved that, "the NC notes DH's failure to write document on the crisis" and a second motion was also passed that noted his "failure to write draft programme". In August 1952 Hallas himself wrote: "Our organisation must be improved—and we in Manchester are amongst the worst offenders in this respect." Last, but not least, the minutes of the National Committee in November 1952 record that a motion was moved that Hallas be given one month to pay dues or have his membership reduced to sympathiser status.

Perhaps Stan Newens summed it up best for me when he said Don was "intellectually brilliant but sometimes dilatory".[32]

Notwithstanding his approach to political work at this time, Hallas produced two extremely important internal documents for the group. The first, and most famous one, "The Stalinist Parties", can rightly be considered as one of the founding texts of the IS Tradition. Indeed, the inclusion of the document in the 1971 book, *The Fourth International, Stalinism and the Origin of the International Socialists: Some Documents* endorses that view.[33] We have reproduced the document in full in this volume.

It was Don Hallas himself who, at the SRG National Committee in December 1950, proposed that three documents be written for discussion. One of these, "The Nature of the Stalinist Parties", was allocated to Ellis Hillman to write.[34] He duly produced his document in May 1951. The original is closely typed on foolscap paper and runs to 17 pages. Ian Birchall's brief description of the document's most dangerous assertion, namely that united front work with the CP is to be rejected, is appropriate:

> ...drawing heavily on work of the Johnson-Forest Tendency,[35] [Hillman] argued that Stalinist parties were not part of the working class movement. As a result, "The tactic of the united fronts with the CP which was considered a weapon to separate the rank and file from the bureaucratic leadership must be rejected on *principle*". This was a disastrous conclusion which would have made any serious trade union activity impossible since the Communist Party was still by far the most important left-wing force within the unions.[36]

In truth Hillman's document is much more than this one conclusion but, suffice to say, it was not well received![37] Hallas was tasked to write a reply and the conclusion to his document puts the correct and only possible political position for the SRG in the early 1950s, well:

> Our approach to...the Stalinist parties proper, must be based upon a practical, concrete programme of struggle against the bourgeoisie. Outside the Russian Empire and Yugoslavia it is sheer nonsense to assert that "the struggle against Stalinism is, in fact, the sharpest and highest expression of the class war". Exactly the opposite is the case. It is the struggle against the bourgeoisie and its social-democratic agents that is the decisive one. The struggle against Stalinism is subsidiary to that major conflict and flows naturally from it. Without in any way underestimating the difficulties and dangers of unity in action with the Stalinist workers we have to say that such unity is an absolutely essential step towards

the goal of breaking up Stalinism. We have broken with the paralysing conception of workers' statism. We are in no danger at all of falling into pro-Stalinism: we are in considerable danger of following Shachtman and Co. in the no less dangerous mistake of Stalinophobia.[38]

Fortunately, it was the Hallas policy that the SRG's members pursued. As Stan Newens once told me:

As Duncan Hallas makes clear, anyone working within the trade union movement was likely to encounter CPGB members and to refuse to work with them on issues which concerned the whole workforce would have been divisive and counterproductive.

I became involved in the Briggs/Ford strike at Dagenham in 1952, as the result of giving a series of NCLC lectures to the NUGMW branch. When they told me that the lectures had to be cancelled because the members were taking strike action, I offered my assistance, which was readily accepted. I could not have said, I was not willing to work with CPGB members of other unions taking part in the strike, without giving offence and I would not have dreamt of taking such a line. I sold *Socialist Review* but formed friendships with CP members which lasted many years—until his death, in the case of shop steward (later convenor) Sid Harraway.[39]

The importance of Don's document for trade union and united front work was recognised to be such that when the document was discussed at the SRG National Committee in November 1951 it was agreed that it should be used in discussion with the group's contacts.

Hallas may have been censured at the February 1952 National Committee for his failure to write a draft programme for the SRG, but he corrected that omission in July 1952. The opening sentence of his "Programme for Action" document gave his conception of the current situation of the SRG:

> Since the inception of our group we have pursued a policy of propaganda and education amongst advanced workers, many of them already influenced by Trotskyist ideas. We have concentrated on building a cadre rather than on influencing the class struggle. In spite of occasional attempts at political action, that is to say, intervention in specific struggles with concrete slogans, we have remained in the main, a purely propaganda group.

Hallas was calling for a step change. Later in the document he explains:

> To say that we must now enter into serious political work means that we must shift our emphasis from propaganda to agitation. To do this we need two things, a programme and a perspective. Again to avoid misunderstanding by a programme I do not mean a document reiterating the fundamentals of Communism—though such a document one should certainly also have—I mean a list of things we tell the workers *to do now*, by a perspective I do not mean an analysis of the decline of British capitalism—again this is a necessary weapon in our armoury—I mean a concrete plan of work to build the group.[40]

And Hallas goes on to lay out both a programme and a perspective.

In the contemporaneous letter to Edward Grant of August 1952 mentioned previously, Don expressed his thoughts on the SRG's situation and his proposals as follows:

> I want to put my own conception of our difficulties. As a group we are not developing. No doubt this is in part the result of inertia, routinism and so on. But this

answer cannot account for very much. Basically, we are not developing because our methods of work are not *politically* orientated. We are a propaganda group and as such have reached, more or less, the limit of our growth... We are pursuing the propaganda, small circle line that was necessary from 1946-1950 at a time when we should be putting out a concrete agitational programme. But we are very small? Yes, but the WIL started out with 12 members, one of whom was a police agent. Nevertheless, it did the job.

Perhaps all this sounds very remote from the present problem. In reality, it is not so. Periods of stagnation or decline invariably bring to the surface personal conflicts, squabbles about minor questions and so on.

We are now entering a favourable period. Some comrades have been forecasting this period for so long they can't recognise it when it arrives. If we seize our opportunity most of our internal problems will be greatly eased. This, in my opinion, is the real question.[41]

The debate on the "Programme" took place at a two-day SRG National Committee in August 1952. Manchester branch was represented by Ted Morris. To cut a long story short I have written elsewhere:

Tony Cliff put the nail in the Hallas coffin by stating quite specifically that "agitation was not our work" and then moving a motion "that the *Socialist Review* continue as a propaganda organ". Cliff's motion was carried five for and two against.[42]

Whilst Hallas failed to win his call for a change in political focus the episode shows how Don was always striving to relate concrete facts on the ground to concrete action in an organisation. He returned to the question of the differing roles of agitation and propaganda in a famous article written in 1984, an article that remains an important component of SWP education to this day.[43] Notwithstanding his defeat, the organisation introduced a new programme early in 1953, which did indeed have its roots in the one suggested by Don.

Even at this early age Don was a great intellectual and practical help to his comrades. Stan Newens relates:

> I was particularly interested in the application of Marxist ideas to the history of ancient Rome and ancient Greece. Duncan Hallas, a member of the Socialist Review Group, advised me to read Gibbons' *Decline and Fall of the Roman Empire.*[44]

Hallas had, and retained, an enormous interest and knowledge in history, archaeology, anthropology and beyond—and he was always willing to share it with others. When, in 1993, he was asked to name his favourite books he said:

> Gordon Childe's *Man Makes Himself* heads the list... The content is the enormous creativity of ancient classless agricultural societies, the discovery and development not only of agriculture and stock breeding but of spinning and weaving, of pottery, of boat craft and brick making, stone masonry and cosmetics and many, many other things—all before the growth of classes and class society. Childe's subsequent *What Happened in History* is also a lovely book (although the first chapter is obsolete and should be disregarded)...
>
> A second choice is J M Robertson's *Short History of Christianity*... Robertson's little book exposes brilliantly the mixture of delusion and fraud, forged documents and vested interests that still today buttress the Anglican, Papist and Orthodox churches...
>
> A better book by Archibald Robertson (no relation) *The Bible and Its Background* gives a Marxist analysis of the origins of Judaism and its Christian and

Islamic offshoots...

I have never read all the voluminous works of Marx and Engels...what sticks in my mind and makes me re-read again and again is the trilogy on 19th century France: above all, *The Eighteenth Brumaire of Louis Bonaparte*. Each time I read it I learn something more about politics, as opposed to the crude reductionism that passes for "Marxism" in some circles.

Which leads me to Trotsky's *The History of the Russian Revolution.* Nobody, not even Marx, has ever written such a graphic, analytical and, especially, concrete description of an actual revolutionary process. It is not a particularly easy book but it is one that every serious revolutionary should read...

We can learn too, and get pleasure from, some of the works of the best bourgeois writers in the years of their ascendancy. One of my favourite books is Macaulay's *History of England*...

This has all been non-literary. It reflects my own (depraved?) tastes. I devour detective stories in vast amounts, most of them rubbish. I therefore finish with Voltaire's *Candide.* Published in English translation by Penguin in 1910, it is the best pre-Marxian critique of society I have ever read and re-read.[45]

Heading North

Given his insatiable thirst for knowledge and his undoubted ability as a communicator it was perhaps inevitable that Duncan would, at some stage, turn to a role in education. It was also perhaps inevitable that the role would be with that bastion of working class education, the National Council of Labour Colleges (NCLC). He was duly appointed as their East of Scotland Organiser in May 1953 and he and Irene moved to Edinburgh.

The life would have been a busy round of lectures, meetings and educational courses, with the bonus of the chance to engage directly with a very large number of active trade unionists and socialists. Years later, veteran socialist Harry McShane recalled attending NCLC talks by Hallas.[46] The NCLC had long been a favoured arena for left-wing activists and the Trotskyists were no exception. During Duncan's time with the NCLC, Jock Haston, the former General Secretary of the RCP (but now definitely an ex-Trotskyist) was one of the two London Regional Organisers. Sid Bidwell, for many years a member of the SRG, was the other. Very long-time Trotskyist John Archer was a North Regional Organiser based in Leeds. The following newspaper reports would represent a pretty typical selection of Don's meetings:

Fifeshire Advertiser (Saturday 03 October 1953).
WAGES, PRICES AND PROFITS. The Federation of Shipbuilding and Engineering Industry held a well-attended public meeting in the Library Hall on Wednesday night. Mr A Wiscombe, who presided, explained the object of the meeting and introduced Mr D Hallas, Organiser of the East of Scotland NCLC. Mr Hallas then gave an interesting address in which he dealt with wages, prices and profits.

Falkirk Herald (Saturday 18 September 1954).
CO-OP WOMEN'S GUILD. The fortnightly meeting of the Falkirk and District Co-operative Women's Guild (Falkirk No. 1 Branch) held on Wednesday evening, took the form of a lecture and film show given by Mr D Hallas of the National Council of Labour Colleges on "The Food Distribution of the World". Following the film show Mr Hallas answered a number of interesting questions put to him by Guild members.

Falkirk Herald (Saturday 08 October 1955).
AUTOMATION. "The Automation Age" was the subject of a lecture by Mr D Hallas of Edinburgh held at the Labour Hall, Grangemouth, on Tuesday, under the auspices of

the National Council of Labour Colleges. Hallas dealt with the effect of automation, especially on British industry and a large number of questions were asked during the discussion which followed the talk.

Don was certainly still a member of the SRG when he arrived in Scotland but he was now geographically isolated from other members. Stan Newens recalls taking Tony Cliff on the back of his motorcycle on a tour of the north of England and Scotland sometime in 1953 or 1954 where they met T Dan Smith in Newcastle,[47] Harry McShane in Glasgow, and Don Hallas in Edinburgh. Stan still remembers the blocked sink at Don's home! He also specifically remembers that at the time Don was still an SRG member—albeit inactive. He was certainly a member in early 1954 as a letter written by Ray Challinor in January 1954 exists that states in terms of the SRG, "Don is plodding along as usual in Edinburgh". Cliff merely reports that Hallas "had left the organisation in 1954".[48]

Don left the NCLC early in 1956 and according to Nigel Harris in 2004 this was because he was sacked for his excessive political activity. Certainly, his boss, J P M Millar, was no friend of the left. Don entered Edinburgh University to take a BSc in Chemistry in September 1956 and this coincided with the start of an upturn in the fortunes of the tiny Trotskyist left in Britain. What became known as the New Left was born.

The seeds of the British New Left were sown in the political earthquakes of 1956. Khrushchev's "secret" speech, Soviet troops crushing the Hungarian Revolution and the British invasion of Egypt aiming to seize the Suez Canal were seismic events. Ten thousand members left the Communist Party. New publications, the *New Reasoner* and *Universities & Left Review*, were founded in 1957 together with an array of socialist forums and political discussion groups. In 1960 these publications merged to become *New Left Review*. A newer, younger element was also becoming politicised—the Campaign for Nuclear Disarmament (CND) was formed in 1958, the first Aldermaston march took place in 1959 and, in 1960, the Labour Party launched its youth organisation, the Young Socialists.

The Socialist Review Group not only engaged with, but was highly active in this new milieu, but engagement and activity did not mean uncritical adherence. Socialist Review Group members were the key driving force in bringing forth the new journal *International Socialism (IS)*, an explicitly Marxist journal with a non-sectarian composition and a link to action. The journal was launched in 1958 and relaunched in 1960. Michael Kidron used the second relaunched issue to review the New Left book, *Out of Apathy*, in which he defined at length the IS view of the New Left.[49] The review provoked an exchange between E P Thompson[50] and Kidron in *New Left Review* (numbers 6 and 7) in which Kidron famously writes:

> I see *IS* in the tradition of political *action*, a paper designed to serve the agent of social change—the working class—and therefore necessarily devoted to problems of class and class consciousness... In a word, to my mind *IS* is geared to action; *New Left Review* is not. Action demands priorities of preoccupation; inaction can do without.[51]

Indeed, Tony Cliff had a joke at the time: "For the New Left, what is theory? A speech by Edward Thompson. And what is practice? Going to hear an Edward Thompson speech."

Don was active in the Edinburgh New Left and seemingly endorsed this SRG viewpoint. Writing in 1974 he said:

> I recall a meeting in Edinburgh in 1957 or 1958. The speaker was E P Thompson. Before any "sectarian dogmatist" had said a word (apart from this reviewer, who as Chairman introduced the speaker), he treated us to a violent denunciation of the sterility, stupidity, ill-faith, and ignorance of the "sects".
>
> In any case, in the light of subsequent events, were not the Marxist critics of the political looseness,

SOCIALIST REVIEW

Neither Washington nor Moscow but international socialism
is unique in British politics.
Like the U. & LR. it interprets the world as it is, not as it was; unlike
—it includes the world of factories, mines and shops.
Like the U. & LR. it is a paper of theory; unlike—it is also a paper of
practice.
Like—it is left; unlike—Marxist.
Like—it appears regularly; unlike—every month
they both cost money,
but the Socialist Review is only eight shillings (post paid).

See the world . . .

through the eyes of the Independent Socialist League in the United
States. A network of correspondents keeps us abreast of the news in
their weekly *Labor Action*, and up to date with socialist views in their
quarterly *New International*. Sixpence and two shillings and sixpence
respectively.

*For these publications write to Stan Newens, 16 Vicarage Lane, North
Weald, Essex.*

SRG and the New Left—Socialist Review *Advert in*
Universities and Left Review *Issue 2 Summer 1957.*

evasiveness and lack of clarity of the New Left leaders
proved to be correct?[52]

John Palmer endorses the position of Hallas at the time:

Stuart Hall[53] told me once (I used to help distribute *New
Left Review* among the Young Socialists) that Duncan
was the equal of Mike Kidron, Alasdair MacIntyre and
Nigel Harris in "the Cliff group" as constructive critics
of the New Left movement. He seemed unaware that
Duncan was not actually in the SRG at that time. Stuart
took them seriously because they shone a critical but
not sectarian eye on the New Left Clubs.[54]

Despite this affinity Hallas was evidently not attracted
"home" to the SRG. Mike Kidron, who was also the editor of
Socialist Review, wrote some letters to Hallas in 1957 and 1958
trying, unsuccessfully, to get him to write for the publication.
It is clear that Don was still receiving and paying for the paper
but the exasperation evident from Kidron indicates that he had

been beating his head against a brick wall for a considerable period. The correspondence does show that Don was Chairman of the University Labour Group. Perhaps most surprising is a letter that Mike Kidron received from James D Young[55] in May 1957 which states:

> Don Hallas won't rejoin SR. He is going to stick to RSL. I was with him from 7.30am (Saturday morning) until 2.00pm and I could *not* persuade him to push SR in the Labour Club. I am seeing Don again on Wednesday and I shall have one last go at him, but I am not very hopeful.[56]

The RSL was the Revolutionary Socialist League—the forerunner of Militant. Whilst at University, as well as overt politics, Don seems to have been involved in an array of activities. He was involved in the University Debates Union where Jack Robertson advises that:

> ...his extraordinary speaking ability was party honed in the national debating competition known as *The Observer Mace* that was run each year for universities by the *Observer* newspaper. The Edinburgh team actually won the competition in 1961.[57]

Don was Honorary Secretary of the Students Representative Council (SRC) 1960-1961 and its First Junior President in 1961-1962. The published *Origins and Purpose* of the SRC tell us that "the most important part of the Council's work is the representations made to the University Authorities on behalf of the student body." Interestingly, when Don was secretary of the SRC its president was David Steel, the future leader of the Liberal Party. Don was the editor of the *Edinburgh University Student's Handbook* in 1960-1961 and its advisory editor in 1962-1963. His Introduction to the 1960-1961 edition concludes with:

Don Hallas's graduation photograph, 1962. Photo courtesy of Edinburgh University

...complaints of misrepresentation, omission, political bias and general incompetence should be addressed to the Editor who is very fond of contentious correspondence. Constructive criticism is also welcome. Now read on.[58]

Chanie Rosenberg says, "he became the student chess champion".[59] Don graduated with a BSc in Pure Science on 27 October 1962.

When Duncan left Edinburgh, he settled in Birmingham for a period and then moved to London. It is from that move that the next episode of his memorable life commenced. He may not have been attracted "home" to his political tradition by the first uptick in the post-war fortunes of the revolutionary left, but the second awakening in the tumultuous year of 1968 was to do the trick.

Heading South

Duncan was now a teacher employed at Sellincourt Junior School in Tooting in the London Borough of Wandsworth. It was from here and his work in the Wandsworth Association of the National Union of Teachers (NUT) that he linked up with his former comrades in the International Socialists. Initially, this happened through the medium of the Teachers' Rank and File organisation; the first issue of their journal being published in April 1968. The introductory editorial to the journal had a quasi-sociological feel:

Rank and File
Teacher *Issue 1,*
April 1968.

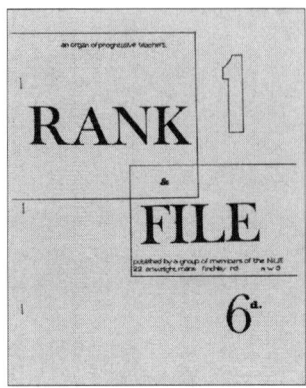

Rank and File is produced by left-wing teachers within the NUT, who believe that the union could, and should, be the most important and effective factor in forcing change and progress, not only in the general sociological-educational field, but also—and most especially—in the struggle for better salaries and conditions for all teachers...[60]

Duncan wrote its first major article, "Salaries—What Can We Do?" that cut much more directly to the chase, not only in answering the specifics of the question posed, but also in its concluding call to arms on the bigger question:

...the union's traditional policy of co-operation with the employers and appeals to public "reasonableness", combined with purely verbal protests, is clearly bankrupt. Our aim must be to convert the NUT into a genuine trade union capable of mobilising teachers in the defence of their interests and those of the educational service. There is no other way out.[61]

Duncan remained at the forefront of the Teachers' Rank and File organisation until he joined IS as a full-timer in 1971.

At Duncan's death Chanie Rosenberg paid this tribute to this aspect of his life and activity:

> We worked closely together in the National Union of Teachers during the huge industrial strike movement of the 1970s, which for teachers lasted from the end of 1969 to 1975. We had to overcome the NUT executive's total opposition to teachers' strikes for half a century. London had to lead the way, as teachers in the capital were much more financially stressed by the low level of the nationally negotiated wage, and its teachers potentially more militant...
>
> When the Rank and File decided to call for pay strikes in 1969 Duncan took over the leadership of the movement and led a terrific, tireless struggle to get the vote for strike action. He was a magnificent debater, and coolly, in a restrained, teacherly manner, thoroughly outwitted all the heads in both knowledge and arguing ability time after time...
>
> This led to the most glorious chapter in the NUT's history, with constant strikes nationally up to 1975, which pushed teachers' salaries up massively both nationally and for London. One of our London Allowance strikes for £350 actually achieved more than we were asking for—£351 (because for some reason the computers could not manage a figure with a nought on the end). Duncan was the chief steward at our demonstrations and rallies. Teachers' social and political consciousness rose sky high, and Rank and File Teacher grew to be a substantial force with a regular broadsheet newsletter till the 1980s (which Duncan edited for many years), many educational and industrial pamphlets, conferences both educational and trade union, and hundreds of new members.
>
> Duncan played a crucial role in the movement, which changed teachers' attitudes from being "ragged

trousered educationalists" who needed two jobs to keep their heads above water to being organised trade unionists and an integral part of the working class.[62]

Strangely, for me, one of the most memorable phrases Duncan ever wrote on education came in the completely different context of the history of the Comintern and the over-reliance of the other Communist Parties on the Russian Communist Party—but it also, I suspect, hides a wider truth about how he saw his own role as an educator in IS:

It was one thing to "go to school" under the Russians but quite another to come to rely on the teachers to solve the complex problems facing the German, Polish, British, United States or whatever parties. The teaching which the Russians could give from their own revolutionary experience was the best available in the early years. *But an important objective of any real education is to emancipate the pupil from excessive dependence on the teacher.*[63]

Outside the NUT, the first time that Duncan came to the attention of the wider IS membership was when he attended the conferences held late in 1968.

These were important conferences for IS as membership had been increasing rapidly and the organisation needed to accelerate the process of transforming itself from a propaganda group into an action-orientated, interventionist one. Cliff summed up Duncan's impact thus:

The most impressive intervention at the conference was by Duncan Hallas. The comrades there did not know who he was, as he had left the organisation in 1954 and had now reappeared. The comrades who argued against Leninist democratic centralism on the grounds that Leninism leads to Stalinism were all very young and inexperienced. Therefore, when Duncan, who was in his forties, spoke with real authority, it was extremely impressive. What he said was short and sharp and included the question, "If Leninism led to Stalinism, why did Stalin kill all the Leninists?" His speech was absolutely riveting. Still, he was heckled by some delegates.[64]

Duncan was persuaded to leave his teaching job and joined IS full-time as "National Secretary" with effect from March 1971. The job description stated that the role was:

> To assist in the political work of the Centre on a day-to-day basis, to ensure effective liaison between the various committees of the Group, to be responsible to the National Committee and the Executive Committee for the execution of decisions taken and for the activities of full-time workers.[65]

His time in this role did not last long. It was clear that Duncan's talents lay in writing, speaking and giving political direction rather than organising. He continued working full-time for the organisation until his retirement in 1995 and had a range of other roles and responsibilities including editing the *Internal Bulletin*, editing the *International Socialism Journal*, guiding the training and education endeavours, sitting on all of the leading committees and being, effectively, the lead editorial writer for the organisation. Over and above these more formal roles, Duncan was one of the major public faces of the organisation. Over many years he travelled the country day in day out speaking at meetings (and spending time in the pub with the members afterwards). Danny Budzak described Duncan's weekly routine when they shared a house in Thistlewaite Road, Hackney for two to three years in the late 1980s and early 1990s:

> He lived a certain pattern of life, often away from Tuesday to Friday, travelling around the country, speaking, meeting people, organising, teaching,

A favourite at Marxism, 1980 Timetable.

learning, listening, talking. When he came back on a Friday, he was tired out. Saturday was reading day with a couple of packets of Player's Navy Cut full strength. We generally went to the pub on a Sunday evening.[66]

Duncan was an immensely popular speaker at the annual Socialist Worker Skegness Rally and at the Marxism Festivals. His range of talks was enormous—some examples from Skegness include: *Marx and Pre-History*; *Marxism and the National Question*; *1688 and All That*; *The French Revolution*, and from Marxism Festival: *Decline of the Comintern*; *Lenin and the Politics of Internationalism*; *1917*; *Bourgeois Revolutions*; *Origins of the SRG*; *Marxism and the Trade Union Bureaucracy*; *Women and Pre-History*; *Trotsky's Legacy*; *Market and Plan*; *Understanding Reformism*; *The State*—the list goes on and on. Very few subjects were beyond benefiting from the Hallas touch. He also made numerous trips overseas speaking to socialists on tours of the US, Canada, Australia, South Africa, and Ireland—and was hugely respected wherever he went.

Duncan's easy style of prose and accessible form of argument were not only inspirational in relating to larger audiences, through speeches or in writing. On the one-to-one level Duncan

always had time to patiently explain sometimes difficult political arguments or concepts—and this he frequently did through
his well-honed knack of making connections between the seemingly obscure and the everyday. One could fill a whole book with
examples and tributes from individual comrades that he influenced or helped, but I will give a few examples:

> Duncan was a great speaker and many thousands have
> heard him talk at the SWP's annual Marxism event on
> subjects as wide ranging as "Marxism and pre-history",
> "Marxist economics" and "Understanding reformism".
> But it was not just the big "showpiece" meetings at
> which he excelled. He was just as brilliant speaking at
> small branch meetings and perhaps even better talking
> to the newest individual member after the meeting had
> formally closed.[67]
>
> Duncan had amassed an astonishing range of
> knowledge covering the natural sciences as well as
> the whole of human history. He had a long practical
> acquaintance with the British trade union movement
> and understood its peculiar strengths and weaknesses.
> For those of us who had come to revolutionary politics
> in the 1960s, he provided a fascinating link with the
> early years of Trotskyism... If you wanted the "Glorious
> Revolution" of 1688, the French Revolution, the General
> Strike, the Spanish Civil War, sectarianism, the united
> front or the theory of surplus value, set out in a couple
> of clear, readable pages, Duncan provided it.[68]
>
> My first memory of him is at a meeting in a living
> room in south London. There were about a dozen of us
> there, almost all students and all in our late teens or
> early twenties—except for this man in his early forties
> with a Manchester accent. We were stunned by the
> clarity of his ideas, the sharpness of his mind and the
> depth of his knowledge of the labour movement—of
> which the rest of us were fairly ignorant. In 1969

and 1971 attempts by first a Labour and then a Tory government to introduce anti-union laws led to the first political strikes in Britain since the year after Duncan's birth, 1926. The Labour government that was elected in 1974 succeeded, with the help of the trade union leaderships, in bringing the wave of workers' struggles to an end. The employing class set about getting its revenge. Much of the left became demoralised in this period. Duncan did not. He never lost his revolutionary optimism as he continued speaking three or four times a week, writing articles, and selling *Socialist Worker* on the streets. Above all he patiently passed on his knowledge of Marxism and the revolutionary tradition to groups of younger people. He managed to visit the Marxism event just a few weeks before his illness struck him down.[69]

And, of course, in remembrance of Duncan's famous capacity for beer drinking, here is the obituary in the *Guardian* newspaper written by former IS National Secretary, Jim Higgins:

Duncan could, on occasion, be quite convivial. I recall him coming to my infant daughter's birthday party. The children had jelly and cake, and the adults a few drinks. Duncan, having imbibed, arranged the children on the stairs, and proceeded to lecture them, eloquently and at length, on the rise and fall of the Comintern, a subject on which he subsequently wrote an excellent pamphlet. One by one the children slipped away, until Duncan was speaking only to our dog, a pedigree Chow, who had little sympathy with the proletariat.[70]

But finally, to highlight the very concrete impact Duncan had on an individual member, John Molyneux has this to say:

I do want to recall two moments where Duncan made a real difference to me personally. The first was through his pathbreaking article "Building the Leadership" in October 1969 which dealt with the political roots of Gerry Healy's Socialist Labour League.

At that time, I was a student at Southampton University and attempting to build on campus and in the town, a branch of the International Socialists. Our main rival amongst students was the Socialist Labour League, who seemed to far outdo us in their confidence, coherence, and fervour. I felt deeply that they were wrong in their authoritarian sectarianism, but I often did not know how to answer their well-trained cadre in debate. Duncan's article gave me exactly what I needed, a Marxist analysis of what they were and how they got that way. Before I read Duncan's article the leading SLLers used to seek me out to try to batter me in arguments. After I read Duncan I noticed, with some satisfaction, that they told their members not to talk to me anymore!

The second was a good many years later sitting in my kitchen in Portsmouth after doing some meeting when we were chatting about art. He said, just in passing, "Of course you can see the transition from feudalism to capitalism on the walls of the National Gallery". Later when I took up lecturing on art history and writing about it those words stuck in my mind and were a starting point for much of my research, including my little book on Rembrandt. These are my examples, but I think thousands of comrades stood in Duncan's debt in similar ways.[71]

Personally, I like to think of Duncan as someone who, in a few pithy sentences, could explain why the SWP became a revolutionary organisation in 1950:

Trotskyism had fought not only to preserve but also to develop and apply the revolutionary ideas of Marx and Lenin which centred around the conception of socialism as the self-emancipation of the working class. And yet we broke with it? No, we did not. We broke with its degeneration in order to preserve its essential core.[72]

Why the SWP remains a revolutionary organisation whether the Labour Party is led by Michael Foot or Keir Starmer—or indeed by Jeremy Corbyn:

We do not believe that the quality of the party leader determines the action of the party when in government. That is, of course, an all too easy way out for many socialists within the Labour Party: blame the leadership. It also follows for them that the only way to change things is to get a better, more left-wing leadership... The performance of the 1974-79 Labour government was not an accident of the leadership, but the outcome of the very nature of the Labour Party and the nature of the social system which we seek to change. You cannot dig a trench with a screwdriver. You must have the right tool for the job.[73]

Maybe, even why Duncan and his comrades (and us) kept at it: "...revolutionaries who cannot withstand temporary popular hatred, as well as official persecution, are worthless".[74]

There was, however, another absolutely indispensable role that Duncan played—as foil and partner to Tony Cliff. Of course, like most relationships the path was not always smooth—internal disputes that had been bubbling in IS since 1973 came to a head in 1974 and 1975. Duncan and others opposed what they saw as Cliff's attempt to use changes to *Socialist Worker* as a Trojan horse to change the political perspective on how and on whom the revolutionary party should focus without the membership debating the issues:

There is a dispute in IS. The majority of the EC members argue that it is solely about *Socialist Worker*.

We believe, to the contrary, that the dispute stems from the political perspective—or lack of it...[75]

He was scathing of Cliff's disregard of the "democratic" part of "democratic centralism":

At the heart of this is the question of democratic centralism. Why are we not in favour of five people running the organisation? Because the whole tradition and experience shows the organisation cannot lead unless it has healthy internal life and there is debate on issues and feedback from that debate... Never again must we permit an affair like the *Socialist Worker* affair. The membership was not involved in the discussions until it was finished, and administrative changes then were made behind the back of the National Committee. It cannot be tolerated because it makes a mockery of democratic centralism.[76]

However, prior to the 1974 IS Conference Duncan unexpectedly "changed sides". His reasoning has never been fully, even adequately, explained. John Palmer, one of those most closely involved in this episode with Duncan tells me:

Duncan did say that there was no way we would win in the long run and that we should wait for another opportunity to raise the issue in the future. He never gave any further reason. I think he could not contemplate a split and a return to small group status which he had experienced in the post-war years after the dissolution of the RCP.[77]

Be that as it may, Ian Birchall has made two interesting comments on this symbiotic relationship between Cliff and Hallas:

Whilst not an original thinker in the style of Cliff, Hallas was a man of enormous intellectual breadth. If Cliff resembled Lenin in his remorseless focus on the political, Hallas took after Engels in his vast range of interests in the natural and social worlds.

And:

[Hallas] was a powerful speaker and prolific writer, with a prodigious range of knowledge. He played an important part in the internal discussions, often engaging in the patient persuasion for which Cliff sometimes did not have the time or inclination.[78]

It was this combination of Duncan's immense knowledge combined with, for the want of a better expression, his "people skills" that made him such an indispensable part of building and holding the organisation together. It was the combination of his broad experience and his fine-tuned antennae as to how political history, political theory and political organisation needed to be brought to bear on current day events that made him the organisation's number one polemicist. It was the combination of his utter belief in the cause of socialism and his unflinching desire to bring it about that made him, in the words of Ian Birchall, "one of the finest socialist propagandists of his generation".[79] It would take a full-length political biography to do justice to all of Duncan's achievements in the SRG, IS and the SWP. I hope that one day, someone will be in a position to undertake that task.

Duncan retired from his full-time role in the SWP in 1995 when ill-health had got the better of him. He suffered physically in his last years, confined to a wheelchair, but fortunately never losing his intellectual curiosity. Those who knew him best know that he never lost his belief in his class.

Duncan died on 19 September 2002 at the Homerton Hospital in Hackney. But what a life.

Notes

1   Duncan was an intensely private and modest person. Only rarely did he talk about his past life or his past achievements. The potted political biography and appreciation that follows has been pieced together from the fragments of Duncan's own records that exist plus the views and recollections of many of those who knew him best. He led a full life and this record is therefore necessarily selective.

2   Duncan Hallas, "A Soldier's Story: An Interview with Clare Fermont and Chris Nineham", *Socialist Review,* 186 (May 1995) www.marxists.org/archive/hallas/works/1995/05/soldier.htm

3   Nigel Harris, "Duncan Hallas: Death of a Trotskyist", *Revolutionary History,* Vol 8, No 4 (2004) www.marxists.org/history/etol/writers/harris/2004/xx/hallas.html

4   Crispin Hull, "Falklands Best Things for Tories Since Sliced Bread", *The Canberra Times* (29 May 1982).

5   Nigel Harris, "Duncan Hallas: Death of a Trotskyist", p261.

6   Duncan Hallas, "A Soldier's Story", p13.

7   Mick Bennett, *Youth and the War* (London: Young Communist League, 1940), p10. emphasis in the original.

8   Duncan Hallas, *The Comintern* (London: Bookmarks, 1985) p157. www.marxists.org/archive/hallas/works/1985/comintern/index.htm

9   Fred Eastwood, *Youth and the Trade Unions* (London: Young Communist League, 1942), p15.

10   Duncan Hallas, "A Soldier's Story", p13.

11   Duncan Hallas, "A Soldier's Story", p13.

12   Duncan Hallas, "A Soldier's Story", p11.

13   Danny Budzak, personal communication, December 2020

14   Jim Nichol, personal communication, December 2021.

15   Duncan Hallas, "A Soldier's Story", p12.

16   For more on Duncan's wartime experiences see also the interview "Swimming Against the Tide: Duncan Hallas on his Experiences in Egypt", *Revolutionary History*, Vol 8, No 2 (2002), www.marxists.org/archive/hallas/works/2001/02/egypt.htm

17   David Renton, "Bread and Freedom", *Revolutionary History,* Vol 8, No 2 (2002), www.marxists.org/history/etol/revhist/backiss/vol8/no2/renton.html

18   Frank Henderson, *Life on the Track: Memoirs of a Socialist Worker* (London: Bookmarks, 2009) p39.

19   Anon, "Political Life in Britain 1940-48: The Rise and Fall of Trotskyism", *Special Supplement to Correspondence*, Vol 1, No 31, 27 November 1954 (Detroit, Michigan: 1954). (NB: The article is anonymous but a minimal amount of detective work proves it was written by Alan Christianson).

20   Duncan Hallas, "Letter to Edward Grant dated 6 August 1952", Hull History Centre: Papers of Dr Edward Grant.

21   Raymond Challinor, "Unpublished memo on Socialist Review group, Duncan Hallas and Tony Cliff dated 24 November 2002", Society for the Study of Labour History collection at Warwick Modern Records Centre.

22   Harry Ratner, *Reluctant Revolutionary: Memoirs of a Trotskyist 1936-1960* (London: Socialist Platform Ltd., 1994) p189.

23   Anon, "Filey Notebook", *Socialist Advance. The Organ of the Labour Party League of Youth, June 1949* (London: Transport House, 1949) p11.

24   Sam Levy, "Letter to Brian Deane dated 7 September 1950", Warwick Modern Records Centre.

25   Bill Donnelly, Ted Morris & Don Hallas. "To All Members", Internal SRG document dated 28 February 1951.

26   Duncan Hallas, "Problems of Rearmament", *Socialist Review,* Vol 1, No 2 (January 1951) pp1–5, www.marxists.org/archive/hallas/works/1951/01/rearm.htm

27   Duncan Hallas, "The Permanent Crisis", *Socialist Review,* Vol 2, No 2 (June–July 1952), www.marxists.org/archive/hallas/works/1952/06/crisis.html

28   Gonzalo Pozo, "Reassessing the Permanent Arms Economy",

International Socialism, 127 (Summer 2010): p122, http://isj.org.uk/ reassessing-the-permanent-arms-economy/

29 Duncan Hallas, "The Significance of Nationalisation", *Socialist Review,* Vol 1, No 4 (May 1951), www.marxists.org/ archive/hallas/works/1951/05/nat. html

30 Duncan Hallas, "The Significance of Nationalisation".

31 Duncan Hallas, "The Significance of Nationalisation".

32 Stan Newens (1930-2021) personal communication, December 2015. Stan Newens was an early member of the SRG. He later became a Labour MP.

33 Tony Cliff et al, , *The Fourth International, Stalinism and the Origin of the International Socialists: Some Documents.* (London: Pluto Press, 1971).

34 Ellis Hillman (1928-1996) had been in the RCP but was only an SRG member for a short period.

35 J R Johnson and Freddie Forest were the pseudonyms of C L R James and Raya Dunayevskaya. They spent time in both the Workers Party of the USA and the US Socialist Workers Party. In September 1950 the Tendency published State Capitalism and World Revolution in the SWP's internal Discussion Bulletin.

36 Ian Birchall, *Tony Cliff: A Marxist for His Time* (London: Bookmarks Publications, 2011) p143.

37 See John Rudge, "Hillman, Hallas and the Stalinist Parties" for a fuller look at this episode of SRG history. *Grim and Dim website*, http://grimanddim. org/tony-cliff-biography/hillman-hallas-and-the-stalinist-parties/

38 Duncan Hallas, "The Stalinist Parties", Internal SRG document (July 1951, www.marxists.org/archive/hallas/ works/1951/xx/stalparty.htm

39 Stan Newens, personal communication, August 2016.

40 Duncan Hallas, "A Programme for Action", Internal SRG document (6 July 1952) *Grim and Dim website*, http://grimanddim.org/ tony-cliff-biography/duncan-hallas-and-the-1952-programme-for-action/

41 Duncan Hallas, "Letter to Edward

Grant dated 6 August 1952", Hull History Centre: Papers of Dr. Edward Grant.

42 John Rudge, "Duncan Hallas and the 1952 'Programme for Action'", *Grim and Dim website*, http://grimanddim. org/tony-cliff-biography/ duncan-hallas-and-the-1952-programme-for-action/

43 Duncan Hallas, "Agitation and Propaganda", *Socialist Review,* No 68 (September 1984) p10, www.marxists. org/archive/hallas/works/1984/09/ agitprop.htm

44 Stan Newens, *In Quest of a Fairer Society* (Washington, England: The Memoir Club, 2013) p66.

45 Duncan Hallas, "My Favourite Books," *Socialist Review,* No. 163 (April 1993) p25, www.marxists.org/archive/ hallas/works/1993/04/books.htm

46 Harry McShane (1891-1988) was a lifelong Glasgow socialist who at certain periods worked with the SRG/ IS/SWP.

47 T Dan Smith (1915-1993) was a Trotskyist for a period. He was later better known for his role in local politics in Newcastle and his imprisonment for corruption.

48 Tony Cliff, *A World to Win: Life of a Revolutionary* (London: Bookmarks, 2000) p101.

49 Michael Kidron (1930-2003) was a Marxist theoretician, economist, and editor of *International Socialism*.

50 E P Thompson (1924-1993) was a Marxist historian and author of *The Making of the English Working Class*, who left the CPGB in 1956 and became one of the founders of the New Left.

51 Michael Kidron, "Intellectual Liberalism?", *New Left Review*, No 7 (January-February 1961) p59.

52 Duncan Hallas, "The Socialist Register 1973 (book review)" *International Socialism*, 1: 69 (May 1974) p29, www.marxists.org/archive/hallas/ works/1974/05/register.htm

53 Stuart Hall (1932-2014) was a leading light in the New Left and a founder of *New Left Review*.

54 John Palmer personal communication, 3 May 2022. John Palmer joined the SRG in 1959.

55 James D Young (1931-2012) was an

SRG member for a short period. Later a well-known labour historian.

56   Letter to Mike Kidron from James D Young, May 1957.

57   Jack Robertson, personal communication, 25 November 2021

58   Introduction, *Edinburgh University Student's Handbook*, 1960-1961.

59   Chanie Rosenberg, "An Agitator of the Best Kind", *Socialist Review*, 268 (November 2002) p20, www.marxists.org/history/etol/writers/rosenberg/2002/11/hallas.html

60   Editorial, *Rank and File Teacher,* No 1 (April 1968).

61   Duncan Hallas, "Salaries—What Can We Do?", *Rank and File Teacher*, No 1 (April 1968) p6.

62   Chanie Rosenberg, "An Agitator of the Best Kind", *Socialist Review,* 268 (November 2002) p20.

63   Duncan Hallas, *The Comintern* (London: Bookmarks, 1985) p70-71, (my emphasis)

64   Tony Cliff, *A World to Win: Life of a Revolutionary* (London: Bookmarks Publications Ltd, 2000) p101.

65   Minutes of IS National Committee Meeting, 27 March 1971.

66   Danny Budzak, personal communication, 4 December 2021.

67   Frank Henderson, "An Agitator of the Best Kind", *Socialist Review,* 268 (November 2002), https://socialistworker.co.uk/socialist-review-archive/duncan-hallas-agitator-best-kind/

68   Ian Birchall, "An Agitator of the Best Kind", *Socialist Review*, 268, (November 2002), https://socialistworker.co.uk/socialist-review-archive/duncan-hallas-agitator-best-kind/

69   Chris Harman, "Obituary: Duncan Hallas 1925-2002", *Socialist Worker*, 1819 (28 September 2002).

70   Jim Higgins, "Duncan Hallas: Revolutionary socialist striving to build a mass workers' party", *Guardian*, 30 September 2002.

71   John Molyneux, "On Duncan Hallas", personal communication to John Rudge, 16 January 2022.

72   Duncan Hallas, "Introduction" to *The Fourth International,* (London: Socialist Workers Party, 1988) p1.

73   Duncan Hallas, *The Labour Party: Myth and Reality* (1st edition) (London: Socialist Workers Party, February 1981) p4.

74   Duncan Hallas, *The Comintern* (London: Bookmarks, 1985) p17.

75   Duncan Hallas, Jim Higgins, John Palmer & Roger Protz, "Socialist Worker—Perspectives and Organisation", *IS Internal Bulletin* (April 1974) p18.

76   Hallas in the Minutes of 11 May 1974 IS National Committee meeting

77   John Palmer, personal communication, 21 May 2022.

78   Ian Birchall, *Tony Cliff: A Marxist for His Time* (London: Bookmarks, 2011) p301.

79   Ian Birchall, "Speak One More Time (Book Review)" *Revolutionary History*, Vol 9 No 1 (2005) p281, www.marxists.org/history/etol/writers/birchall/2005/xx/higgins.html

The Stalinist Parties
Duncan Hallas
(July 1951)[1]

*This was Duncan's first major internal party document. In it he
provides the theoretical underpinning to the united front work
of the Socialist Review Group.*

In my opinion, Comrade Hillman's document is not a satisfactory
basis for this very important discussion. Therefore, I submit
this alternative. It is not a polemic against Comrade Hillman; to
deal with all the questions raised in *The Nature of the Stalinist
Parties*, some of which have only a remote connection with the
subject, would necessitate a document of formidable dimensions.
I cannot find the time to write such a document, and, much more
important, I suspect that many comrades would not find the
time to read it. The following, then, is a bare outline of my own
conceptions. (All unidentified quotations are taken from *The
Nature of the Stalinist Parties* by E Hillman.[2])

Trotsky's Analysis of the Stalinist Parties
Trotsky did not assume that "in some unspecified way,

the Stalinist parties were parties of the working class". His conception was perfectly specific. He designated them as centrist parties of a particular kind. Later (after the Seventh Congress of the Comintern) he decided that they had evolved into neo-reformist parties. These clear and concrete descriptions have become blurred by the use of the meaningless term "degenerated workers' parties", a term which may tell us something of their origin, but which tells us nothing at all of their present role, a term which covers all kinds of different analyses—hence its popularity within the FI in the post-war period. To avoid any possible confusion, I give Trotsky's definition in his own words:

> The ruling faction of the Comintern represents, not centrism "in general" but a quite definite historical form of centrism, which has its social roots, rather recent, but powerful. First of all, the matter concerns the *Soviet Bureaucracy*... The party as a self-controlling vanguard of the proletariat no longer exists. The party apparatus has been fused with the administration. The most important instrument of the "general line" within the party is the GPU [intelligence service]. The ruling and uncontrolled position of the bureaucracy is conducive to a psychology which in many ways is directly contradictory to the psychology of a proletarian revolutionary... In the course of a number of years the Stalinist faction demonstrated that the interests and psychology of the "strong peasant", engineer, administrator, Chinese bourgeois intellectual and British Trade Union functionary were much closer and more comprehensible to it than the psychology and needs of the unskilled labourer, the peasant poor, the uprising Chinese national masses, the English strikers, etc. But why, in that case, didn't the Stalinist faction lead to the very end of its line of national opportunism? Because it is the bureaucracy of a *workers' state*. Hence is derived the dual psychology

and policies of the Stalinist bureaucracy. *Centrism*, but centrism on the foundations of a *workers'* state, such is the sole possible expression for this duality.[3]

(Notice that Trotsky does not distinguish between the CPSU and the other parties of the Comintern. In fact, the article quoted from is concerned with, chiefly, the German Communist Party.)

A centrist tendency is, by definition, evolving either towards or away from Marxism. Trotsky believed that the fundamental evolution of the Comintern was towards classical reformism, just as the evolution of the Russian bureaucracy was towards the restoration of private (i.e. monopoly) capitalism. Hence he believed that the ultra-left line of the "Third Period" (1928–34) must inevitably be replaced by an ultra-opportunistic one.

> The Brandlerites, including the leaders of the SAP, remaining even today the theoretical pupils of Thalheimer, saw only "ultra-leftism" in the policies of the Comintern and denied (and continue to deny) the very meaning of bureaucratic centrism. We, on the other hand, were able to forecast with absolute precision the inevitability of a new opportunistic turn. The present (Fourth Period), when Stalin is pulling the European workers' movement on the hook of the Comintern to the *Right* of official reformism, demonstrates how shallow and opportunistic is the official philosophy of Thalheimer-Walcher and Co.[4]

The Seventh Congress of the Comintern in 1935 was, for Trotsky, the culmination of the evolution of Stalinism towards reformism.

> The "defence of the USSR" is the excuse—not the reason but the excuse—for the capitulation of the Cachins,

Jacquemottes, Gottwalds, etc., to the "public opinion" of "their own" bourgeoisie.[5]

The same idea is repeated several times in the fundamental document of the FI, e.g.:

The *definite passing over of the Comintern to the side of the bourgeois order*, its cynically counter-revolutionary role throughout the world particularly in Spain, France, the United States and other "democratic" countries, created exceptional supplementary difficulties for the world proletariat.[6]

Finally, in the event of war, the Stalinists would behave no differently from the reformists of 1914.

No less traitorous is the role played by social democracy and Stalinism in the face of the imminent war danger... They have neither the desire nor the possibility of organising the struggle against the coming imperialist war. On the contrary, completely corrupted by social patriotism and flying the pirate flag of "democratic" imperialism, they are already acting as recruiting sergeants of imperialism.[7]

This then is Trotsky's position. Bureaucratic centrist parties swinging right (1923), left (1924), right (1925–27), left (1928–33), right (1934) and finally ending up on the side of the bourgeois order (in its "democratic" form) from 1935 onwards. This conception is clear and unambiguous. We can now see that it is clearly and unambiguously wrong. The early war period (1939-41) cast doubt upon it. The postwar period (especially 1947 onwards) has finally disproved it. Today nobody but an imbecile can maintain that the Stalinist parties are capitulating to "their own" bourgeoisie. And nobody—not even the IS [The International Secretariat of the Fourth International]—does so. Hence we have to re-investigate the question. We cannot maintain our old position. It simply isn't there to maintain. What, then, are the Stalinist parties?

Workers' Parties?

Comrade Hillman—and also Shachtman[8]—is anxious to show that the Stalinist parties are not workers' parties. What is meant by this term? A party can be defined according to its composition, its leadership, or its programme—the real, not the formal programme—or according to a combination of these three factors. Comrade Hillman—and also Shachtman—take the leadership and (real) programme of the Stalinist parties and conclude that they are not workers' parties. In the case of Shachtman, the question of composition is ignored. In the case of Comrade Hillman an attempt is made to show that the composition is not predominantly proletarian, or that, if it is, workers become "declassed" when they join the party. Let us apply this method to a reformist party.

The leadership of, say, the British Labour Party (BLP) is not proletarian. It consists of trade union functionaries, lawyers, clergymen, doctors, professional "liberal" politicians, company directors, ex-civil servants, ex-university teachers, scions of the nobility, etc. It is formed of *various sections of the middle classes,* including an important (but numerically declining) group from the bureaucracy of the TUs. It is a *petty-bourgeois* leadership in ideology as well as in composition. The (real) programme of the party is neo-liberalist class collaboration and pro-imperialism. It is diametrically opposed to the struggle for the unity and emancipation of the workers in Britain or anywhere else. It is a petty-bourgeois programme—and a very reactionary one at that. Finally, the internal regime of the party is not democratic. The democratic façade conceals the dictatorship of the parliamentary leadership and the TUC bosses. All these facts are well known and beyond dispute. The conclusion that would have to be drawn from them, working by the Hillman-Shachtman method, could only be that the BLP is not a workers' party. But it is not only the BLP that has to be considered. All the other reformist parties have similar features; in some cases, without even the proletarian membership of the BLP (e.g. the SFIO). But practically the entire international working class is lined up behind the Stalinists and the reformists, or behind semi-fascist nationalist movements (Peron, Vargas, etc), or behind "democratic" bourgeois parties (MRP, Democratic Party of the USA, etc). Therefore, the logical conclusion to be drawn from the Hillman-Shachtman thesis is that there are no workers' parties at all in the world today. In one sense this is perfectly true, of course, for, if we define a workers' party by programme and leadership, then the only workers' parties are proletarian revolutionary, Communist Parties. That these do not exist (on any scale) is obvious.

However, this does not elucidate the question of the nature of the Stalinist parties. The whole discussion of "workers' parties" or "not workers' parties" is in fact a red herring. The only meaningful definition of a workers' party is in terms of composition. A party which bases itself mainly upon the working class is a workers' party. The nature of its leadership and programme has nothing to do with the question. Naturally, such a party cannot have *any* programme. It cannot have the programme (openly) of the Economic League or Hitler. Naturally also, such a party, with a petty-bourgeois leadership, must play a dual role corresponding to the conflict of interests between the leadership and the membership. All this is obvious. The reason we (as revolutionaries) are concerned with the question at all is because, in order to win the working class, it is necessary to approach such parties in a certain way. That is to apply the united front tactic to them in order to win the proletarian rank and file from the bourgeois ideologies of the leadership. No one has yet shown any other way of doing this.

However, Comrade Hillman (and also Shachtman) have another argument up their sleeve. Whereas the reformist parties have their basis in the bureaucracy of the trade union and co-operative movement and are tied to, are part and parcel

of, *bourgeois democracy*, Stalinism, like fascism, is a totalitarian movement which can only come to power by destroying
the workers' organisations. Since Stalinism is in an entirely
different category from reformism, the united front tactic
cannot be used against them any more than against the fascists.
Logically, one would suppose, the tactical approach to them
should be expressed in the slogan "Smash the Stalino-Fascists".
(Why not, Comrade Hillman?) This thesis, absurd as it appears
on the surface, contains *elements* of truth and must be carefully
examined.

Social-Fascist Parties?

This is in reality a theory of "social-fascism". It makes no
difference whether one calls the Stalinist parties "bureaucratic-
collectivist parties", "Red Fascism", "totalitarian state-capitalist
parties", or any other name. (We will leave Comrade Hillman's
personal aberration "totalitarian state-capitalist societies in
embryo" for another occasion. In reality, Comrade Hillman
draws his conclusions not from this conception but from the
social-fascist thesis.) The essence of this theory is that the
Stalinists, like the fascists, seek to, and under certain conditions
are able, to seize power, smash the working class and establish
a totalitarian society.

The theoreticians of this school are unquestionably correct
when they state that this is the aim of the Stalinist leaderships. They
are also correct when they say that the methods of Stalinism in
dealing with opposition are identical with those of fascism. Whenever it is able to do so, Stalinism reinforces its slander machine
with thugs and gunmen. Conditions permitting, the beating-up
and murder of opponents (especially revolutionaries) is a normal
Stalinist tactic. In this respect there is no distinction between the
storm-troopers of Hitler and the storm-troopers of Stalin.

There is a further analogy in the internal structure of their
parties and in the character of their propaganda and agitation. For all their pseudo-Marxism, the ideology of Stalinism
is as much based on leader-worship as that of fascism. The

psychology of Stalinism is similar to that of fascism (summed up in Mosley's slogan "ACTION!") and so on.

The fundamental defect in the social-fascist thesis is that it ignores the class struggle. Given that the Stalinist parties are social-fascist—and the description is not wholly inaccurate—the question is: *Can these parties take power in the same way as the fascists can (and have)?* The question has only to be posed to see the fallacy of the idea. Fascism in Germany, for instance, was a movement of petty-bourgeois and lumpen-proletarian radicals which *was lifted into power by the big bourgeoisie* in order to preserve monopoly capitalism or state-monopoly capitalism. In *no case whatever* did fascism seize power against the big capitalists—it could not do so. The only way to do so is to lead the masses into head-on conflict with the state machine and thereby smash it. But these same masses would not then permit the fascist bosses to enslave them. The result would not be fascism but socialism.

Now, unlike fascism, Stalinism seeks, not to preserve monopoly or state-monopoly capitalism, but to establish the "Russian System" (it is immaterial, for this argument, whether this system is called "bureaucratic collectivism", "bureaucratic state-capitalism", or what have you) and this system involves the liquidation of the big bourgeoisie (as a class) and their replacement by a single bureaucratic corporation. We can therefore say with complete confidence, that the big bourgeoisie will not lift Togliatti and Reimann into power as they lifted Mussolini and Hitler. (For notwithstanding Comrades Hillman and Shachtman the bourgeoisie is by no means baffled by "this movement that has hitherto defied logical explanation").

There are two other possible roads to power. The road of revolutionary struggle—from which the Stalinists are barred for exactly the same reason as the fascists—and the road of becoming gauleiters[9] for a foreign conqueror. This last road is the only real one (except under certain conditions discussed later). This is the reason, as Johnson (quoted by Hillman) correctly states, for their "loyalty" to the Kremlin—"sheer naked self-interest".

The objection will be raised that the theory that Stalinism cannot seize power against the bourgeoisie has been disproved in practice in two cases—Yugoslavia and China. In fact, the "exceptions" do not disprove the case but they do raise an extremely important issue. What had China and Yugoslavia in common? The simultaneous existence of an extremely weak and impotent bourgeoisie which did not control the state machine (in Yugoslavia the state machine was simply a shadow of the Wehrmacht, in China the state machine was in the hands of the Bonapartist clique of Chiang Kai-shek) and an extremely weak, scattered and impotent proletariat in a predominantly peasant country. Under these circumstances, it was possible for the Stalinists to build a Bonapartist military-state machine based on the peasantry and to conquer, by military means, a disintegrating opponent.

The resulting regime is bureaucratic state-capitalism imposed upon a primitive peasant agriculture. Obviously, then, we have to admit the possibility of the Stalinist parties taking power in other areas given similar conditions. In those countries where the bourgeois revolution was never achieved Stalinism represents a possible means of destroying the old society, given the impotence of the working class. The theory of Permanent Revolution has therefore to be modified to meet this case as also to meet the case of the bourgeoisie, again under exceptional conditions, achieving the main essentials of a bourgeois revolution. The theory then appears as a statement of revolutionary strategy and not as a law of development. This does not involve any modification of the conception that the Stalinists cannot seize power by a revolutionary struggle. The decisive battle for socialism must necessarily take place in the areas of proletarian concentration, i.e. in the advanced countries. The colonial revolts are only an auxiliary, an important auxiliary but only an auxiliary force.

The nature of Stalinism

Stalinism is a unique phenomenon. Like fascism, it is a "thing in itself" and not some variety of any well-known movement.

It is, as Hillman and Johnson stress, a product of the defeat and demoralisation of the working class. The Stalinist parties are, like both fascism and social-democracy, petty-bourgeois in their ideology and leadership. Like the social-democratic parties but unlike the fascist parties, they base themselves in the advanced countries upon the working class, i.e. they are "workers' parties". Like the fascist parties but unlike the social-democratic parties, they are totalitarian in structure and aim. Like social-democracy, Stalinism exists by virtue of the absence of a revolutionary proletarian movement. Marx said that society was more and more splitting into two great classes. This is true but it is also an oversimplification.

State-monopoly capitalism creates a whole series of inter-mediate castes or sub-classes whilst at the same time preserving large sections of the "old" petty-bourgeoisie (shopkeepers, small businessmen, etc) as its captives. The most easily recognised of these castes is the labour bureaucracy—the real backbone of "classical" reformism. But other castes, not tied fundamentally to bourgeois democracy, are also created—professional administrators, technicians of all kinds, some socially necessary engineers, chemists, etc, others purely parasitic—advertising agents, insurance brokers, etc. It is the aspirations of these strata that are reflected, in varying conditions, by both Stalinism and fascism. (Both movements gain substantial support also, from pre-capitalist survivals—especially the peasantry—in countries where these classes are numerically important.)

These groups do not invariably support either of the totalitarian ideologies—quite the reverse, they are often supports for social-democracy or "democratic" conservatism. But under conditions of great social conflict, given the absence of the revolutionary party, they are impelled against the working class either directly (fascism) or indirectly (Stalinism). There are considerable differences in the ideological content (apart from the obvious difference in form) of fascism and Stalinism corresponding to their differences in aim. Stalinism reflects more the "pure" managerial outlook of the "new petty-bourgeoisie" and the totalitarian labour bureaucrats with their contempt for bourgeoisie and proletariat alike. Hence its pseudo-rationalism and "marxist" phraseology. It is the most up-to-date "scientific" totalitarianism. Whereas fascism, with its irrationalism and Blood and Soil nonsense, has only violence to offer as a solution to the crisis of civilisation, Stalinism, proposing a radical reorganisation of class society in order to save class society, is able to dominate the working class, under favourable conditions, and thus it is the most reactionary (because most effective) of all the petty-bourgeois ideologies. On the other hand, its weakness, as compared to its rivals, is its inability to take power and its dependence upon the Kremlin bureaucracy. The fact that it is a "workers' party" (in the sense described) is its achilles heel as well as its strength. It is this vital distinction that enables it to be disintegrated by a growing revolutionary tendency instead of, as in the case of fascism, necessitating a frontal assault.

The struggle against Stalinism

The weakness of the "neo-reformism" conception of Stalinism is shown clearly by its inability to explain the facts of life. Its proponents are compelled to construct a dream world for themselves and thus become completely disorientated. This was the fate of the IS [the International Secretariat] and its adherents. Their latest lurch into pro-Stalinism is the result. The weakness of the "social-fascism" conception, on the other hand, becomes clear only when the question of a practical struggle against a mass Stalinist party is posed. Since this is not an issue in the USA, the falsity of Shachtman's line is not so clear as the stupidity of Cannon's. Once the question is faced—how do we win the workers from Stalinism?—the error of "social fascism" is obvious. The workers, far from ceasing to be such on joining the party, join (in the main) because for them the CP is the party of working-class struggle. They will break with Stalinism only in the course of struggle. Our whole future perspective is based on the conception that, in the long run, the class struggle will prove stronger than the most solid party apparatus. It is from this fact that the conclusions must be drawn. From this flows our line for the struggle against Stalinism—the tactic of the united front. Of course, this is not an immediate slogan. To demand that someone form a united front with us presupposes that we dispose of a force of our own—which we do not! Comrade Hillman is probably correct when he says that our forces will come, in the first instance, from left social-democracy—at least in many cases though not necessarily in all (e.g. in Germany our obvious line is to assist the leadership of the UAPD, Stalinist in origin, to a revolutionary position).[10]

But having got a cadre party, the question remains—how do we win the workers from Stalinism? The only serious answer is—in the same way as we win them from social-democracy, the united front tactic. Comrade Hillman says (correctly), "When the Stalinists operate a united front it is invariably *led* by them and is invariably bureaucratic, counter-revolutionary..." etc., etc. Of course. But this is not the question at all. The united front tactic presupposes also that the leadership of the anti-revolutionary organisation is against a united front. The whole point of the tactic is to unite the workers in spite of their leaders either by forcing them (by the pressure of their membership) into united action (the best variant) or by tearing away sections of their following. That this is more difficult in the case of a Stalinist organisation with its monolithicism, discipline and leader-cult than with the more heterogeneous social democracy, is indisputable.

To say that it is impossible is to ignore the dual character of the Stalinist party and to lose, in advance, any prospect of winning the workers away from it. The "social fascist" theory ignores the fact that every successful action by the working class enhances its self-confidence and its will to fight—and to that extent undermines the basis of Stalinism. An upsurge of the masses creates the possibility of building a revolutionary party. A defeat, as Comrade Hillman himself tells us, produces reaction and demoralisation. Obviously then we work to strengthen the upsurge—by trying to force the reactionary leadership into the fight. If the Stalinist leadership itself is prepared to conduct a struggle within certain limits (for its own reasons, of course) so much the better. Neither Comrade Hillman nor anyone else has told us any other method of participating in and helping forward the class struggle. Adherents of the "social-fascist" conception should ask themselves—why is it that the Stalinist leaderships are always against a united front with revolutionaries? Because it will strengthen Stalinism?

There is no doubt that the GPU is a serious threat in disturbed conditions—but the only way to fight it is by gaining a mass base. Moreover, the use of terrorism against revolution-aries is not avoided by a sectarian attitude towards Stalinism—it is enhanced as the revolutionaries have less contact with the Stalinist-influenced workers. To murder Erwin Wolf was simple, to murder Nin a great deal of trouble, to murder Vasquez impos-sible.[11] It is not a question of defensive precautions (necessary as these are) but of a mass base.

I have not dealt at all with the question of the struggle against Stalinism in power. This is simply the class struggle itself. There are many problems involved, of course, but they have no particular reference to this discussion.

Conclusion

The above is only an outline of a position. It does not deal with a great many minor difficulties or with the general prospects for Stalinism. The latter omission is deliberate. It is impossible to make short-term forecasts without fortune-telling and the future of the Stalinist parties depends above all on the development of a revolutionary movement. One topic must be touched upon, however. What is the probable evolution of Stalinist splinter groups? Several such groups have appeared in recent years ("Red Flag" group in Burma, Schappe and Co in Germany, Cuicci-Mangano in Italy, Le Cone in France, etc) and others are inevitable in the future. On the social-fascist theory these are merely rival aspirants for power in the (future) state-capitalist society—like Strasser or Leese in the Hitler and Mosley movements. This again illustrates the error of this theory. The very fact of breaking with the party compels such groups to struggle against the fountain head of Stalinism—and once having been forced into an anti-Moscow attitude they must necessarily rely upon gaining working-class support on a class struggle basis regardless of the needs of Russian diplomacy. The present line of Stalinism, which they have accepted, makes it difficult for them to go over immediately to social democracy and Belgrade is no substitute for Moscow. Thus they become centrist groups evolving towards a revolutionary position. As such, they offer a major possibility for us to win over.

On the other hand, no confidence can be placed in such groups in advance. Their leaders have had many years' training in bureaucratic manoeuvres and in many cases will no doubt prove incapable of freeing themselves from their past. Previous experience leads us to suppose that such elements will evolve towards social-democracy or fascism. But it is essential to remember that this experience was gained in a period of defeat. There is no *a priori* reason why such an evolution is inevitable. Above all the issue depends on the revolutionary forces, upon our ability to demonstrate *in practice* that we are capable of building a serious movement. Our attitude towards such groups must be one of friendly collaboration in practical work, together with firm political criticism. It would be fatal to approach such groups in an ultimatist spirit; no less fatal to ignore or white-wash their errors. Our approach to them, as to the Stalinist parties proper, must be based upon a practical, concrete programme of struggle against the bourgeoisie. Outside the Russian Empire and Yugoslavia it is sheer nonsense to assert that "the struggle against Stalinism is, in fact, the sharpest and highest expression of the class war". Exactly the opposite is the case. It is the struggle against the bourgeoisie and its social-democratic agents that is the decisive one. The struggle against Stalinism is subsidiary to that major conflict and flows naturally from it. Without in any way underestimating the difficulties and dangers of unity in action with the Stalinist workers we have to say that such unity is an absolutely essential step towards the goal of breaking up Stalinism. We have broken with the paralysing conception of workers' statism. We are in no danger at all of falling into pro-Stalinism: we are in considerable danger of following Shachtman and Co in the no less dangerous mistake of Stalinophobia.

Notes

1   From: Duncan Hallas (ed.), *The Fourth International, Stalinism and the Origins of the International Socialists* (London: Pluto, 1971) pp65–75. Marked up by Einde O'Callaghan for the Marxists' Internet Archive.

2   The full text of Hillman's original article is included as Appendix 1 in John Rudge's "Hillman, Hallas and the Stalinist parties", *Grim and Dim website* (September 2017) http://grimanddim.org/ tony-cliff-biography/hillman-hallas-and-the-stalinist-parties/

3   Leon Trotsky, "Centrism 'in General' and the Centrism of the Stalinist Democracy", in *What Next? Vital Questions for the German Proletariat* (January 1932) Ch 10, www.marxists. org/archive/trotsky/germany/1932-ger/index.htm. All emphases in original.

4   Leon Trotsky, "The Soviet Union Today" (footnote), *New International* [New York], Vol. 2, No. 4, (July 1935) pp116–122. www.marxists.org/ archive/trotsky/1935/02/ws-therm-bon.htm. Heinrich Brandler and August Thalheimer were leaders of the German Communist Party who were expelled in 1929 and went on to form the Communist Party Opposition (KPO) and were later centrally involved in the International Communist Opposition (ICO).

5   Leon Trotsky, "On the Seventh Congress of the Comintern", *New*

International, Vol. 2, No. 6 (October 1935) pp177–179. www.marxists.org/ archive/trotsky/1935/09/comintern. htm. Marcel Cachin was a leader of the French CP and editor of its newspaper *L'Humanité* from 1918 to 1958. Joseph Jacquemotte was the general secretary of the Belgian CP from 1934. Klement Gottwald was the leader of the Communist Party of Czechoslovakia from 1929 until his death in 1953. All were prominent members of the Comintern during the 1930s.

6   Leon Trotsky, *Transitional Programme of the Fourth International* (1938), www.marxists. org/archive/trotsky/1938/tp/ (My emphasis—D H)

7   Leon Trotsky, *Transitional Programme of the Fourth International,* 1938.

8   Max Shachtman was one of the founders of Trotskyism in the US. He went on to develop the theory of "bureaucratic collectivism" which defined the Soviet Union as a new form of society. He played a major part in "Third Camp" politics and was a noted polemicist. From the 1950s he moved ever rightward.

9   Gauleiters were regional political leaders of the Nazi Party (NSDAP) in Germany, equivalent to provincial governors. It was the third highest position in the Nazi leadership.

10   The UAPD (in English, the

Independent Workers Party of Germany), was a short-lived split from the Communist Party of Germany who took the side of Tito after the Yugoslavian leader broke with the Soviet Union.

11   Erwin Wolf was one of Leon Trotsky's most trusted secretaries in exile. He was abducted by the GPU (the Stalinist secret police) in Spain in September 1937 and is believed to have been murdered. Andreu Nin was the leader of the POUM (Party of Marxist Unification) a left-wing, anti-Stalinist party in Spain which led a sizable militia during the Spanish Civil War. He was arrested along with the entire leadership of the POUM in 1937, accused of being a fascist agent, and tortured to death by the Soviet secret police. Marià Rodríguez i Vázquez was regional secretary of the Catalan National Confederation of Labor (CNT), an anarcho-syndicalist trade union federation. Later he also held the position of national secretary of the CNT.

Cartoon from Teachers' Rank and File—*Phil Evans.*

Teachers
Duncan Hallas

(*International Socialism*, April/May 1969)

This was a "Survey" piece in which Duncan outlines for militants the key issues facing activists in the National Union of Teachers. In this article Duncan is "loading the bullets". In the same period Duncan wrote articles in Socialist Worker *and* Rank and File *as a militant teacher to make concrete the issues he outlined and turn them into winnable arguments and understandable and achievable objectives. In these other pieces Duncan was "firing the gun".*

When in February a special conference of the National Union of Teachers voted by 130,000 to 90,000 to accept the employer's final salaries offer, it voted to accept, without protest, a cut in real wages for the majority of its members. The increase offered and accepted was 6 percent on the basic scale to operate from 1 April 1969 until 31 March 1971. A 9 percent increase was needed to restore the purchasing power of the basic scale to the level of 1 April 1967!

How was it possible for an apparently representative conference to accept such a settlement? The answer is, in part, political.

The dominant ethos in the higher echelons of the union is liberal, social democratic and there is a strong conservative minority. The alternative to acceptance was strike action against the employers who are backed to the hilt by Her Majesty's "Labour" Ministers and such a struggle is the very last thing the gentlemen of the Executive (in the majority) wish to be involved in. To them the Government is not something you fight; it is something that hands out MBEs, OBEs and even knighthoods.

But of course this is not peculiar to the NUT. The decisive factor in the conference decision was something else. For a small but very influential section of the membership the award was a good one. It will put a lot of extra money into their pockets. They are the headteachers.

The agreement included a section on the alleged abolition of what is called the "primary-secondary differential". The effect of this is to give substantial increases to most primary head-teachers and their deputies and to many secondary heads. It will also create a number of extra above scale payments for assistant teachers—more bones for the rest of us to quarrel over. All this, of course at the expense of the basic scale on which about half the teaching workforce has to live.

The outstanding feature of the NUT is its complete domination at the top by the privileged minority of full-time administrators called headteachers. Not only is the executive completely controlled by them, they also dominate the great majority of local associations outside the London area and hence the national conference. Of course they are not them-selves homogeneous. Their incomes vary greatly according to size of school and other factors, and they include a minority of Leftish Labourites and CPers who identify themselves, in varying degrees, with the rank and file. Nevertheless the union structure is so heavily over-weighted by this group, whose pay and, perhaps more important, whose work situ-ation is radically different from those they are supposed to represent, that the aspirations of the ordinary members are muffled and distorted as effectively in this, on paper, fairly democratic union, as in some of the most bureaucratised workers' organisations.

Headteacher domination rests on a number of factors. The majority of the membership are women and for understandable sociological reasons, they have, in their great majority been relatively inert and passive members. Even today when this situation is beginning to change, a glance at any union conference shows an overwhelmingly male representation. The minority of men in the union provide the vast majority of activists.

Amongst the men a tradition of "deferential" conservatism has been influential, connected no doubt with the well established fact that teaching has been one of the main avenues of upward social mobility for the male children of skilled workers. Political conservatism is on the wane amongst active unionised teachers especially in the big centres, and some of the conservatives are now far from deferential but the old attitudes still retain influence in many areas. There are still plenty who believe "we should be led by those who are best qualified, most experienced and wisest", i.e. the heads.

Another factor of importance is the power of patronage possessed by headteachers. A considerable number of extra payments are available especially in secondary schools. In law, appointment to posts with extra payments is in the hands of the governors or managers of schools. In practice the headteacher is very often in a position to make his own choice and have it rubber-stamped by his nominal masters. It must be emphasised that school staffs have absolutely no say in such matters. Under these conditions, many teachers are cautious about opposing in the union men who can add a little cake to their bread and butter.

The completely autocratic structure of the school situation also reinforces conformity and "deference". The union has absolutely no effective "shop-floor" organisation. The union collector has no right to represent the members; in event of a dispute he must call on the services of the regional full-time official. But the person against whom the complaint is made i.e. the headteacher, will probably be a member of the union, perhaps even a local union officer. A young member in Wandsworth who recently appealed for help against gross discrimination by the head was told by union HQ that the union "could not advise one member against another"! Of course autocratic management in schools is often modified by personality factors. There are democratically-inclined heads and determined assistants who will resist intimidation. Many schools especially big comprehensives, have staff associations of varying degrees of effectiveness and the power of heads in big schools is modified to some extent by their need to work through departmental heads who will occasionally stand up effectively for their subordinates (and for their sectional interests). In spite of these qualifications the general pattern is one of hierarchical subordination to the boss, a pattern which is of course reproduced by the teacher in relation to his pupils and which tends to spill over into the union.

Some of the factors making for the supine and spineless attitude of the NUT are present also in its much smaller rival, the National Association of Schoolmasters, although to a lesser degree. The NAS is basically a reactionary organisation, formed originally to oppose equal pay for woman teachers. In recent years it has proposed various schemes e.g. family allowances and special increments for long and continuous service, which are intended to reintroduce unequal pay by the back door. Only men are admitted to membership and on social and educational issues, it is usually well to the right of the NUT. Notwithstanding these facts and also the absence from its ranks of politically committed militants, practically all of whom are in the NUT, the less "establishment" character of its leadership has allowed a limited militancy on certain issues. These have been for the most part wrong-headed or downright reactionary in their objectives. The current "work to rule" campaign which has led to suspensions of teachers and token strikes, has the aim of securing the reference of the teachers' salaries question to the Prices and Incomes Board or to an "independent" inquiry instituted by the Government! But however absurd the aim, the fact that the NAS has taken even a limited action increases its appeal to many militant but apolitical men teachers. In fact the leaderships of the two organisations feed upon one another; the NAS gains recruits as a result of the flunkyism of the NUT leadership and that leadership benefits from the draining off of militants from its own organisation into the blind ally of NAS sectionalism.

There can be no effective long term alternative programme and leadership in any union which does not have as its basis a political organisation. The opposition and potential alternative in the NUT was based, for many years on the Communist Party. The party had at one time substantial forces in the field. In 1960-61 there were according to an ex-member who was in a leading position in the CP teachers' faction at the time, some 2,000 card-holding party members in the NUT. The party's strategy was based upon the support of "progressive" candidates in union elections and upon the pressing of resolutions at various levels of the organisation. The maximum "unity" was sought around programmes that were acceptable to the more progressive members of the executive and the militants were kept in line by denunciations of sectarianism, adventurism and so on. The result, given the non-participation of the vast majority of the membership was the absorption of the party's leading activists into the union machine. They had some influence on policy, especially educational policy, but it was won at the price of tacitly accepting that policies basically unacceptable to the union leadership should not be pressed. At no time was the basic question of democratising the union, of headteacher domination, even raised. In fact the party's leading figure in the field, Max Morris, was and is a head teacher. The same is true of the prominent fellow travellers.

Today the party is no longer a serious force. Its members are hopelessly split on policy. At a recent meeting of the Inner London Teachers Association (a sort of district committee without any real power) a proposal from the militant Wandsworth Association that the ILTA call an unofficial token strike on the salaries question was narrowly defeated by 28 votes to 25. Many of the prominent CP members supported the motion;

others including the president of the Surrey District of the party voted with the right wing! There are still devoted and self-sacrificing CP militants in the union. There are other CP members who have made their peace with the establishment. The decline of the party is, in the short run, a mixed blessing. It has, undoubtedly, strengthened the right wing. It has also permitted the evolution, as yet on a small scale, of an authentic opposition which is uninhibited by the supposed need to win friends amongst executive members.

The loose grouping of IS, ex-CP, and unaffiliated militants around the journal *Rank and File* is as yet very fragile. The influence of the paper (circulation now around 4,000) is limited but growing. It does constitute a nucleus, the only nucleus in sight, around which the industrial and political militants can crystallise. Already the executive is considering organisational countermeasures. A number of known activists face disciplinary charges. The strategy of *Rank and File* centres around a single issue, democratisation of the schools and of the union. The two are inextricably bound together as this article has tried to demonstrate and, contrary to the shrill criticism of some sectarians, they are *political* issues of the first importance.

The educational structure is an extremely sensitive part of the capitalist state machine and the school system is perhaps even more important in this connection than the higher educational system. The basic function of schools in Britain today is to turn out docile and suitably trained units who will fit into the slots provided by the economy. Docility is the main aim of the authoritarianism dominant in schools. When it is challenged the basis of the whole system is threatened.

The long run prospects of cracking the rigid structure of both school and union structure have been enormously enhanced by the pupil protest movement now developing. This promises to be the axe to the root of the traditional British autocratic school. It challenges the authority of all teachers but above all it challenges the autocratic rule of headteachers. Left wing teachers have the duty to identify with and support this movement. Their struggle is our struggle. There will undoubtedly be victimisation of both pupils and staff. The fight against these will constitute one of the most important aspects of our work.

The next few years will be stormy ones in education. Teachers now face the certainty of declining real wages; pupils are beginning to question the system; the struggle in the schools and in the union will sharpen. Easy optimism would be misplaced. The ideological resources of the system, not to mention its repressive apparatus, are still very great. Whether or not socialist militants can develop the cohesion and determination to make themselves a real force in education is still an open question. If they can the possibilities are enormous.

The Meaning of Marxism, *International Socialists pamphlet, London, 1975.*

Hallas's Marxism
Alex Callinicos

I was fortunate enough to work with Duncan Hallas for close on 20 years, from the mid-1970s till his retirement in 1995, first as his deputy at *International Socialism* and then as a fellow member of the Central Committee of the Socialist Workers Party. Political collaboration with him—together with Tony Cliff and Chris Harman—has been one of the great privileges of my life. What I want in this chapter is to capture something of both his style and substance as a political thinker.[1]

Duncan would probably have laughed at the idea of himself as a political thinker. Though, in some moods at least, immensely self-confident, he was a modest man. But everyone who encountered him was deeply struck by his brilliance. Cliff—who was not easily impressed—told me once that when he first knew Duncan in the 1950s ("we called him Don then," he said), his accomplishments seemed so great that Cliff thought he would be another Trotsky.

Duncan would have laughed at that as well (he had, incidentally, a wonderfully infectious, mischievous laugh). He saw himself, I think, as an educator, someone who passed on the revolutionary Marxist tradition to new generations, most notably those radicalised by the mass movements that swept across the world between the 1960s and the 1980s (and not just in Britain, but also in societies as different as the United States and South Africa). He was indeed an educator—as I will try to show, a supremely accomplished writer and speaker, and certainly was no Trotsky (who is?). But, as Duncan himself well knew, Trotsky used to emphasise that continuing a tradition involves *selection*—in other words, interpreting the tradition to identify those elements that merit passing on. This is a creative process. And Duncan was a highly creative Marxist, who developed an enormous and profound historical knowledge that informed his own attempts to expound and apply this tradition.

But, of course, it's not enough to say that Duncan was both a populariser and practitioner of revolutionary Marxism. He used occasionally to chide me for my interest (which abides to this day) in the work of the French Marxist philosopher Louis Althusser. Althusser was a member of the French Communist Party who struggled unsuccessfully with its Stalinist history and increasingly reformist present, and whose often arcane theoretical writings reflected his distance from practice. Duncan's Marxism couldn't have been more different: from his teens onwards he was a Trotskyist for whom the self-emancipation of the working class was central and theory was empty unless linked organically to the struggle to build a revolutionary party.

Pungent realism

Understanding Duncan's contribution to Marxism therefore must focus centrally on his relationship to Trotsky and Trotskyism. But before I come to that, I want to say something about his *style* as a Marxist. By this I mean something that isn't easy to put one's finger on, but which is important in understanding the kind of Marxism he practised. He himself would have stressed that he didn't make the kind of original intellectual contribution that Cliff made above all in founding the International Socialist tradition, crucially by developing the theory that the USSR was a bureaucratic state capitalist society, and that Harman did in a number of different areas. But that doesn't mean that Duncan wasn't exemplary in *how* he pursued Marxism.

I wrote soon after Duncan's death: "His whole intellectual style was informed by a kind of pungent realism—an insistence on bluntly stating the facts and facing up to their consequences".[2] I had in mind, I think, Bertolt Brecht's concept of "crude thinking" (*Plumpes Denken*). Brecht's friend the great Marxist critic Walter Benjamin elaborated:

> There are many people to whom a dialectician means a lover of subtleties. In this connection it is particularly useful when Brecht puts his finger on "crude thinking" which produces dialectics as its opposite, contains it within itself, and has need of it. Crude thoughts belong to the household of dialectical thinking precisely because they represent nothing other than the application of theory to practice: its *application* to practice, not its *dependence* on practice. Action can, of course, be as subtle as thought. But a thought must be crude in order to come into its own in action.[3]

Perhaps "plain thinking" better captures Duncan's approach, but Benjamin's reference to practice certainly fits. For Duncan the simple, sometimes brutal description of material realities was essential to orienting what Marx calls "revolutionising practice". This was reflected in how Duncan wrote. Like Cliff, he never learned how to type. But, unlike Cliff, who relied on his partner Chanie Rosenberg to type up his writing (in the process turning it into proper English), Duncan would deliver his copy handwritten. It was easily legible by the typesetters and composed (usually with little correction) in short, punchy sentences.

Sometimes, they were almost telegraphic but still conveying much content. Here's a late example, from a review of a book on the military history of the Second World War: "Moreover, Ellis ignores the civilian casualties—British (substantial), German (enormous), Russian (catastrophic), Chinese (worse than that) and Japanese (remember Hiroshima and Nagasaki)".[4]

There was, I think, quite a lot of artifice in this plain style. But it wasn't writing for its own sake, but usually to convey a political point. So here is Duncan defending party-building in an article on sectarianism: "Of course, this may sometimes be attempted in an arrogant or insensitive fashion (not, I hope, by SWP members, or not very often), but that is not so much sectarianism as stupidity".[5] This light-touch admission that SWP members might get things wrong and indeed even be stupid was typical. One thing that Duncan had in common with Cliff was self-deprecation—they might not suffer fools gladly, but they encouraged us not to exaggerate our own importance relative to the powerful class forces that dominate society.

Bragging and bluster are an unfortunate characteristic of many far-left groups, and Cliff and Duncan sought to counter any temptation in this direction—in Cliff's case by self-deflating humour ("Who knows? When the revolution comes I may lie on my bed crying"), in Duncan's by forcing us to confront harsh realities. Occasionally he applied this medicine to Cliff himself. I well remember, at a Central Committee meeting during the early phase of the Great Miners' Strike in spring 1984, Duncan deflating an elaborate speculation by Cliff that the union leadership would strike a compromise with the Tory government by pointing out that it takes two sides to make a deal and there was no sign that Thatcher was interested.

Cliff himself used to say that Marxism was polemical. He meant, I think, that a theory that starts from the fundamentally fractured and antagonistic nature of existing society and orients itself towards revolutionary working-class practice necessarily takes sides and that this partisanship is reflected in how we write and speak. But it was Duncan who was a real master of polemic. In a review of my book *Making History* he chided me for taking the various schools of Analytical Marxism too seriously:

The "Marxist" variant of this trend of thought, e.g. constructions that Alex Callinicos calls Orthodox Historical Materialism (OHM *à la* Cohen), "Rational-Choice Marxism" etc etc, are not to be refuted by logical arguments but, in the first case, by argument from history and experience, and in the second by ridicule—it is exactly on a par with the ultra-right wing theory of "rational expectation" in economics. And is as absurd.[6]

Duncan did ridicule very well. Here he is on the "Post-Althusserian" Paul Q Hirst:

But does that entitle us to dismiss his views on historical writing? On *his* principles, yes. For Hirst says that "writing must be governed by considerations of its political value and not its contribution to the 'discipline' of history."

The political value of this volume is zero.[7]

Or again on John Callaghan's biography of the Stalinist ideologue R Palme Dutt: "It is wearisome to continue an account of the life of this scoundrel. For Callaghan to represent him as a genuine Communist is an insult to the intelligence of his readers".[8]

But most importantly Duncan's distinctive political style was mobilised to persuade. He was a superb speaker, and some of his best performances displayed his pungent realism very effectively. I remember particularly the so-called *Debate of the Decade*, a huge event organised by Peter Hain and the Labour Coordinating Committee (a broad groupiong of the left within Labour) in March 1980. The debate was essentially a confrontation between the Labour left, represented particularly by Tony Benn, Audrey Wise and Stuart Holland, and what was still the extra-parliamentary left, including Paul Foot, Tariq Ali and Hilary Wainwright. The pyrotechnics from the platform were disappointing (partly because of disruptive sectarian stunts), but Duncan was given two minutes to speak from the floor. He started with "Two minutes, two points", and proceeded with highly compressed but remorseless logic to dismantle left Labourism (see Jack Robertson's chapter in this book for the text).

This was at the high point of Bennism, and many in the audience would soon have voted with their feet and joined the Labour Party, if they hadn't already. But those ready to hear Duncan would have been inoculated against the illusions that would all too soon be dashed. I hope readers of this book will be inspired to read some of Duncan's writings and listen to some of his speeches in the Marxists' Internet Archive, experiencing him as directly as is now possible.

Most of Duncan's substantial literary output took the form of pamphlets, articles and book reviews (which contain many of his finest gems). He wrote only two books. The first, *Trotsky's Marxism* (1979), was written under high pressure after Perry Anderson, then editor of *New Left Review (NLR)*, blocked the publication by Pluto Press of a book by Ernest Mandel on Trotsky marking the centenary of his birth. Presumably Mandel, the main leader of the Fourth International, was too highly prized an author for the *NLR* publishing house (soon to become Verso) to let him be poached by a rival, and it was they who brought out his book.

Pluto had originally been, in effect, the IS publishing house, and was still run by two ex-IS members, Mike Kidron and Richard Kuper. Cliff came to their rescue by volunteering Duncan to fill the resulting gap. Maybe Duncan benefitted from the tight deadline imposed by the centenary and from badgering from Cliff. I can bear personal witness that his other book, *The Comintern* (based in part on articles Duncan had originally published in *International Socialism*), required a lot of editorial input from Bookmarks. He was, it seems, happiest writing shorter pieces, and splendid so many of them are.

Where did Duncan's distinctive intellectual style originate? An article called "My Favourite Books" from 1993 is revealing. Some of the list is predictable enough—two books by the Marxist archaeologist V Gordon Childe, Marx's political writings on France, above all *The Eighteenth Brumaire of Louis*

Bonaparte, and Trotsky's *History of the Russian Revolution*. So too is the fiction—detective stories (a taste Duncan shared with Mandel, often a butt of his criticism) and Voltaire's brilliant, witty satire *Candide*. But then there are J M Robertson's *Short History of Christianity*, from the old rationalist anticlerical Thinker's Library, buttressed by a Marxist study by Archibald Robertson "(no relation)", *The Bible and Its Background*, and the Victorian Whig Thomas Babington Macaulay's multi-volume *History of England from the Accession of James the Second*.

Today Macaulay is probably chiefly remembered for his *Minute on Indian Education*, which dismissed the value of the indigenous cultures of colonised India and advocated creating an Anglicised Indian middle class. His *History* focuses on the "Glorious Revolution" of 1688, which consolidated bourgeois rule in Britain. Duncan often praised or quoted the book in conversation and at meetings. Here he writes:

> Most modern academic historians scorn this splendid book. It represents the "Whig interpretation of history" and revolution—even of the very limited revolution of 1688 and is anathema to the academics. We can learn from it, from its class limitations, from its understanding of the revolutionary process and, above all, from the confidence of the mid 19th century bourgeoisie as compared with the wretched, short sighted incompetence of our rulers today.[9]

These literary preferences signal that Duncan was a relatively late example of a tradition of working-class autodidacts who helped to define British Marxism from its emergence in the late 19th century. This tradition had its roots in the older radical-democratic movements of the 18th and 19th centuries, which were infused with the rationalism and anticlericalism of the militant wing of the Enlightenment. Stuart MacIntyre in an important study shows how a layer of socialist and trade union activists, denied access to formal education beyond primary school, would make themselves into worker intellectuals through attending evening classes and lectures, but crucially through their own reading of popular science, anthropology, religious criticism, history, and the Marxist literature that became increasingly available in the first decades of the 20th century:

> And in whichever direction their interests lay, these autodidacts exhibited a characteristic intellectual tone: they were great respectors of fact and intellectual authority; earnest, even reverential, in their treatment of the text; and they brooked no short cuts in the search for knowledge. Alongside this deference to literary authority, one must put the fact that it remained their education, for they defined both the purpose and the boundaries of their intellectual exploration and the books they read assumed significance in this light. Thus an original interest in the doctrine of the creation could lead from the *Freethinker* to Darwin or Huxley, and thence to Haeckel's *Riddle of the Universe*, Morgan's *Ancient Society* and sometimes Engels's *Origin of the Family, Private Property and the State*; or an interest in history might commence with Gibbon, Macaulay, Lecky or Buckle and subsequently assume an increasingly sharp focus on the basis of the current social order, thus leading to Marx's historical writings.[10]

The range and seriousness of this proletarian self-education is astonishing. I remember once seeing in the library of Stirling University the huge and intellectually very diverse collection of books that a Glasgow engineering worker had donated. This tradition declined in the second half of the 20th century— Marxism became more or less the monopoly for a while of the Communist Party, which was able, particularly from the 1930s onwards, to attract and use the skills of relatively large numbers of middle-class graduates; post-war university expansion and the associated increase in social mobility provided greater working-class access to formal education. This was the context in which, thanks to the radicalisation of the 1960s, a much more plural Marxism (albeit often of a highly academic kind) became relatively widely available in universities.

Duncan, a Manchester engineering worker who went to university as a mature student and became a schoolteacher, stood in many ways at the cusp of these changes. In any case, thanks both to his own abilities and the stimulating intellectual environment offered even by the Trotskyist micro-groups of the 1940s and 1950s, he developed into a worker-intellectual who was in no sense deferential to the books he read so voraciously. But in the range of his reading and his insistence on writing and speaking in a popular and accessible style he recalled those earlier working-class autodidacts.

History and freedom

Duncan made what he read his own. The most important example of this is offered by his interpretation of historical materialism as a theory of freedom. Here he is in 1987, commenting on Chris Harman's important article, "Base and Superstructure":

> "There is a confusion at the very centre of Marxism" (p4).[11] This is a mistaken formulation. There is indeed a contradiction between two sides, two aspects, of our attempt to grasp reality in order to change it; but that is by no means the same thing as a confusion. The contradiction is rooted in the reality and cannot be solved by theoretical refinements, but only by transforming that reality and then only by a certain, although large, degree.
>
> On the one hand "freedom". "History does nothing, it possesses no immense wealth, it wages no battles. It is man, real living man that does all that... History is nothing but the activity of man pursuing his aims" (Marx and Engels in *The Holy Family*). All that happens in society is the result of human action.

This is surely right and the only scientific approach; anything else leads to mysticism, God or that kind of mechanical materialism which denies the essential distinguishing characteristics of the human species.

On the other hand "constraint". "In the social production of their life, men enter into definite relations which are independent of their will, relations of production which correspond to a definite stage of development of their material productive forces.

This too is surely right. It is a foundation, a central pillar of historical materialism.

The contradiction between "freedom" and "constraint" can be solved *formally* in a statement. Nobody has ever done this better than Marx himself in a famous passage in *The Eighteenth Brumaire of Louis Bonaparte*:

"Men make their own history, but they do not make it just as they please; they do not make it under circumstances chosen by themselves, but under circumstances directly encountered, given and transmitted from the past."

Yet this statement, this formal solution, does not predict a determinate outcome. Nor could it, or any variant or elaboration of it, because of an inherent limitation in the nature of our knowledge... There is therefore an element of indeterminacy in Marxism (and in any conceivable scientific theory of society). And that element of indeterminacy is not simply a matter of our relative ignorance but is inherent in the nature of our understanding; of our interaction with other forces in society.[12]

This statement highlights what is distinctive to Duncan's Marxism. In the first place, he rejects any understanding of historical materialism as a deterministic theory of history. Marxism isn't about the development of the productive forces inevitably bringing about revolution by what Karl Kautsky called "natural necessity", but about how human beings, constrained by their place in concrete social relations, above all structures of class exploitation and domination, struggle to free themselves. The brilliant Albanian Marxist philosopher Lea Ypi made the same point in her own way much more recently:

> Each year, I begin my Marx course at the London School of Economics by telling students that many people think of socialism as a theory of material relations, class struggle or economic injustice but that, in reality, something more fundamental animates it. Socialism, I tell them, is above all a theory of human freedom, of how to think about progress in history, of how we adapt to circumstances, but also try to rise above them.[13]

Secondly, a theory of freedom is necessarily political. In Duncan's case, there is surely a direct connection between his understanding historical materialism in this way and his commitment to Marx's conception of socialism as the self-emancipation of the working class. But because freedom is exercised under constraint, "under circumstances directly encountered, given and transmitted from the past", we need to understand these circumstances—in other words, to study history. Duncan's vast erudition essentially encompassed the whole course of human history, from the earliest hunter-gatherer societies to the global capitalism of the late 20th century, but with a practical political intent.

Thirdly, history is an open process where our actions make a difference. Duncan elaborated on this last point in his little book on Trotsky:

> "Men make their own history," Marx said, "although they do not do so under conditions of their own choosing." The "voluntary" acts of millions and tens of millions of people who are, of course, themselves historically

conditioned, pressing against constraints imposed by the whole course of previous historical development (of which the millions are, typically, unaware) produces effects more complex than the most far-sighted theorist can foresee. The degree of *on s'engage, et puis... on voit* (get stuck in, and then we'll see), which was Napoleon's aphoristic description of his military science, must always be considerable for revolutionaries engaged in a conscious attempt to shape the course of events.[14]

Duncan is quoting Lenin here, though his translation of Napoleon is, typically, punchier (an example of Brecht's *Plumpes Denken*, perhaps). Looking back, close to the end of his active life on the Bolsheviks' gamble on world revolution in seizing power in October 1917, Lenin scornfully dismissed Menshevik criticisms of the revolution based on a deterministic reading of Marx. He wrote: "Napoleon, I think, wrote: *'On s'engage et puis... on voit.'* Rendered freely this means: 'First engage in a serious battle and then see what happens'".[15] So revolutionaries make choices in circumstances where much is uncertain. Duncan's stress on the limits of our knowledge would sometimes irritate Cliff, who was always adamant that we had to pursue single-mindedly whatever the leadership—and usually he—had correctly (or so he thought) identified as the key tasks of the day. Duncan was temperamentally more cautious, but his understanding of history gave an essential role to the conscious, organised action undertaken by human beings.

Their Trotskyism and ours

The political tradition to which Duncan was won in his teens and to which he adhered for the rest of his life was Trotskyism. The first organisation he joined—the Workers International League, later Revolutionary Communist Party (RCP), which played an important role in British workers' struggles during the Second World War—left an abiding mark:

Our own tendency was formed during these debates and emerged as the Socialist Review Group in 1950–51. It was necessary, in the process, to reject much of the RCP's theoretical baggage. One thing the Socialist Review Group did inherit was the model (even if only as an aspiration at times) of an active, flexible, interventionist (where possible) organisation whose fixed point of reference was working-class struggle. And that was vital.[16]

But Duncan's debt to his initial Trotskyist formation made it important to understand what it meant to be a Trotskyist in the decades after its founder's murder by a Stalinist agent and the fragmentation of his movement into rival tendencies. This was the context in which the IS tradition emerged. It defined itself by, simultaneously, the refusal to follow the Fourth International leadership in transforming the analyses of capitalism and Stalinism Trotsky had developed during the 1930s into an unchallengeable orthodoxy and the insistence nevertheless on continuing the revolutionary Marxist tradition as a means of understanding and transforming the world.[17]

Now the heavy lifting here was, as I have already noted, done by Cliff. It was he who developed the theory of state capitalism as an alternative to Trotsky's conception of the USSR as a degenerated workers' state and applied it to Russia itself and later to Eastern Europe, China and Cuba. The other crucial contribution to our theory in the 1950s and 1960s, the analysis of the role of arms expenditure in stabilising Western capitalism after the Second World War, though implicit in Cliff's *State Capitalism in Russia*, was developed by Kidron and later extended and updated to address the return of serious economic crises from the 1970s onwards by Harman.

It is noteworthy, however, that Duncan's first article in *Socialist Review* was about the Labour government's massive rearmament programme—a symptom of "the drift towards the third world war".[18] Writing 18 months later, he argued that, though "rearmament is not the cause of the crisis, in a sense it is a solution." For "the root cause of all economic difficulties in capitalist society is the problem of what the economists call "effective demand"; in other words, how to sell the people more goods than they have money to buy, and to do this at a profit to boot!" From this perspective, "Rearmament is like a snowball; once an arms race has begun, governments can never have enough".[19]

Duncan thus anticipated by five years Cliff's own study of the permanent arms economy (PAE).[20] But both were hampered by their reliance on an underconsumptionist theory of crises, according to which they are caused by a shortage of effective demand. One of the great strengths of Kidron's version of the PAE analysis was that he placed it firmly within the framework of Marx's law of the tendential fall in the rate of profit.[21] Duncan nevertheless developed a deep understanding of Marxist and bourgeois political economy that is reflected, for example, in an incisive 1970 review of Kidron's *Western Capitalism since the War*.[22]

Once the initial break with the Fourth International (FI) was accomplished, Cliff showed little interest in any further appraisal of Trotskyism. He concentrated on making sense of what was going on and on spotting and acting on opportunities to build an initially minuscule revolutionary group. As our moment came during the great upturn of the late 1960s and early 1970s, Cliff's theoretical focus was on Lenin, the master party-builder, to whom he devoted a three-volume biography. Only in his last years did he return to Trotskyism with his massive four-volume biography of Trotsky (1989-93) and *Trotskyism after Trotsky*, published in 1999, the year before his death. This left Duncan to play the decisive role in defining where we stood in relation to Trotskyism.

This was especially important after Duncan returned to IS in 1968. Thanks to the explosive growth of the student movement, the group more than doubled in size to about 1,000 members in the course of that miraculous year. Absorbing this intake of enthusiastic but unruly young revolutionaries required both politically educating them and turning them towards a confident and well-organised working class in increasing conflict with first Labour and then Tory governments seeking to curb their militancy and cut their wages. Duncan played a critical part in this process, in the first instance in the debates that convulsed IS in 1968 over whether or not the group should adopt democratic centralism, in effect, embracing the Leninist model of revolutionary party-building. Appearing from nowhere, visibly of a different generation with his short back and sides and tweed jacket among the denim-wearing long-hairs, overwhelmingly knowledgeable and eloquent, Duncan had an electric effect.[23]

But it was also politically vital to define our relationship to Trotskyism. Trotskyist tendencies dominated the British far left; Maoism, very influential elsewhere in Europe and the rest of the world, had only a marginal presence here. The main Trotskyist organisation in Britain during the 1950s and 1960s was the Socialist Labour League (SLL, soon to become the Workers Revolutionary Party). Its leader, Gerry Healy, had presided over the destruction of the RCP in the late 1940s. He developed a political style combining dogmatic catastrophism, tactical opportunism, the brutal repression of internal dissent and (so it proved) sexual exploitation.

The big fish in the small pool of the British far left at the height of the Cold War, the SLL lost its dominance amid the upsurge of workers' and students' struggles in the late 1960s. The tiny circle that stayed loyal to the FI leadership were able to connect much more effectively with the mood of the time as the International Marxist Group, drawing on the prestige of their French comrades such as Alain Krivine and Daniel Bensaïd for their role in the events of May-June 1968, and winning Tariq Ali, the main leader of the Vietnam Solidarity Campaign. Meanwhile, still burrowing away within the Labour Party Young Socialists was the Militant Tendency, dominated by yet another RCP leader, Ted Grant, which would become a major force in the 1980s.

So where did we stand in relation to these different Trotskyist currents? Were we Trotskyists at all, and if we were what kind of Trotskyists were we? It was Duncan who answered these questions. He did so in two ways. First and most obviously through his writings and secondly through his practice. His writings on the subject started with "Building the Leadership", a critique of the SLL published in *International Socialism* in 1969, then two articles on the history of the Fourth International that Duncan as editor published in *International Socialism* in 1972-3, the book *Trotsky's Marxism* (1979), and an important 1982 account of the Trotskyist experience of "entrism" in the Labour Party, once again in *International Socialism*.

Trotsky's Marxism

Trotsky's Marxism stands out among these texts. It is a remarkable achievement of concise but rich exposition and critique. Duncan made clear the grandeur of Trotsky's achievement—leadership in the Russian revolutions of 1905 and 1917 and the Civil War of 1918-21; theorist of permanent revolution; and indomitable critic and analyst of the Stalinist degeneration of the 1917 Revolution. But he also pointed to the limits of Trotsky's assessment of the global situation in the years leading up to the outbreak of the Second World War in September 1939.

Trotsky argued that the Great Depression of the 1930s marked capitalism's inability further to develop the productive forces. The widely anticipated war would stimulate another revolutionary upheaval, perhaps even greater than that in which the First World War had ended. This would sweep away both the reformist labour bureaucracy and the Stalin regime in the USSR. The Fourth International, which had a few thousand followers when it was launched in September 1938, would rapidly become a mass force: "During the next ten years the programme of the Fourth International will become the guide of millions and these revolutionary millions will know how to storm earth and heaven".[24]

The actual outcome of the war was of course very different. On the one hand, the development of the permanent arms economy thanks to the Cold War made possible the strongest and most sustained boom in capitalism's history, which gave reformism a powerful new lease of life. On the other hand, Duncan wrote:

> The USSR emerged from the war stronger than before (relative to other powers) with the bureaucracy firmly in the saddle on the basis of nationalised industry. Moreover, it imposed regimes along the lines of the Russian model in Poland, Czechoslovakia, Hungary, Rumania, Bulgaria, East Germany and North Korea... "indigenous" Stalinist regimes came to power in Albania, Yugoslavia and, a little later, in China and North Vietnam *without* significant direct intervention by the Russian army. Stalinism, evidently, was not in its "death agony" but was, in the absence of proletarian revolution, an alternative means of capital accumulation to "classical" state monopoly capitalism.[25]

Duncan identified two main sources of Trotsky's error. Theoretically, he confused the construction of a state owned industrial economy in the Soviet Union during the 1930s with the transcendence of capitalism. State ownership, not workers' power, for him made a society a workers' state, albeit, in the case of Stalinist Russia, one where the party-state bureaucracy led by Stalin had "politically expropriated" the working class.[26] Trotsky refused to admit the possibility that the USSR had become a state capitalist society. But, Duncan pointed out:

> For Marx, the bourgeoisie's significance was as the personification of capital. In the USSR the bureaucracy fulfils this function. This last point Trotsky directly denied. For him, the bureaucracy was merely "a gendarme" in the process of distribution, determining

who gets what and when. But this is inseparable from the direction of the process of capital accumulation. The implication that the bureaucracy does not direct the accumulation process, that is, does not act as the "personification" of capital, will not stand a moment's examination. If not the bureaucracy, then who? Certainly not the working class.[27]

One might add that Trotsky's dismissal of the idea of state capitalism facilitated his prediction that the system had hit the buffers economically. For Cliff had already shown in *State Capitalism in Russia* that it was the pressure of military competition with Western imperialism—Britain in the 1920s, Germany in the 1930s, the United States during the Cold War—that enforced the priority of capital accumulation on the Stalinist bureaucracy.[28] Nikolai Bukharin had shown during the First World War that the geopolitical rivalries between the major imperialist powers promoted the growth of militarised state capitalism in the Western economies. After 1945, the new phase of these rivalries in the form of the Cold War gave rise to the PAE that allowed capitalism a new lease of life.[29]

Duncan's presentation of the theory of state capitalism in *Trotsky's Marxism* is of course hugely indebted to Cliff. But in one respect it improves on the original. Cliff had argued that labour power was not a commodity in the USSR.[30] Without explicitly contradicting him, Duncan writes:

The form of property (state ownership in this case) cannot be considered independently of the social relations of production. The *dominant* relation of production in the USSR (especially after industrialisation) was the wage labour/capital relationship characteristic of capitalism—and still is. The worker in the USSR sells a commodity, labour power, in the same way as a worker does in the USA. Nor is he or she paid in rations like a slave, or in a share of the produce like a serf, but in money which is spent on commodities, goods produced for sale.[31]

Duncan was entirely right in this. Cliff's main argument to the contrary, that workers in the USSR confronted a single capital in the shape of the state and thus lacked the freedom of their Western counterparts to change jobs, ignored the considerable competition for workers by individual *enterprises* that made possible a high level of labour mobility. Duncan would go on a little later to criticise the revival of Cliff's argument by Peter Binns and Mike Haynes.[32] Here, then, he strengthened the theory of state capitalism.

Duncan had already made an independent contribution to the theory. In his classic essay "The Stalinist Parties" (1951) he criticised the argument of followers of Max Shachtman, who argued that the USSR was a "bureaucratic collectivist" society, and the Communist parties reactionary tools of totalitarianism. Duncan showed that the latter were bureaucratically led workers' parties that would be pulled in different directions by the class struggle and challenged by the use of the united front tactic—something that we were able to start to undertake in the 1970s.[33]

Duncan also defended the theory of state capitalism. As editor of *International Socialism* in 1976, he devoted most of an entire issue to a response, written by him and Binns, to a clumsy attack on the theory by an economist from the Eurocommunist right wing of the Communist Party. It was a sign of IS's growing influence in the mid-1970s that the CP, then still the strongest force on the radical left in Britain, began to mount critiques of our theory. Duncan led our counter-attack with great relish.

The article shows his polemical skills working at full throttle. But it also makes another important theoretical contribution, developing Marx's conception—most fully stated in the "Critique of the Gotha Programme"—of the dictatorship of the proletariat as marking the transition from capitalism to the "higher stage of communist society" that would be governed

*The CP attack the theory
of state capitalism.*

*The International
Socialists reply.*

by the principle: "From each according to their abilities, to each according to their needs!"[34]

> A working class in power cannot introduce socialism by decree. Bourgeois right (in the original German the word—*Recht*—also means law) has an objective basis—scarcity and men moulded by scarcity—which cannot be abolished by edicts. The proletarian revolution is necessarily an abrupt and rapid overturn. The period transitional to socialism, the period of workers' states, is necessarily a prolonged period of *gradual* transformation of the relations of production and *of the producers themselves.*
>
> In a workers' state, or in a group of workers' states, wage labour, commodity production, money and the rest persist, with diminishing force, for a period which may be quite lengthy—depending on world developments. So, therefore, does alienation, social inequality (within certain limits), the division between manual and mental labour and state repression (the function also of a *workers'* state). In Marx's words:

"What we have to deal with here is a communist society, not as it has *developed* on its own foundations, but, on the contrary, just as it *emerges* from capitalist society; which is thus in every respect, economically, morally and intellectually, still stamped with the birth marks of the old society from whose womb it emerges".[35]

But the *trend*, the direction, in a workers' state is towards reducing the importance of these *capitalist* features, which it inevitably inherits. Thus, there is a progressive expansion in the range of goods and services which are supplied on a non-monetary basis—from public libraries, sanitation, hospital care, education (which are *already*, under developed capitalism in Britain, supplied in a distorted quasi-"communist" way—this is what Engels meant by "*the invading socialist society*") to public transport, housing, basic foodstuffs, clothing and so on. And so to a progressive reduction of the importance of money and so to a progressive erosion of real income differences and so to the gradual "withering away" of the wages system, of commodity production and of the state. The workers remain wage earners but they are no longer, strictly speaking, proletarians.

They have political power and political and economic categories gradually fuse.[36]

Here again, without any fanfare, Duncan was developing our theory in a way that showed his materialist realism. Somewhat ironically, given Duncan's hostility to Althusser, the only counterpart to his approach to the dictatorship of the proletariat with which I am familiar was written at more or less the same time by Althusser's close collaborator Étienne Balibar.[37] But Duncan's treatment of state capitalism shares with those of Cliff and Harman an important weakness: as Sheila McGregor has pointed out, they failed to build on Trotsky's analysis of how the Stalinist degeneration of the October Revolution involved the restoration of heteronormative family structures oppressing women as the main mechanism for reproducing labour power.[38]

Nevertheless, Duncan's improvements on Cliff's original theory underline that he was much more than the transmitter of ideas formulated by others. Delving in the treasure trove of his writings uncovers other examples. There is, for instance, "In a Class of Our Own", one of the articles included in this book. Here, writing in his column in *Socialist Worker* in 1975, Duncan deftly explains the nature of the modern working class—setting out Marx's conception of capitalist exploitation, finessing theoretical complications such as productive and unproductive labour, and analysing the nature of white-collar work, with clarity, concision and authority. Re-reading this text I was humbled to see how Duncan in a few hundred words solved the problem that a few years later I devoted thousands to addressing in an article on the "new middle class". This was typical of how Duncan quietly but decisively demonstrated that Marxism could make sense of the contemporary world.

The second source of Trotsky's mistaken predictions, and especially what Duncan called "the element of near-messianism" in his expectations for the Fourth International, was socio-political:

> Inevitably, his enforced isolation from effective participation in the workers' movement, in which he had once played so big a part, affected to some extent his understanding of the ever-changing course of the class struggle. Not even his vast experience and superb tactical reflexes could substitute entirely for the lack of feedback from the militants engaged in the day-to-day struggle that is possible only in a real communist party. As the period of isolation lengthened, this became more apparent.[39]

What was an almost inescapable consequence of Trotsky's circumstances in the 1930s became politically catastrophic when his heirs had to grapple with the very unexpected situation that confronted them after the Second World War. In his *International Socialism* articles Duncan paid tribute to what the generally tiny Trotskyist groups had been able to achieve "swimming against the stream" during the gigantic wartime clash of military and class forces. After all, one of these groups had provided Duncan with his own baptism in revolutionary politics. But he was relentless in anatomising the inability of Trotsky's epigones to respond effectively to the geopolitical and economic transformations that unfolded at the end of the war.

This involved in the first instance denying reality. Thus Mandel tried to explain away the signs of post-war economic recovery in Britain, and got skewered by Cliff, replying on behalf of the RCP leadership.[40] The US Trotskyist leader James P Cannon went even further, announcing in November 1945, long after Germany and Japan had surrendered:

> Trotsky predicted that the fate of the Soviet Union would be decided in the war. That remains our firm conviction. Only we disagree with some people who carelessly think the war is over. The war has only passed through one stage and is now in the process of regroupment and reorganisation for the second. The war is not over, and the revolution which we said would issue from the war in Europe is not taken off the agenda. It has only been delayed and postponed, primarily for lack of a sufficiently strong revolutionary party.[41]

This was followed by the transformation of what the Fourth International had inherited from Trotsky into what Cannon called "orthodox Trotskyism". The crucial move came in the attempt to overcome the contradiction arising from the fact that the new Stalinist regimes rapidly developed politico-economic structures identical to those in the USSR—statised economies underpinned by the Communist Party's monopoly of power, while their origins lay, not in a workers' revolution that had undergone bureaucratic degeneration, as Trotsky had argued with respect to the Soviet Union, but, in the case of Central and Eastern Europe and North Korea, military conquest by the Red Army, and in Yugoslavia, Albania, China, and North Vietnam, the victory of Communist-led peasant armies. Eventually, the FI leadership affirmed that they too had broken with capitalism:

> The lead was taken by Michael Pablo [of the FI secretariat]. Yugoslavia, he decided, was a workers' state, deformed yes, but a workers' state. And if Yugoslavia, then by the same token Bulgaria, Poland, East Germany, China, in fact all the Stalinist regimes. That is to say 40 percent of the world's population now live in workers' states and, except for the USSR, these states have not been created by working-class revolutions. Orthodoxy had now given rise to the most gigantic revisionism. Not only Trotsky but Marx and Lenin too had been wrong in thinking that only the working class could overthrow capitalism.[42]

Cliff pointed out in 1950 that this involved the abandonment of Marx's conception of socialism as the self-emancipation of the working class:

> Marx repeated hundreds of times that the proletarian revolution is the conscious act of the working class itself... Therefore, if we accept that the "People's Democracies" [in Central and Eastern Europe] are workers' states, what Marx and Engels said about the socialist revolution being "history conscious of itself" is refuted.[43]

As this concluding act brings out, the failure of orthodox Trotskyism was at once intellectual and political. Politically, the fundamental problem lay, as Cliff and Duncan stressed, in the idea that socialism could be achieved by forces other than the working class—a conclusion that licensed all sorts of adventurism and opportunism. Intellectually the problem was not primarily that of specific errors in analysis—everyone commits these, but of method. Immunising Trotsky's theories from refutation encouraged an intellectual style that refused to address changed realities. Sectarians of the likes of Healy took this to extremes, but even a figure as talented and erudite as Mandel became skilled in evading inconvenient facts. As both Gramsci and Cliff pointed out in different ways, the biggest cost of such dishonesty is that one deceives *oneself*—failing to start from a realistic appreciation of the situation and of revolutionaries' usually highly precarious place within it.[44]

The test of practice

This brings me to the second way that Duncan showed us what kind of Trotskyists we were—by example. He held Trotsky in enormous respect.

The last sentence of *Trotsky's Marxism* declares: "To all those Marxists for whom Marxism is a synthesis of theory and *practice*, and not merely more or less learned commentary, it [Trotsky's heritage] is an indispensable contribution to that synthesis today".[45] But this respect was, as we have seen, never uncritical, any more than we have been uncritical of Marx himself, Engels, Lenin, Luxemburg, Gramsci and the rest. And we rejected what Duncan called the "theoretical baggage" of orthodox Trotskyism.

One implication of this rejection was the political choice to stay away from the orthodox Trotskyist milieu and its sectarian controversies. Our orientation was always on real movements and not the internecine squabbles of the far left. It was Cliff who set the norm here. His reference point was always what was happening in the more powerful forces on the reformist left, in the Labour Party and (till its demise after 1989) the Communist Party. Duncan in his public role maintained the same stance, though he often enjoyed a chuckle at some other group's discomfiture.

When the Fourth International organised a rally at Friends Meeting House in Central London in January 1977 to denounce

Healy's campaign to brand the American Trotskyist leader Joseph Hansen a KGB agent, the SWP Central Committee wouldn't let Duncan join the platform of notables. He still sneaked upstairs to enjoy from the gods what proved to be a night of sectarian fun as Mandel denounced "Thomas Gerald Healy" as "a stupid little rascal" and Tariq Ali in the chair refused to allow Healy, surrounded by a phalanx of bodyguards, to speak from the floor.[46] (Readers may have guessed that I too gave way to temptation.)

How then to continue the Trotskyist tradition, particularly in the light of such negative examples? Here Duncan's style, discussed above, was invaluable. It involved at once a consistent orientation on practice, the refusal to inflate our own importance and influence ("Big Flame—big mouth, more like it" was his devastating dismissal of an autonomist group active for a while in the car industry), and the careful study of the empirical situation, embracing both its objective tendencies and the state of the class struggle. His deep knowledge, moreover, of the history and politics of the British working-class movement was also invaluable.

Duncan's time in the IS/SWP leadership embraced a series of sharp shifts in the class struggle—the upturn of the late 1960s and early 1970s that forced the Tories from office in 1974, the Portuguese Revolution of 1975-6, the rise and fall of Eurocommunism, the shift in the balance of class forces in Britain in the second half of the 1970s that paved the way for an all-out capitalist offensive under Margaret Thatcher during the 1980s, a decisive step in the global imposition of neoliberalism, the collapse of the Stalinist regimes in 1989-91 and the emergence of New Labour under Tony Blair and Gordon Brown.

Navigating these upheavals, assessing the state of consciousness in the working-class movement, and steering the organisation through what were often difficult tactical turns were demanding tasks. Duncan's influence was at its greatest during the 1970s. This was a time of great hope and great disappointment. The massive workers' struggles against the Tory government of 1970-4 were one of the high points of the global upturn.

They provided the context in which IS could not simply grow numerically but create a number of factory branches that made it a real workers' organisation.

But Labour's return to office in March 1974 dramatically changed the situation. In particular, the left-wing ministers who were strongly represented in the new government—above all Michael Foot and Tony Benn—could command the loyalties not just of powerful trade union leaders such as Jack Jones and Hugh Scanlon but of the shop stewards who had led the struggles of the past few years on the ground. Initially, we thought the Labour government would enjoy a brief "honeymoon" before the class confrontation would resume at a more intense pitch. We were badly mistaken, and underwent a series of internal crises that continued till after Margaret Thatcher's election victory in May 1979.

The start of this turbulent period saw Duncan pitted against Cliff. In the heady climate of the anti-Tory struggle, Cliff had adopted a misguided policy of giving free rein to a group of young and talented organisers who had led the construction of the factory branches. For them Duncan (who was briefly removed from the full-time leadership) represented a conservative small-group past that needed to be swept away; indeed one of this group, Andreas Nagliatti, influenced by Italian "Mao-centrism" (particularly the big far-left organisation Avanguardia Operaia), proposed a frontal critique of the entire Trotskyist tradition.

Duncan led the challenge to this policy from a section of the old leadership. It became public after Labour's return to office and forced Cliff to retreat. He later told me that Nagliatti had demanded that he expel Duncan. Cliff replied that if he did this, we would end up with 500 members. Nagliatti said it didn't matter. To which Cliff responded: "Yes, but you won't be one of the 500." The exchange shows both Cliff's good judgement of people and his awareness of Duncan's importance. Duncan proved to have much more staying power than these supposed "hard men", who, once rebuffed by Cliff, rapidly exited revolutionary politics.[47]

Duncan also played his part in the next crisis the SWP experienced in those years, in 1977-9. When our expectation that Labour's honeymoon would be short-lived was dashed, we were thrown into disarray. Cliff was the first in the leadership to develop an analysis that brought together the increasing bureaucratisation and incorporation of rank-and-file workplace organisations with the grip that reformist ideology continued to exercise at every level of the workers' movement. But Duncan quickly lent his own authority in support.

It is an important weakness of Ian Birchall's otherwise excellent biography of Cliff that his account of this crisis is mistaken in claiming that Cliff's analysis of the downturn only became a major issue in 1979.[48] In fact Cliff first put it forward at the meeting of the SWP National Advisory Committee in February 1978, where it was attacked as a manoeuvre to justify our ceasing to run candidates in elections (one of the issues under debate then). Typically realistic in his assessment of the working-class movement, Duncan backed him up: he had already noted "the incapacity and unwillingness to fight of the reformist plant leaderships" under Labour.[49]

He was the only member of the Central Committee (CC) openly to side with Cliff at this meeting. As a new member of the CC, I was too timid to speak, but I agreed with Cliff as well, and commissioned and conducted the interview where he set his analysis in the first issue of the new *Socialist Review*.[50] What is true is that Cliff hadn't really worked out the implications for our practice. These only emerged in 1982-3 when Andy Strouthous as Manchester district organiser pioneered what became known as the "propaganda perspective" of large branches focusing on discussing the Marxist tradition. This was a good example of how to learn from practice; Duncan must have been pleased it happened in his native city.

In the 1980s he moved to a more backseat role. My personal hunch is that the time he spent living with Cliff and Chanie for whatever reason damaged the relationship between the two men, and also undermined Duncan's self-confidence. The dynamics on the Central Committee also changed, particularly after Chris Harman resumed the editorship of *Socialist Worker* in 1982 while managing also to continue writing a stream of important books and articles. Chris offered another powerful source of intellectual authority that was especially attractive to the younger members of the CC.

Duncan receded somewhat into the background, though he still wrote. His book *The Comintern* (1985) paid tribute to the Communist International and traced its later decline. Trotsky had sought to defend its achievements after the October Revolution against the Stalinist bureaucracy as it started to crystallise in the early 1920s. The book shows Duncan working at full power, demonstrating his usual grasp of historical detail, clarity in presentation—and capacity for robust argument. It has introduced thousands of militants to the authentic communist tradition as it was in its years as a mass force.[51]

Many more pamphlets, articles and reviews continued to pour from Duncan's pen (indeed, of his texts on the *Marxists Internet Archive*, 78 were written between 1951 and 1979, and 67 between 1980 and 2002). And he remained ever in demand as a speaker. In my obituary I recalled "a magical evening in Dublin a decade or so ago. Duncan and I were due to speak for our Irish sister organisation. While the two of us waited for the meeting to start, I sat rapt as Duncan discoursed on the origins of class society".[52] I was only one of many to enjoy this experience.

Duncan set what would now be called a benchmark—in his speeches at the endless branch meetings he spoke at as well as the Marxism annual festivals, in the articles he wrote in *Socialist Worker* and *Socialist Review*, in his interventions at conferences and other national meetings of the SWP, and in conversation, especially pint in hand in the pub. In his fidelity to the Marxist tradition, while refusing to make a religion of it, and in his practice of what Gramsci called "good sense", he showed how to be a working-class revolutionary in the last decades of the 20th century.

Notes

1   I'd like to thank Colm Bryce, Sheila
McGregor, Jack Robertson, John
Rudge, and Dave Sherry for their very
helpful comments on this chapter in
draft. I'm particularly grateful to John
Rudge, who came up with the idea
of this tribute, worked tirelessly to
achieve it, and enriched it with his
research into Duncan's life and into
the illustrations.

2   Alex Callinicos, "Duncan Hallas—
Thinker, Orator, Revolutionary",
Socialist Review, 267 (October 2002),
www.marxists.org/archive/hallas/
biog/callinicos-sr.html

3   Walter Benjamin, *Understanding
Brecht* (London: NLB, 1973), p81.

4   Duncan Hallas, "Running a
Temperature", *Socialist Review,* 172
(February 1994) www.marxists.org/
archive/hallas/works/1994/02/ww2.
htm

5   Duncan Hallas, "Sectarianism",
Socialist Worker Review, 75 (April
1985) www.marxists.org/archive/
hallas/works/1985/04/sectar.htm

6   Duncan Hallas, "Unworthy
Opponents", *Socialist Review*, 107
(March 1988), www.marxists.org/
archive/hallas/works/1988/03/
unworthy.htm

7   Duncan Hallas, "Zero Rating", *Socialist
Worker Review*, 74 (March 1985)
www.marxists.org/archive/hallas/
works/1985/03/zero.htm

8   Duncan Hallas, "The Shyster Lawyer",
Socialist Review, 167 (September 1993).

9   Duncan Hallas, "My Favourite Books",
Socialist Review, 163 (April 1993),
www.marxists.org/archive/hallas/
works/1993/04/books.htm

10   Stuart MacIntyre, *A Proletarian
Science: Marxism in Britain,* 1917-1933
(Cambridge: Cambridge University
Press, 1980), p71. This fascinating book
attracted both praise and criticism
from Duncan: Duncan Hallas, "The
Proud Tradition", *Socialist Worker
Review*, 98 (May 1987) www.marxists.
org/archive/hallas/works/1987/05/
prolesci.htm

11   Duncan is quoting here from Chris
Harman, "Base and Superstructure",

International Socialism 2: 32 (Summer
1986), www.marxists.org/archive/
harman/1986/xx/base-super.html

12   Duncan Hallas, "Comments on Base
and Superstructure", *International
Socialism*, 2: 34 (Winter 1987),
www.marxists.org/archive/hallas/
works/1987/xx/basesuper.htm

13   Lea Ypi, *Free: Coming of Age at the
End of History* (London: Allen Lane,
2021), p305.

14   Duncan Hallas, *Trotsky's Marxism*
(London: Pluto Press, 1979), p18.

15   V I Lenin, (1923) "Our Revolution
(Apropos of N Sukhanov's Notes)",
in *Collected Works*, Vol 33 (Moscow:
Progress, 1965), available at www.
marxists.org/archive/lenin/
works/1923/jan/16.htm

16   Duncan Hallas, "The Sad Fate of
British Trotskyism", *Socialist Review*,
91 (October 1986) p21, www.marxists.
org/archive/hallas/works/1986/10/
brittrot.html, reviewing Sam
Bornstein and Al Richardson, *War
and the International: A History of
the Trotskyist Movement in Britain*
1937-1949 (London: Socialist Platform,
1986). I have removed what was
presumably an editorial interpolation
that replaced *Socialist Review* with
Socialist Worker Review—an ill-
judged name change for the magazine
during the 1980s. The group's history
and metamorphosis into first the
International Socialists and later
the Socialist Workers Party can be
followed in some detail in Ian Birchall,
Tony Cliff: A Marxist for His Time
(London: Bookmarks, 2011).

17   See my own account of this process,
enormously indebted to Duncan's
writings: *Trotskyism* (Milton Keynes:
Open University Press, 1990),
available at www.marxists.de/
trotism/callinicos/index.htm

18   Duncan Hallas, "Problems of
Rearmament", *Socialist Review*, 1:2
(January 1951), www.marxists.org/
archive/hallas/works/1951/01/rearm.
htm

19   Don Hallas, "The Permanent Crisis",
Socialist Review, 2: 2 (June–July 1952),

www.marxists.org/archive/hallas/
works/1952/06/crisis.html

20   Tony Cliff, "Perspectives of
the Permanent War Economy",
Socialist Review, 6: 8 (May 1957),
www.marxists.org/archive/cliff/
works/1957/05/permwar.htm

21   Joseph Choonara, "The Monetary
and the Military: Revisiting Kidron's
Permanent Arms Economy",
International Socialism 171 (Summer
2021), http://isj.org.uk/kidron-pae/

22   Duncan Hallas, "Western Capitalism:
The Latest Phase", *International
Socialism* 1: 44 (July/August 1970),
www.marxists.org/archive/
hallas/works/1970/xx/westcap.
htm, reviewing Michael Kidron,
Western Capitalism since the War
(Harmondsworth: Penguin, 1970).

23   See the account of IS in 1968 in
Birchall, *Tony Cliff,* ch7.

24   Leon Trotsky, *Writings* 1938-39 (New
York: Pathfinder, 1974), p87.

25   Hallas, *Trotsky's Marxism,* p112.

26   Leon Trotsky, *The Revolution Betrayed:
What is the Soviet Union and Where
is it Going?* (New York: Pathfinder,
1972), available at www.marxists.org/
archive/trotsky/1936/revbet/

27   Hallas, *Trotsky's Marxism,* p110.

28   Tony Cliff, (1948) *State Capitalism in
Russia* (London: Bookmarks, 2022),
ch7. www.marxists.org/archive/cliff/
works/1948/stalruss/ch07.htm. Cliff's
original document, "The Nature of
Stalinist Russia", has been published
in Cliff, *Selected Writings,* Volume 3
(London: Bookmarks, 2003).

29   The connections are well brought
out in Chris Harman, *Explaining the
Crisis: A Marxist Reappraisal* (London:
Bookmarks, 1984), ch3, www.
marxists.org/archive/harman/1984/
explain/03-today.html

30   Cliff, *State Capitalism in Russia,* pp241-
3.

31   Hallas, *Trotsky's Marxism,* p110.
Duncan had first put this argument
forward a few years earlier in Peter
Binns & Duncan Hallas, "The Soviet
Union: State Capitalist or Socialist?",
International Socialism, 1: 91
(September 1976).

32   Duncan Hallas, "Eastern European
Class Societies", *International

Socialism,* 2: 9 (Summer 1980),
www.marxists.org/archive/
hallas/works/1980/xx/eeursoc.
htm, commenting on Peter Binns
and Mike Haynes, "New Theories
of East European Class Societies",
International Socialism, 2: 7 (Winter
1980), www.marxists.org/history/
etol/writers/binns/1980/xx/
newtheories.html I also criticised this
article in "Wage Labour and State
Capitalism: A Reply to Peter Binns
and Mike Haynes", *International
Socialism 2:* 12 (Spring 1981), www.
marxists.org/history/etol/writers/
callinicos/1981/xx/wagelab-statecap.
html. Cliff's own views are a bit of a
mystery, since, as Duncan points out
in his reply to Binns and Haynes, he
demonstrated the high level of labour
mobility even under high Stalinism in
a piece first drafted only slightly after
"The Nature of Stalinist Russia", "The
Theory of Bureaucratic Collectivism:
A Critique", in Cliff, *State Capitalism in
Russia,* pp369-73, www.marxists.org/
archive/cliff/works/1948/xx/burcoll.
htm#s7.

33   Duncan Hallas, "The Stalinist
Parties", www.marxists.org/
archive/hallas/works/1951/xx/
stalparty.htm I am indebted here
to the scholarship of John Rudge
in recovering the original 1949
version of Cliff's "Bureaucratic
Collectivism" article and comparing
it with the published version,
probably drafted in the early 1960s.
The original does not contain the
discussion of the Stalinist parties
in the later version: John Rudge,
"Tony Cliff and Bureaucratic
Collectivism", http://grimanddim.
org/tony-cliff-biography/tony-cliff-
and-bureaucratic-collectivism/

34   Karl Marx and Friedrich Engels,
Collected Works, Vol 24 (Moscow:
Progress, 1989), p87 (translation
modified).

35   Marx and Engels, *Collected Works,* Vol
24, p85.

36   Binns & Hallas, "The Soviet Union:
State Capitalist or Socialist?", replying
to David Purdy, *The Soviet Union—
State Capitalist or Socialist? A Marxist
Critique of the International Socialists*

(London: Communist Party of Great Britain, 1976).

37   Étienne Balibar, *On the Dictatorship of the Proletariat* (London: New Left Books, 1977), esp chV.

38   Sheila McGregor, "Sexism, Socialism, and the State: Women and the Eastern Bloc", *International Socialism,* 2: 170 (Spring 2021), http://isj.org.uk/eastern-bloc-women/, and Trotsky, *The Revolution Betrayed,* ch7.

39   Hallas, *Trotsky's Marxism,* p95-96.

40   Tony Cliff, (1947) "All That Glitters is not Gold: A Reply to Germain's 'From the ABC to Current Reading: Boom, Revival or Crisis?'", in Cliff, *Marxist Theory after Trotsky, Selected Writings, Volume 3,* (London: Bookmarks, 2003), www.marxists.org/archive/cliff/works/1947/09/glitters.htm. Mandel's document can be found here: www.marxists.org/archive/mandel/1947/11/abc-reading.html

41   James P Cannon, *The Struggle for Socialism in the "American Century"* (New York: Pathfinder, 1977), p200.

42   Duncan Hallas, "Building the Leadership", *International Socialism,* 1: 40 (October/November 1969), www.marxists.org/archive/hallas/works/1969/xx/building.htm

43   Tony Cliff, (1950) "On the Class Nature of the 'People's Democracies'", in Cliff et al, *The Fourth International, Stalinism, and the Origins of the International Socialists: Some Documents* (London: Pluto, 1971), available at www.marxists.org/archive/cliff/works/1950/07/2.htm#con

44   See my account of how these tendencies played out in some varieties of orthodox Trotskyism in Callinicos, *Trotskyism,* ch3. One of Mandel's own comrades, Daniel Bensaïd, wrote quite a stringent critique of his quasi-Kautskyan historical outlook: "Thirty Years After: A Critical Introduction to the Marxism of Ernest Mandel", (2007) www.marxists.org/archive/bensaid/2007/07/mandel.htm

45   Hallas, *Trotsky's Marxism,* p117.

46   The official text of Mandel's speech—preserved here www.marxists.org/archive/mandel/1977/01/frameup.html—is somewhat bowdlerised.

47   There is a good account of this conflict and the relationship between Duncan and Cliff in Birchall, *Tony Cliff,* chs8 and 9.

48   Birchall, Tony Cliff, ch9 and 10. I'm grateful to Jack Robertson, like me a neophyte CC member at the time, for confirming my chronology of the downturn debate.

49   Duncan Hallas, "Editorial", *International Socialism* 1: 85 (January 1976), www.marxists.org/history/etol/newspape/isj/1976/no085/editorial.htm

50   Tony Cliff, "Where Do We Go from Here?", *Socialist Review*, 1 (April 1978), www.marxists.org/archive/cliff/works/1978/04/interview.htm

51   Duncan Hallas, *The Comintern* (London: Bookmarks, 1985), available at www.marxists.org/archive/hallas/works/1985/comintern/index.htm

52   Callinicos, "Duncan Hallas".

Trotskyism Reassessed
Duncan Hallas

(*International Socialism*, July 1977)[1]

I'll try to go through every idea that we are talking about and try to show the roots—where did it come from? Well let's start from when we broke from traditional Trotskyism. Now we broke on one simple thing, on the Russian question. That was the central issue of our time.

Now what did we accept from Trotsky? We accepted from Trotsky first of all that the working class is the agent of the socialist revolution; that the working class is the subject, not the object, but the subject of the socialist revolution; that the criterion to every change in society is what role the working class is playing actively in it...

The second thing we took straight from Trotsky is opposition to all rising bureaucracies. Thirdly we took from Trotsky the theory of the impossibility of socialism in one country, the fact that the pressure of world capitalism distorts development in every workers' state, in this case the Russian workers' state. We also accepted from Trotsky the question of the international nature of the revolution. These things we accepted from him. Now what were the defects, where didn't we agree? Now what we thought was wrong with Trotsky was this, that if it was true that the working class was the agent of socialist revolution then the form of property is a bloody stupid criterion for deciding whether a state is a workers' state or not... What the worker as an active agent cares about is the relations in production, in other words what place the worker is in the process of production; whether the worker comes to a state enterprise like the railways or private enterprise like ICI, he doesn't come in relation to it as regards the form of property... Trotsky was not consistent enough in his own criteria of approach.

Second of all, planning is not a criterion for judging the nature of the state because the question is who is being planned and who is doing the planning... The central thing is quite simply that we came to the conclusion that workers' control is the decisive thing in evaluating a workers' state... and therefore a workers' state is a state where the workers control their destiny. It cannot be given to them. They have to do it themselves. Once you abolish the element of workers' control, you abolish the essence of the workers' state.

This was really the first theoretical thing we were faced with and we are still [faced] with it, and when we are faced with new phenomena and new backward countries in the process of industrialisation we use the same criteria and the same general approach, and therefore for us it is not a surprise what happened to Nkrumah, whatever happens in China...

(Tony Cliff, from a speech on *Revolutionary Traditions*, 1967)[2]

Trotskyism has come to mean many different things in the 37 years since Trotsky's death. Widely differing and often mutually hostile groupings describe themselves as Trotskyist and it is not very profitable to attempt to set up a standard of orthodoxy to judge them by. There are many Trotskyisms. Moreover, those of them that have persisted in an organised form over any considerable period of time have undergone profound and sometimes repeated changes. For example, the Mandel tendency is a very different political current today than it was 10 years ago; and 10 years ago its political content was markedly different from what it had been 10 years before that.

This article is mainly concerned with Trotskyism as a body of revolutionary theory and practice as developed by Trotsky in the decade of his third exile (1929-40). I shall argue first that Trotsky fought to preserve the authentic communist tradition, the tradition of the early Communist International, in the only way that it could or can be preserved, by developing it and embodying it in a living moment; second, that the extremely unfavourable circumstances of the time not only defeated his efforts so far as immediate large-scale results were concerned, but also led to characteristic distortions and deformations of the tradition itself as it came to be embodied in the various Trotskyist groupings; third, that while Trotsky was aware of this and fought vigorously against certain of the deformations, he himself contributed to fostering some of them.

By "tradition" I mean the doctrine, strategy, and tactics developed by the Comintern in Lenin's time, a development in which Trotsky played a prominent part.

In 1932 Trotsky summarised the matter as follows:

> The International Left Opposition stands on the ground of the first four Congresses of the Comintern. This does not mean that it bows before every letter of its decisions, many of which had a purely conjunctural character and have been contradicted by subsequent events. But all the essential principles (in relation to imperialism and the bourgeois state, to democracy and reformism; problems of insurrection; the dictatorship of the proletariat; on relations with the peasantry and the oppressed

nations; soviets, work in the trade unions; parliamentarianism, the policy of the united front) remain even today the highest expression of proletarian strategy in the epoch of the general crisis of capitalism.[3]

There is an important omission here, the nature of the communist party—an active, conscious section of the working class. Otherwise, it is an accurate condensation of the indispensable theoretical basis of a revolutionary Marxist movement.

The post-1923 Comintern deviated rapidly from the line of the first four congresses, first in an opportunist direction (1924-28, with a partial "left" oscillation in 1924), then in an ultra-left direction (1928-34), and finally completely abandoned the whole basis of communist politics with the lurch into popular frontism from 1935 onwards.

Trotsky's superb analysis of these developments and untiring struggle to reintegrate the authentic tradition with the actual movement was an enormously important achievement. Our own politics rest upon it. All the more reason, then, to look critically at the weaknesses of the Trotskyist heritage.

The most glaring, of course, is that referred to by Cliff in the speech quoted here. Until late 1933 Trotsky had maintained that the working classes of the USSR had the possibility of "recapturing" the bureaucratised state by peaceful and legal means, "without a new revolution, with the methods and on the road of *reform*".[4]

However unrealistic in fact, this position enabled Trotsky to reconcile the Marxist conception of the working class as the active agent of the socialist revolution with his description of the USSR under Stalin's dictatorship as a workers' state.

Once this "reformist" perspective was abandoned, as it was in October 1933, there was a built-in contradiction in Trotsky's theoretical system. At the time it did not have any very important practical consequences. The USSR, which indisputably originated from a genuine proletarian revolution, could be regarded as a very special case.

After the Second World War, the creation, by means other than proletarian revolution, of a whole series of states of the same general type exploded the contradiction. The theoretical coherence of Trotskyism—of Trotsky's own Trotskyism—was shattered. In the late forties and early fifties, the Trotskyist movement—more or less united until then—splintered into fragments, largely, though not wholly, under the impact of the enormous upsurge of Stalinism with the emergence of the "socialist camp," and the inability of the Trotskyists to emancipate themselves from Trotsky's error.

But there were other defects in the tradition, too, defects whose seeds were sown in Trotsky's lifetime. They now flourish like rank weeds in the various Trotskyisms.

Propagandism and its price

The opposition is now taking shape on the basis of principled ideological demarcation, and not on the basis of mass actions... Mass actions tend as a rule to wash away secondary and episodic differences and to aid the fusion of friendly and close tendencies. Conversely, ideological groupings in a period of stagnation or ebb tide disclose a great tendency towards differentiation, splits and internal struggles. We cannot leap out of the period in which we live. We must pass through it. A clear, precise ideological differentiation is unconditionally necessary. It prepares future successes.

(Leon Trotsky, *The Groupings in the Communist Opposition*, 1929)[5]

The first problem facing Trotsky at the outset of his last exile was how to pull together a coherent oppositional movement within, or at any rate oriented on, the Communist International.

An *independent* movement, a movement seeking to build directly in the working class, was ruled out. "The cry about a second party and a Fourth International is merely ridiculous... We do not identify the Communist International with the Stalinist bureaucracy".[6]

The perspective was to influence the course of the Communist Parties in the hope that the combined effect of events and the criticism of the left opposition could shift them towards realistic revolutionary policies. As in the USSR, Trotsky's aim was *reform* of the existing communist movement, not the creation of a new movement.

The policy failed. The destruction of the German labour movement by the Nazis in 1933, as a result in large part of the criminal lunacy of the Comintern's "Third Period" ultra-leftism, which paralysed the German Communist Party, marked the end of any realistic hope of its success.

Yet it was certainly correct to try. There was no chance at that time of building independent parties. The enormous prestige of the Russian revolution, still a recent event, had been inherited by Stalin, and some of it had rubbed off onto the Stalinist leaders of the Comintern sections. Moreover, these were the years of the greatest slump in the history of capitalism, and *simultaneously*, of the first five-year plan. The contrast between mass unemployment and industrial decline in the West and the feverish expansion of Russian industry was stark and clear to millions of workers.

And there was Germany—"the key to the international situation" as Trotsky rightly said. Here was a highly industrialised country with the biggest working class in Europe and the biggest Communist Party in the world (for as Trotsky also said, the CPSU was no longer a party, but a bureaucratic apparatus) plunging into a prolonged social crisis that could be resolved only by the proletarian revolution or the fascist counter-revolution.

To write off the KPD (which claimed 250,000 members in 1932) was to concede victory to Hitler in advance. The KPD, however, like all the Comintern sections, maintained that the social democrats—re-christened "social fascists" since 1929— were the main enemy, not the Nazis, and denounced Trotsky's call for a workers' united front against fascism as "the theory of an utterly bankrupt fascist and counter-revolutionary".[7]

The brilliance and cogency of Trotsky's writings on the German crisis has rarely been equalled and has never been excelled by any Marxist, not excluding Marx and Lenin. But ideas become a force only to the extent that they move people; socialist ideas become significant only to the extent that they become rooted in the working class.

The contrast between Trotsky's writings and the state of the German Trotskyists on the ground was painful. They were a handful. And they were almost all socially marginal people quite outside the workers' movement. The German opposition, Trotsky noted in 1932, had failed to recruit even "ten native factory workers." It consisted largely of "individualistic, petty-bourgeois and lumpen elements who cannot tolerate discipline".[8]

The power of the Stalinists had forced the German Trotskyists—and not only the Germans as we shall see—into a political ghetto which also had a definite *social* location: the fringes of the intellectual section of the petty bourgeoisie. This is the most important simple fact about Trotsky's followers. They originated, for the most part, within a petty-bourgeois milieu, and with rare exceptions they could not break out of it. The political consequences of this fact profoundly distorted their development.

One of the exceptions, partially at any rate, was the American group. They had in their ranks one of Trotsky's most considerable non-Russian followers, [James] Cannon, an ex-CP leader of working-class background and considerable experience in the movement, and one or two others—[Vincent] Dunne, [Arne] Swabeck, [Hugo] Oehler—of similar origin.

Yet here is Cannon's own description of the membership in the early thirties:

We began to recruit from sources none too healthy... Freaks always looking for the most extreme expression of radicalism, misfits, windbags, chronic oppositionists, who had been thrown out of half a dozen organisations... Many people came to us who had revolted against the Communist Party not for its bad sides but for its good sides; that is, the discipline of the party, the subordination of the individual to the decisions of the party in current work. A lot of dilettantish, petty-bourgeois minded people who couldn't stand any kind of discipline, many of the newcomers made a fetish of democracy... All the people of this type have one common characteristic; they like to discuss things without limit or end... They can all talk; and not only can but will; and everlastingly, on every question.[9]

In more moderate terms—too moderate, for the French section was one of the worst of the lot—a historian of French Trotskyism describes the main French group in Paris. "The Paris region included a large proportion of intellectuals, former communist cadres now cut off from their base".[10]

Trotskyism had been *forced* into this milieu and Trotsky was acutely aware of the need to break out of it. Objective conditions made it extremely difficult. Subjective circumstances—the social nature of the Trotskyists—became an additional obstacle. But Trotsky compounded the difficulties. He denounced "closed circles," "literary arrogance," "conceit and grand airs". Yet at the same time he insisted: "The cadres can only be educated if all questions are debated by the *whole* Opposition... Questions of general revolutionary tactics and internal questions should be the property of every member of the Opposition organisation".[11]

This approach inevitably further strengthened the "intellectualist" tendencies to which the petty-bourgeois nature of the movement gave rise and made effective involvement in the workers' movement still more difficult. It further strengthened the trend towards "natural selection" of those who wished to "discuss things without limit," the trend to the "one continuous stew of discussion" of which Cannon complained.

Trotsky encouraged the various sections of the opposition to interest themselves in each others' activities, he wrote interminable circulars and epistles explaining, say, to the Belgians why the French fell out, to the Greeks why the German comrades were in disagreement, to the Poles what were the points at issue between different sets of the Belgian or of the American opposition, and so on and so forth. He did all this in the belief that he was educating and training a new levy of communists, new "cadres of revolution".[12]

Some of this was doubtless unavoidable, a necessary consequence of the propagandist stance which, in turn, was politically correct at the time. Some, but by no means all. Trotsky's method legitimised and encouraged the pretensions of people who, though they could not gain so much as a toe-hold in their own working-class movement, felt able to pronounce on the details of policy and tactics all over the world. It fostered the very "conceit and grand airs" that was such an obstacle to serious work. It helped to give the Trotskyist groups an exotic, hothouse atmosphere remote from the world of working-class militants and thus perpetuated the petty-bourgeois nature of the groups. To all this, Trotsky contributed, in spite of quite opposite intentions. The basic fallacy was that cadres can be trained outside the class struggle. And the baleful influence of this tradition was to persist; a poison in the bloodstream of the movement long after propagandism had been officially abandoned as a struggle orientation.

One particular aspect of the evil, factionalism, took a strong hold in the early period and was never subsequently entirely eliminated. Some factional struggles are an inevitable overhead cost in the growth of any serious revolutionary organisation. Permanent, persistent factionalism, however, is not an overhead cost, but a disease.

As Cannon wrote later: "There is no greater abomination in the workers' political movement than a permanent faction. There is nothing that can demoralise the internal life of a party more efficiently than a permanent faction".[13]

A light-minded toleration of factionalism certainly cannot

be attributed to Trotsky. His approach to the development of cadres nonetheless encouraged it precisely because it enabled petty-bourgeois cliques to justify their existence on "theoretical" grounds.

Entrism and its outcome

The period of existence as a Marxist circle ingrafts invariably habits of an abstract approach to the problems of the workers' movement. He who is unable to step in time over the confines of the circumscribed existence becomes transformed into a conservative sectarian... To a Marxist, discussion is an important but a functional instrument of the class struggle. To the sectarian, discussion is a goal in itself.

(Leon Trotsky, *Sectarianism, Centrism and the Fourth International*, 1935)[14]

After Hitler gained power, Trotsky abandoned the reformist orientation towards the Communist Parties. It was necessary, given the utter bankruptcy shown by the failure to even attempt seriously to resist the Nazis, to create new revolutionary parties. Again the political judgement was inescapable. Within two years the Comintern had swung from the ultra-left pseudo-radicalism of the "Third Period" to Popular Frontism—collaboration with the social democrats and "progressive" bourgeois parties on the basis of "defending democracy". The struggle for socialism was thrown out of the window.

How could new revolutionary parties (and a new international) be created? It was, and is, an immensely difficult task. Social democracy had been built in the late 19th and early 20th centuries when, so to say, there was a clear space, when rival *workers'* parties were not, in most cases, significant. The communist parties came out of the splits in the social democracy on a rising revolutionary tide.

Neither of these conditions existed in the thirties. At the same time, in these years, the anti-Trotskyist campaign orchestrated from Moscow reached its height. Trotsky was an agent of Hitler and the Japanese Emperor—as the line in the period of the Moscow trials goes, "The Trotskyists were fascist agents in the workers' movement."

Any realistic assessment of the failure of Trotskyism to take root, of the failure of successive attempts to break out of isolation, must put overwhelming emphasis on the profoundly unfavourable situation in which the Trotskyists were placed.

In 1939, on the eve of the war, and after many failures, Trotsky frankly surveyed the situation:

> We are not progressing politically. Yes, it is a fact which is an expression of a general decay of the workers' movement in the last fifteen years. It is the more general cause. When the revolutionary movement in general is declining, when one defeat follows another, when fascism is spreading over the world, when the official "Marxism" is the most powerful organisation of deception of the workers, and so on, it is an inevitable situation that the revolutionary elements must work against the general historical current even if our ideas, our conceptions, are as exact and wise as one can demand. But the masses are not educated by prognostic theoretical conception, but by the general experience of their lives. It is the most general explanation—the whole situation is against us.[15]

It was true. The blemishes of the Trotskyists in these circumstances are of significance only in so far as they became institutionalised and transmitted to later generations. Three issues of that period are still significant.

To restate the problem as it was, the groups were weak, petty bourgeois, and more or less outside the workers' movement. How to break out of the ghetto, proletarianise Trotskyism, and pull significant numbers of workers into new communist parties?

After initial attempts to "re-group" with various left social-democratic/centrist formations (mainly unsuccessfully), Trotsky proposed entry into the social-democratic parties. Strictly speaking, this was argued for specific cases—France at first—but it came to be generalised in practice. The argument was that the social democrats were moving left creating a more favourable climate for revolutionary work, that they were attracting new layers of workers, and were an incomparably more proletarian environment than the propaganda groups Trotskyism inhabited.

The operation was conceived as a short-term one: a sharp, hard fight with the reformists and centrists to rally the potentially revolutionary forces, then split and found the party. "Entry into a reformist-centrist party in itself does not include a long-term perspective. It is only a stage which under certain conditions can be limited to an episode".[16]

The first issue was that of the internal democracy of the Trotskyist groups. It was an issue because in many if not most sections, the opponents of the "French Turn" (entry) were the majority. Democratic centralism was part of their creed. But what did it mean? An open reciprocal relationship between the revolutionary party and its working-class base, a relationship which requires a correspondingly open party regime?

That, of course, was what it was supposed to mean, but very obviously that did not apply to the Trotskyist groups. They were not parties and they were not working class. Or did it mean commitment to accept the majority decision of a petty-bourgeois group?

In practice Trotsky was extremely ruthless. While insisting, rightly, on the maximum feasible internal democracy for *educational* reasons, he insisted on purges and splits with those of his cadres who were deeply wedded to the intellectual milieu. "A revolutionary organisation cannot develop without purging itself, especially under conditions of legal work when not infrequently chance, alien and degenerate elements gather under the banner of revolution".[17] And again, "The (French)

League is passing through a first crisis under the banner of clear revolutionary criteria. Under these conditions, a splitting off of a part of the League will be a great step forward. It will reject all that is unhealthy, crippled and incapacitated; it will give a lesson to the vacillating and irresolute elements; it will harden the better section of the youth...".[18]

This approach was denounced by sundry opponents as undemocratic, authoritarian, and so on, all of which was a reflection of the unwillingness of these opponents to break from their background. Because, in the end, entry failed in its strategic aim, because much of the Marxist movement remained petty bourgeois, these attitudes, "making a fetish of democracy" without analysis of the *class* and *political* content, recurred again and again and still recur today.

The second issue was the re-emergence of propagandism under a new guise—programme fetishism. The arguments with reformists and centrists pushed Trotskyists in the direction of defending the fundamentals of communism rather than applying them in actual working-class struggles. The defence of "the programme" inevitably loomed very large, and for some, came to have an almost mystical significance. Some of Trotsky's own formulations (though not his practice) lent some colour to this deviation. But Marxism is a synthesis of theory and practice. No programme is of any value unless it leads to practical activity necessary to achieve its aims. Again, it has to be stressed that circumstances forced a degree of programme fetishism on the Trotskyist groups. But this fetishism—the attribution of *independent* power to an inanimate object, a body of writings—did not always disappear when the conditions fostering it had altered. It is still very much alive among some of the Trotskyist grouplets of today.

In particular, one document, *The Death Agony of Capitalism and the Tasks of the Fourth International*, the 1938 *Transitional Programme*, came to acquire a status close to that of Holy Writ in the eyes of many Trotskyists. It is a blend of concrete political analysis, which proved to be faulty in a number of important respects; tactical recipes related to the analysis; history; and basic communist ideas. That it was a misleading guide is much less important than the fact that most of Trotsky's followers proved incapable of a critical reappraisal. They did not learn from Trotsky's own unhesitating rejection of positions he had long held when they were clearly inapplicable.

In the end, of course, fetishism too has material roots. Forced back into the specific social environment in which they had begun, powerless to affect the course of events, some succumbed to a quasi-religious faith—for that, after all, is what programme fetishism is, no matter how stridently its adherents proclaim their atheism.

The third issue was parasitism. The entrist operates inside an alien body. A certain degree of adaptation to the norms of that body is unavoidable. Adaptation, however, can mean not only care in language, etc., but a shift in political emphasis. Already, in the original short-term entry in France, this occurred. Trotsky wrote of "those (in R Molinier's circle) who, exhilarated by the initial successes, were anticipating a long perspective of untroubled activity within the reformist party. And it was precisely these elements, leaning on new allies and semi-allies on the right, who began to exercise a very big influence on the political line of our group".[19]

When, in the 1950s and subsequently, long-term entry, the so-called "entry sui-generis" or "deep-entry", was adopted by certain Trotskyist groups, the political adaptation of the parasite to the host went very far. It became hard to tell the entrist from his prey. This was accompanied by another sort of mysticism, the belief in "profound historic forces" for socialism, *independent* of actual working-class action.

Here is a specimen, taken from a "World Congress" resolution, of the Pablo-Mandel tendency in 1957:

> The fundamental change in the international situation
> and in the internal situation within the USSR, charac
> terised on the one hand by the world-wide upsurge

of the revolutionary forces since 1943 and especially since the victory of the Chinese revolution, and on the other hand by the spectacular successes of planification which made the USSR the second power in the world, destroyed the objective bases for the full sway and power of the Soviet bureaucracy. The evolution of the international correlation of forces in favour of the anti-capitalist social strata was paralleled by an evolution of the correlation of forces inside the USSR in favour of the proletariat and at the cost of the bureaucracy.[20]

And the conclusion?

The concrete march of the world revolution throughout the world after the Second World War has made of the Chinese and colonial revolutions the principal motor of the world revolution. In reaching the USSR and the countries dominated by the Soviet bureaucracy, the revolutionary wave makes of the political revolution against this bureaucracy the second most powerful motor of the world revolution.[21]

Great historic forces are very comforting things! This deformation, too, is still present in various Trotskyisms.

The heritage
When all is said, the struggle carried on by Trotsky and his followers (with all the weaknesses) did preserve an authentic communist current, if not in the working class, then at least on the fringes. The Fourth International, as a serious proposition, was still-born, but a degree of continuity from the revolutionary period of the Comintern was maintained in the teeth of near-insurmountable difficulties. We are part of that continuity today; the tradition Trotsky fought for is our tradition.

Traditional Trotskyism, that of Trotsky himself, became partially irrelevant in the same way that Lenin's "democratic dictatorship of the proletariat and peasantry" became irrelevant in 1917. The various Trotskyisms of today are deformed in several ways and unlikely to be capable, in most cases, of further positive development. But the revolutionary essence of Trotsky's politics survives. That is the important thing.

Notes

1   First published in *International Socialism*, 1: 100, (July 1977).

2   From a speech at Wortley Hall, Sheffield, 22 April 1967, to an aggregate meeting of the International Socialism group. Originally published in David Widgery, *The Left in Britain, 1956–1968* (London: Harmondsworth, 1976) pp92–7.

3   Leon Trotsky, *Writings*, 1932-1933 (New York: Pathfinder, 1972) pp51-52. www.marxists.org/archive/trotsky/works/index.htm

4   Leon Trotsky, *Writings*, 1930-1931, (New York: Pathfinder, 1973) p.225, Trotsky's emphasis.

5   Fourth International, *A Documentary History of the Fourth International*, Vol.4, No.5 (May 1946) pp154-156. www.marxists.org/archive/trotsky/1929/03/commopp.htm

6   Isaac Deutscher, *The Prophet Outcast* (London: Oxford University Press, 1963) p143.

7   Isaac Deutscher, *The Prophet Outcast*, p206.

8   Leon Trotsky, *Writings*, 1930 (New York: Pathfinder, 1972) p293.

9   James P Cannon, *History of American Trotskyism* (New York: Pathfinder, 1972) pp92-93.

10 Yvan Craipeau, *Le Mouvement Trotskiste en France* (Paris: Ed Syros, 1972) p39.

11 Leon Trotsky, *Writings*, 1930 (New York: Pathfinder, 1972) p297. Trotsky's emphasis.

12 Isaac Deutscher, *The Prophet Outcast*, p60.

13 James P Cannon, *Speeches to the Party* (New York: Pathfinder, 1973) p185.

14 *New Militant*, Vol. II No. 1, (4 January 1936) p3. www.marxists.org/archive/trotsky/1935/10/sect.htm

15 Leon Trotsky, *Writings*, 1938-39 (New York: Pathfinder, 1972) pp251-2.

16 Leon Trotsky, *Writings*, 1935-36 (New York: Pathfinder, 1972) p31.

17 Leon Trotsky, *Writings*, 1933-34 (New York: Pathfinder, 1972) p90.

18 Leon Trotsky, *Writings*, 1933-34 (New York: Pathfinder, 1972) p91.

19 Leon Trotsky, *Writings*, 1935-36 (New York: Pathfinder, 1972) p3l.

20 SWP (US) *The Development and Disintegration of World Stalinism* (New York: SWP, 1970) p28.

21 SWP (US) *The Development and Disintegration of World Stalinism*, p47.

Towards a Revolutionary Socialist Party
Duncan Hallas

(from *Party and Class*, 1971)[1]

The events of the last 40 years largely isolated the revolutionary socialist tradition from the working classes of the West. The first problem is to reintegrate them. The many partial and localised struggles on wages, conditions, housing, rents, education, health and so on have to be co-ordinated and unified into a coherent forward movement based on a strategy for the transformation of society.

In human terms, an organised layer of thousands of workers, by hand and by brain, firmly rooted amongst their fellow workers and with a shared consciousness of the necessity for socialism and the way to achieve it, has to be created. Or rather it has to be recreated. For such a layer existed in the twenties in Britain and internationally. Its disintegration, initially by Stalinism and then by the complex interactions of Stalinism, Fascism and neo-reformism, reduced the authentic socialist tradition in the advanced capitalist countries to the status of a fringe belief. As it re-emerges from that status, old disputes take on new life. The nature of the socialist organisation is again an issue.

That an organisation of socialist militants is necessary is common ground on the left, a few anarchist purists apart. But what kind of organisation? One view, widespread amongst newly radicalised students and young workers, is that of the libertarians. In the nature of the case this is something of a blanket term covering a number of distinct tendencies. The essence of what they have in common is hostility to central-ised, co-ordinated activity and profound suspicion of anything smacking of "leadership". On this view nothing more than a loose federation of working groups is necessary or desirable. The underlying assumptions are that centralised organisations inevitably undergo bureaucratic degeneration and that the spontaneous activities of working people are the sole and suffi-cient basis for the achievement of socialism.

The evidence for the first assumption is, on the face of it, impressive. The classic social-democratic parties of the early 20th century are a text-book example. It was the German social democracy that furnished Robert Michels with the material from which he formulated the "iron law of oligarchy". The commu-nist parties, founded in the first place to wrest the politically conscious workers from the influence of conservative social-democratic bureaucracies, became in time bureaucratised and authoritarian to a degree previously undreamt of in working class parties. Moreover, the basic mass organisations, the trade unions, have everywhere become a byword for bureaucratisa-tion and this, apparently, irrespective of the political complexion of their leadership.

From this sort of evidence some libertarians draw the conclusion that a revolutionary socialist party is a contradiction in terms. This is, of course, the traditional anarcho-syndicalist position. More commonly it is conceded that a party may, in favourable circumstances, avoid succumbing to the embraces of the establishment. However, the argument goes, such a party, bureaucratised by definition, inevitably contains within its structure the embryo of a new ruling group and will, if successful, create a new exploitative society. The experience of Stalinist parties in power is advanced as evidence here.

Much of the plausibility of views of this sort derives from their highly abstract and therefore universal character. It would be unfair to equate them with the currently fashionable "naked apery" but there is certainly some similarity in their psychological appeal. Writers like Morris and Ardrey[2] dispense with the difficult and complicated job of analysing actual societies and actual conflicts in order to deduce from an allegedly unchanging human (or animal) nature the "inevitability" of this or that. In the same way much libertarian thinking proceeds from very general ideas about the evils of formal organisation to highly specific conclusions without much effort to investigate the actual course of events. Thus, Stalinism is seen as the "inevitable" consequence of Lenin's predilection for a centralised party. A few general notions, a few supposed "universal truths" which are easily mastered in half an hour, become the substitute for serious theoretical equipment. Since the real world is a very complicated place it is highly reassuring to have at one's disposal the ingredients for an instant social wisdom. Unfortunately, it is also highly misleading.

The equation "centralised organisation equals bureaucracy equals degeneration" is in fact a secularised version of the original sin myth. Like its prototype it leads to profoundly reactionary conclusions. For what is really being implied is that working people are incapable of collective democratic control of their own organisations. Granted that in many cases this has proved to be true; to argue that it is necessarily, inevitably true is to argue that socialism is impossible because democracy, in the literal sense, is impossible.

This is precisely the conclusion that was drawn by the "neo-Machiavellian" social theorists of the early 20th century and which is deeply embedded in modern academic sociology. It lies at the root of modern social democratic theory, such as it is. Of course, libertarian socialists will have none of this. The essence of their position is rejection of the tired old cliché that there must always be élites and masses, leaders and led, rulers and ruled. Nevertheless, the opposite conclusion is implicit in their approach to organisational questions for the simple reason that formal organisations are an essential feature of any complex society.

In fact, useful argument about the problems of socialist organisation is impossible at the level of "universal" generalisations. Organisations do not exist in a vacuum. They are composed of actual people in specific historical situations, attempting to solve real problems with a limited number of options open to them. Failure to take adequate account of these rather obvious considerations vitiates discussion. This is particularly clear in the disputes about the origins of Stalinism.

That Bolshevism was the father of Stalinism is an article of faith with most libertarians. It is also the view of the great majority of social-democratic, liberal and conservative writers and, of course, in the purely formal sense that the Stalinist bureaucracy emerged from the Bolshevik party, it is incontestable. But this does not get us very far. By the same reasoning Jesus Christ was the father of the Spanish Inquisition and Abraham Lincoln the father of United States imperialism, but nobody, one hopes, imagines that statements of this type lead to any useful conclusion. The question is how and why Stalinism emerged and what role, if any, the structure of the Bolshevik party played in the process.

Daniel Cohn-Bendit's[3] treatment of the matter in his book *Obsolete Communism* is instructive. He sets out to show that "far from leading the Russian Revolution forwards, the Bolsheviks were responsible for holding back the struggle of the masses between February and October 1917, and later for turning the revolution into a bureaucratic counterrevolution—in both cases because of the party's very nature, structure and ideology".[4]

The first point is not relevant here and will be discussed later. The second is developed by means of quotations, suitably selected to establish the calculated malevolence of Lenin and Trotsky. It is shown, correctly, that in 1917 Lenin favoured management of enterprises by elected committees of workers and that in 1918 he came out strongly for one-man management, that Trotsky in 1920 called for the militarisation of labour and that the suppression of the Kronstadt revolt in 1921 was an important turning point in the process by which the Russian workers lost power. What is really astonishing about Cohn-Bendit's account of these events is his complete omission of any consideration of the circumstances in which they took place. The ravages of war and civil war, the ruin of Russian industry, the actual disintegration of the Russian working class; all this, apparently, has no bearing on the outcome. True it is conceded in passing that Russia was a backward country and was isolated by the failure of the German revolution but, we are told, "these general factors can in no way explain the specific turn it (the revolution) took".

Now it is usually supposed that there is some sort of connection between the type and level of the production of the necessities of life and the kinds of social organisation that are possible at any stage. No doubt it is very unfortunate that this should be so. Otherwise, mankind might have leapt straight from the old stone age to socialism.

If, however, it is conceded that one of the preconditions for socialism is a fairly highly developed industry with a high productivity of labour then some of the "general factors", so casually dismissed by Cohn-Bendit, assume a certain importance. Russia at the time of the revolution was not just a backward country. By the standards of the developed capitalist countries of the time it was very backward indeed. 80 percent of the total population was still engaged in agriculture; the comparable figure for Britain was 4.5 percent of the work force. The economist Colin Clark estimated the real income per head per occupied person in Russia in 1913 as 306 units; the comparable figure for Britain was 1,071 units. Indeed, on Clark's calculations, the figure for Britain as early as 1688, some 370 units, was higher than that for

Russia in 1913. All such assessments contain a large margin of error no doubt, but even if the maximum allowance is made for this the prospects for an immediate transition to a non-coercive society in early 20th century Russia were very slender indeed. True, man does not live by bread alone, the cultural heritage is also important. And the cultural heritage of Russia was Tsarist barbarism. Not surprisingly there was no tendency whatever in the pre-revolutionary Russian Marxist movement that believed that socialism was on the agenda for an isolated Russia, though this illusion had, it is true, been entertained by the Narodniks.[5]

Yet the economic level of 1913, miserable as it was, repre-sented affluence compared to what was to come. War, revolu-tion, civil war and foreign intervention shattered the produc-tive apparatus. By May 1919 Russian industry was reduced to 10 percent of its normal fuel supply.[6] By the end of that year 79 percent of the total railway track mileage was out of action—and this in a huge country where motor transport was practically non-existent. By the end of 1920 the output of all manufactured goods had fallen to 12.9 percent of the 1913 level.

The effect on the working class was catastrophic. As early as December 1918 the number of workers in Petrograd had fallen to half the level of two years earlier. By December 1920 that city had lost 57.5 percent of its *total* population. In the same three years Moscow lost 44.5 percent.

The number of industrial workers proper was over three million in 1917. In 1921 it had fallen to one and a quarter million. The Russian working class was disappearing into the countryside to avoid literal starvation. And what a countryside! War, famine, typhus, forced requisitioning by red and white alike, the disappearance of even such manufactured goods as matches, paraffin and thread—this was the reality in the Russia of 1920–21. According to Trotsky even cannibalism was reported from several provinces.

In these desperate conditions the Bolshevik party came to substitute its own rule for that of a decimated, exhausted working class that was itself a small fraction of the population, and within the party the growing apparatus increasingly edged the membership from control. All this is incontestable, but it seems reasonable to suppose that the actual situation had rather more influence on these developments than the "very nature, structure and ideology" of the party. As a matter of fact, the party regime was astonishingly liberal in this period.

The most balanced summary of the matter is that of Victor Serge, himself a communist with strong libertarian leanings, an eyewitness and a participant:

> It is often said that "the germ of all Stalinism was in Bolshevism at its beginning". Well, I have no objection. Only, Bolshevism also contained many other germs—a mass of other germs—and those who lived through the enthusiasm of the first years of the first victorious revolution ought not to forget it. To judge the living man by the death germs which the autopsy reveals in a corpse—and which he may have carried in him since his birth—is this very sensible?[7]

Given the backwardness of Russia, which germs flourished and which stagnated, which of the several potential outcomes actually materialised, depended above all on the international situation.

The Bolshevik seizure of power took place in the context of a European revolution. The revolutionary movements proved strong enough to overthrow the German Kaiser, the Austrian Emperor and the Turkish Sultan as well as the Russian Tsar. They proved strong enough to prevent a foreign intervention sufficiently massive and sustained to overthrow the Soviet regime, assisted of course by the conflicts between the remaining great powers. But they were aborted or crushed before the critical transition, the establishment of working class power in one or two advanced countries, was reached. The failure of the German revolution in 1918–19 to pass beyond the stage of the capitalist-democratic republic seems,

in retrospect, to have been decisive. The defeat of the Sparta-
cists sealed the fate of working class rule in Russia, for only
substantial economic aid from an advanced economy, in practice from a socialist Germany, could have reversed the disintegration of the Russian working class.

The actual outcome, the transformation of what Lenin, in
1921, called a "workers' and peasants' State which is bureaucratically deformed" into a totalitarian State capitalism, was
itself complex and lengthy. The point that is relevant to this
discussion is that an essential part of that process was the
destruction of all the wings and tendencies of the Bolshevik
party. It was not sufficient for the counter-revolution to liquidate the various oppositions of left and right. So little was the
party suitable as an instrument "for turning the revolution into
a bureaucratic counter-revolution" that most of the original
Stalinist cadre too had to be eliminated before the new ruling
class stabilised its position.

By 1934, the year of the 17th Party Congress, all open
opposition in the party had long been suppressed. The fate
of the delegates to that Congress, Stalinists almost to a man,
was revealed by Khrushchev in 1956. "Of the 1,966 delegates,
1,108 were arrested... Of the 139 members and candidates of
the party's central committee elected at the Congress 98, i.e. 70
percent, were arrested and shot".[8] In short, the vast majority of
those who had any roots in the Bolshevik past—80 percent of
the 17th Congress delegates had joined by 1921—were liquidated and replaced by new personnel "uncontaminated" by
even the most tenuous ties with the working class movement.

These events, which have had such profound and lasting
consequences, are facts of an altogether different order of magnitude from the deficiencies, real or alleged, of Bolshevik organisational practice. To suppose otherwise is to fall into that extreme
voluntarism which many libertarians share with the Maoists.

It does not follow that the last word in organisational wisdom
is to be found in the Bolshevik model. In the very different conditions of late 20th century capitalism arguments for or against

Lenin's position of 1903 are not so much right or wrong as irrelevant. The "vanguard partyism" of some of the Maoist and Trotskyist sects is the obverse of the libertarian coin. Both alike are based on a highly abstract and misleading view of reality.

What is in dispute here is in part the usefulness of the analogy. It is clear that any substantial revolutionary socialist party is necessarily, in one sense, a "vanguard". But there is no substance in the argument that the concept is elitist. The essence of elitism is the assertion that the observable differences in abilities, consciousness and experience are rooted in unalterable genetic or social conditions and that the mass of the people are incapable of self-government now or in the future. Rejection of the elitist position implies that the observed differences are wholly or partly attributable to causes that can be changed. It does not mean denial of the differences themselves.

The real objection to the emphasis on the "vanguard party" is that it is often part of an obsolete world outlook that directs attention away from contemporary problems and leads, in extreme cases, to a systematic false consciousness, an ideology in the strict Marxian sense of that term.

A vanguard implies a main body, marching in roughly the same direction and imbued with some sort of common outlook and shared aspiration.

When, for example, Trotsky described the German Communist Party of the 1920s and early thirties as the vanguard of the German working class, the characterisation was apt. Not only did the party itself include, amongst its quarter of a million or so members, the most enlightened, energetic and self-confident of the German workers; it operated in a working class which, in its vast majority, had absorbed some of the basic elements of Marxist thought and which was confronted, especially after 1929, with a deepening social crisis which could not be resolved within the framework of the Weimar Republic.

In that situation the actions of the party were of decisive importance. What it did, or failed to do, influenced the whole subsequent course of European and world history. The sharp polemics about the details of tactics, history and theory, which were the staple output of the oppositional communist groups of the period, were entirely justified and necessary. In the given circumstances the vanguard was decisive. In Trotsky's striking metaphor, switching the points could change the direction of the whole heavy train of the German workers' movement.

Today the circumstances are quite different. There is no train. A new generation of capable and energetic workers exists but they are no longer part of a cohesive movement and they no longer work in a milieu where basic Marxist ideas are widespread. We are back at our starting point. Not only has the vanguard, in the real sense of a considerable layer of organised revolutionary workers and intellectuals, been destroyed. So too has the environment, the tradition, that gave it influence. In Britain that tradition was never so extensive and influential as in Germany or France but it was real enough in the early years of the Communist Party.

The crux of the matter is how to develop the process, now begun, of recreating it. It may be true, as Gramsci said, that it is harder to create generals than to create an army. It is certainly true that generals without an army, are entirely useless; even if it is supposed that they *can* be created in a vacuum. In fact, "vanguardism", in its extreme forms, is an idealist perversion of Marxism, which leads to a moralistic view of the class struggle. Workers are seen as straining at the leash, always ready and eager to fight but always betrayed by corrupt and reactionary leaders. Especially pernicious are the "left" leaders whose radical phraseology conceals a fixed determination to sell the pass at the first opportunity.

Such things certainly happen of course. Corruption in the literal sense is not unknown in the British labour movement and in its more subtle manifestations it is widespread. But it is grotesquely one-sided to suppose that, for example, the history of Britain since the war can be explained in terms of "betrayals" and it is idiotic to imagine that all that is necessary is to "build a new leadership" around some sect or other and then offer it as an alternative to the waiting workers.

The reality is much more complex. The elements of a working class leadership already exist. The activists and militants who actually maintain the shop floor and working class organisations from day to day are the leadership in practical terms. That they are, typically, more or less under the influence of reformist or Stalinist ideas or ideas more reactionary still, is not to be explained in terms of betrayal. It is to be explained both in terms of their own experience and in terms of the absence of a socialist tendency seen as credible and realistic.

The first point has been crucial. Reformist policies have been successful in the advanced economies in the last 20-odd years. Not always or for everyone but for enough people enough of the time to create a widespread belief in reformism as a viable proposition.

As conditions change the second point becomes increasingly important and excessive emphasis on the vanguard concept can become a real barrier to the process of fusing the tradition and the activists.

One of the negative features of the leadership/betrayal syndrome is the assumption that the answers to all problems are known in advance. They are contained in a programme which is definitive and final. To safeguard the purity of the programme is seen as one of the main tasks of the selected few. That there may be new problems which require new solutions, that it is necessary to learn from one's fellow workers as well as to teach, are unwelcome ideas. And yet they are fundamental. Omniscience is no more granted to organisations than to individuals. A certain amount of modesty, of flexibility, of awareness of limitations is necessary.

It is, on the face of it, rather unlikely that a programme written in, let us say, 1938 contains the complete solution to the questions of the 1970s. It is certainly the case that in the process of recreating a considerable socialist movement many old concepts will have to be modified. Ideas, at least useful, operative ideas, have some sort of relationship to facts and it is a platitude that the world in which we work is changing at an unparalleled rate.

As a matter of fact, the development of a programme, in the sense of a detailed statement of partial and transitional aims and tactics in all important fields, is inseparable from the development of the movement itself. It presupposes the participation of a large number of people who are themselves actively engaged in those fields. The job of socialists is to connect their theory and aims with the problems and experiences of militants in such a way as to achieve a synthesis that is both a practical guide to action and a springboard for further advance. Such a synthesis is meaningful to the extent that it actually guides the activities of participants and is modified in the light of practice and that change in circumstances which it itself produces. This is the real meaning of the "struggle for a programme" that is so often turned into a fetish.

Similar considerations apply to internationalism. Internationalism, the recognition of the long-run common interests of workers everywhere and of the priority of this interest over all sectional and national considerations is basic to socialism. Today, with the increasing weight and influence of great international big business concerns, this is more obvious than ever. There cannot be a purely national socialist organisation. It is one of the merits of the Trotskyist groupings to have consistently emphasised this fundamental truth.

Yet the conclusion often drawn from it—"one must start with the International"—is another example of the distorting influence of overconcentration on "leadership". An "International" which consists of no more than a grouping of sects in various countries is a fiction. It is a harmful fiction because, as experience has shown, it leads to delusions of grandeur and hence to evasion of the real problems. The ludicrous situation in which no less than three bodies exist, each claiming to be the Fourth International and exchanging mutual anathemas like rival mediaeval popes, is a sufficient indication of the bankruptcy of ultra-vanguardism in the international field.

To develop a real current of internationalism—and without such a current all talk of an International is self-deception—it is necessary to start by linking the concrete struggles of workers in one country with those of others; of Ford workers in Britain and Germany for example, of dockers in London and Rotterdam and so on. This means starting where such workers actually exist, namely in the various countries. It means putting aside grandiose ideas of "International leadership", "World Congresses" and the like, in favour of the humdrum tasks of propaganda and agitation in one's own country together with the development of international links which, however limited at first, are meaningful to advanced workers outside the sectarian milieu.

Meetings and discussions between socialist grouplets in the various countries are essential, theoretical discussion is essential but above all the creation of real links between groups of workers is essential. Only after this has been done on a considerable scale will the preconditions for the recreation of the International be achieved. In the existing situation the analogy of Marx and the First International is in some ways more relevant than that of Lenin and the Third. Neither provides a blueprint that can be followed mechanically.

Of course, after all the dross is discarded, there is an important grain of truth in the "vanguard" analogy. It lies in the recognition of the extreme unevenness of the working people in consciousness, confidence, experience and activity. A rather small and constantly changing fraction of the working class is actually involved, to any extent, in the activities of the existing mass organisations. A larger fraction is episodically involved and the vast majority are drawn into activity only in exceptional circumstances. Moreover, even when largish numbers of workers are engaged in actions, in strikes or rent struggles, etc, these actions are typically sectional and limited in their objectives. The only major exception which occurs more or less regularly, the act of voting for a party seen as, in some sense, the working man's party, is itself increasingly ritualistic in character. And even at this level it has to be remembered that at every election since the war something like one-third of the working class has voted Tory.

To state these well-known facts is sometimes regarded as something of a betrayal, a slander against the working class. And yet it is merely a statement, not only of what exists, but also of what must exist for capitalist class society in its "democratic" form to continue at all. Once large numbers of people actually act directly, collectively and continuously to change their conditions they not only change themselves; they undermine the whole basis of capitalism. The relevance of a party is, firstly, that it can give the real vanguard, the more advanced and conscious minority of workers and not the sects or self-proclaimed leaders, the confidence and the cohesion necessary to carry the mass with them. It follows that there can be no talk of a party that does not include this minority as one of its major components.

The problem of apathy has to be seen in this context. As has often been pointed out, the essence of apathy is the feeling of powerlessness, of inability to change the course of events in more than a marginal way, if that. The growth of apathy, the increase in "privatisation", in turning one's back on the world, is naturally closely connected with the decline in the ability of reformist politics to deliver the goods as the power of the international capitalist firms to evade "national" restrictions grows steadily. This is why apathy can be very rapidly turned into its opposite if a credible alternative is presented.

That alternative must be more than a mere collection of individuals giving general adherence to a platform. It must also be a centre for mutual training and debate, for raising the level of the raw activist to that of the experienced, for the fusion of the experiences and outlook of manual and white collar workers and intellectuals with ideas of scientific socialism. It must be a substitute for those institutions, special schools, universities, clubs, messes and so on, through which the ruling class imbues its cadres with a common outlook, tradition and loyalty. And it must do this without cutting off its militants from their fellow workers.

That hoary red herring, the question of whether socialist consciousness arises "spontaneously" amongst workers or is imposed by intellectuals from the "outside" has absolutely no relevance to modern conditions. It is strictly a non-question because it assumes the existence of a more or less autonomous working class world-outlook into which something is injected. Whether the relatively homogeneous working class outlook, so lovingly described by writers like Hoggart,[9] was ever so autonomous as has often been supposed may be questioned. In any case it is dead, killed by changing social conditions and above all by the mass media. It is rather ridiculous to argue about whether one should bring ideas from "outside" to workers who own television sets. Certainly most workers and especially the activists see things rather differently than the denizens of the stockbroker belt. Their whole life experience ensures this. But workers are not automata responding passively to the environment. Everyone has to have some picture of the world, some frame of reference into which data are fitted, some assumptions about society. The whole vast apparatus of mass communications, educational institutions and the rest have, as one of their principal functions, what sociologists call "socialisation" and what the old Wobblies called head-fixing. The assumptions convenient to the ruling class are the daily diet of all of us. Individuals, whether bus drivers or lecturers in aesthetics, can resist the conditioning process to a point. Only a collective can develop a systematic alternative worldview, can overcome to some degree the alienation of manual and mental work that imposes on everyone, on workers and intellectuals alike, a partial and fragmented view of reality. What Rosa Luxemburg called "the fusion of science and the workers" is unthinkable outside a revolutionary party.

Such a party cannot possibly be created except on a thoroughly democratic basis; unless, in its internal life, vigorous controversy is the rule and various tendencies and shades of opinion are represented, a socialist party cannot rise above the level of a sect. Internal democracy is not an optional extra. It is fundamental to the relationship between party members and those amongst whom they work.

The point was well illustrated by Isaac Deutscher in discussing the Communist Parties in the late twenties and early thirties:

> When the European communist went out to argue his case before a working class audience, he usually met there a Social Democratic opponent whose arguments he had to refute and whose slogans he had to counter. Most frequently he was unable to do this, because he lacked the habits of political debate, which were not cultivated within the party, and because his schooling deprived him of the ability to preach to the uncon-verted. He could not probe adequately into his oppo-nent's case when he had to think all the time about his own orthodoxy... He could propound with mechanical fanaticism a prescribed set of arguments and slogans... When called upon, as he often was, to answer criticism of the Soviet Union, he could rarely do so convincingly, his thanksgiving prayers to the workers' fatherland and his hosannahs for Stalin covered him with ridicule in the eyes of any sober-minded audience. This ineffec-tiveness of the Stalinist agitation was one of the main reasons why over many years, even in the most favour-able circumstances, that agitation made little or no headway against Social Democratic reformism.[10]

Latter-day parallels will spring to mind.

The self-education of militants is impossible in an atmos-phere of sterile orthodoxy. Self-reliance and confidence in one's ideas are developed in the course of that genuine debate that takes place in an atmosphere where differences are freely and openly argued. The "monolithic party" is a Stalinist concept. Uniformity and democracy are mutually incompatible.

Naturally a party cannot be a hold-all in which any and every conceivable standpoint is represented. The limits of member-ship are democratic collective control by the working class over industry and society. Within these limits a variety of views on aspects of strategy and tactics is necessary and inevitable in a democratic organisation. The heresy hunting characteristic of certain sects is self-defeating; an atmosphere of quasi-religious fanaticism is incompatible with the reintegration of the socialist tradition with a broad layer of workers.

The discipline that is certainly necessary in any serious organisation can arise in one of two ways. It can arise from a system of artificial unanimity enforced by edicts and prescriptions, a system that is counter-productive in a socialist group. Or it can arise from a common tradition and loyalty built on the basis of common work, mutual education and a realistic and responsible relationship to the spontaneous activities of workers.

Spontaneity is a fact. But what does it mean? Simply that groups of workers who are not active with any political or even trade union organisation take action on their own behalf or in support of others. From the point of view of organisations the action is "spontaneous"; from the point of view of the workers concerned it is conscious and deliberate. Such activity is constantly occurring and reflects the aspirations for self-government that are widespread even amongst workers commonly regarded as "backward". It is an elemental expression of the class struggle. Without it, conscious militants would be suspended in a vacuum. To use the hackneyed but useful analogy, it is the steam that drives the pistons of working class organisation.

Pistons without propellants are useless. Steam unchannelled has only a limited effect. Spontaneity and organisation are not alternatives; they are different aspects of the process by which increasing numbers of workers can become conscious of the reality of their situation and of their power to change it. The growth of that process depends on a dialogue, on organised militants who listen as well as argue, who understand the limitations of a party as well as its strengths and who are able to find connections between the actual consciousness of their fellows and the politics necessary to realise the aspirations buried in that consciousness.

It sometimes happens that even the best militants find themselves overtaken by events and occupying a position, for a shorter or longer time, to the right of previously unmilitant workers. The experience is familiar to active rank-and-file trade unionists. Slogans and demands that were yesterday acceptable only to the more conscious people can quite suddenly be too limited for the majority when a struggle develops beyond the expected point. Inevitably the greater experience and knowledge of the activists induces a certain caution, normally appropriate, but which, in a rapidly changing situation, can sometimes become a real barrier to advance. The same tendency is bound to occur with an organisation. This is the valid element in Cohn-Bendit's critique of socialist parties.

The danger is inherent in the nature of the environment. Sudden changes of consciousness amongst this group or that cannot always or even usually be predicted. What can be predicted is the need for the sensitivity to detect them rapidly and the flexibility to react appropriately.

Neither the existence of such spontaneous changes of mood, unexpected upheavals nor the frequent tendency towards caution amongst the layer of experienced and committed socialists constitute an argument against a party. On the contrary, given the unevenness of consciousness and the industrial and geographical divisions of the working class, a party, indeed a centralised party, is essential to give to various actions of different groups that cohesion and co-ordination without which their effect will be limited to local and sectional gains.

It is an argument against that bureaucratic caricature of a party that Stalinism has caused many on the left to confuse with the genuine article. One of Cohn-Bendit's chosen illustrations of party conservatism, the fact that in July 1917 the Bolshevik party lagged behind the workers of Petrograd and tried to restrain and limit their demonstrations, illuminates the point. The party was caught in a dilemma inherent in the uneven development of the movement in Russia as a whole. As Trotsky wrote "there was the fear that Petrograd might become isolated from the more backward provinces; on the other hand there was the hope that an active and energetic intervention by Petrograd might save the situation".[11] This "conservatism" was a reflection of the pressure of the party members in other centres who, in turn, transmitted the mood of working class circles in these centres. The fact that there was a party sufficiently flexible to react to that pressure probably prevented a repetition of the Paris Commune in 1917. This, of course, was the most extreme situation possible but similar problems are inevitable at every stage of development.

A revolutionary socialist party is necessary then; but such a party has been necessary for a long time. Why should it be supposed that it is possible to create it in the 1970s? Basically the case rests on the analysis of the world crisis developed in *International Socialism*, and particularly on the thesis that, in the changing conditions of capitalism, reformist policies will be less and less able to provide those partial solutions to the problems confronting the working class that they have been able to provide in the decades since the Second World War. This is the objective factor.

The most important subjective factor is the decline in the ideological power of Stalinism. The past influence of Stalinism on the left and its effects, direct and by reaction, in effectively excluding the building of an alternative are difficult to exag gerate. For 15 years that power has been eroded, slowly at first and then more and more quickly. Today it is in full disintegration. This ideological decomposition is not to be confused with the organisational decline of Communist parties. Though the British party has certainly declined this is not the decisive consideration. The party still commands the allegiance of a good many industrial militants. But it no longer commands it on the old basis. It is no longer a Stalinist party. All kinds of tendencies exist within it and now that the papal infallibility of Moscow is gone forever the monolithic party cannot be restored.

The dominant group in the party, the Gollan leadership, is effectively reformist. Whether, as some of its critics suspect, the leadership aims to liquidate the party into the Labour Party, or whether, as seems more likely, it clings to the illusion that there is room in British politics for a second reformist workers' party, makes little difference. As an obstacle to regroupment on the left the party is a rapidly waning force.

Nor is the Labour Party left the force it used to be. In part this is a reflection of the decline of the Communist Party, for every significant left wing in the Labour Party in the past has leaned heavily on the Communist Party's trade union base. In part it is an effect of the decline of the Labour Party's own membership organisations—youth, wards, constituencies—which has become so marked in recent years. There are still genuine socialists active in the Labour Party as there are also amongst the passive card-holders. But it seems unlikely, though it is not inconceivable, that any fairly massive socialist current will develop in the party.

The basis for the beginnings of a revolutionary socialist party exists amongst those industrial militants who used to look to the Communist Party, amongst increasing numbers of radicalised young workers and students and amongst the revolutionary groups.

The latter are an important but difficult problem. The root cause of the sort of sectarianism that has plagued the British left is the isolation of socialists from effective and influential participation in mass struggles. The isolation is rapidly diminishing but its negative effects—the exacerbation of secondary differences, the transformation of tactical differences into matters of principle, the semi-religious fanaticism which can give a group considerable survival power in adverse conditions at the cost of stunting its potentiality for real development, the theoretical conservatism and blindness to unwelcome aspects of reality—all these persist. They will be overcome when, and only when, a serious penetration and fusion of layers of workers and students outside sectarian circles has been achieved. The International Socialism group intends to make a significant contribution to that penetration. Without having any illusions that it is "the leadership" the group exists to make a theoretical and a practical contribution to the regeneration of socialism in Britain and internationally.

Notes

1   This article was published near simultaneously in 1971 as "The Way Forward" in the collection "World Crisis: Essays in Revolutionary Crisis" (London: Hutchinson & Co Ltd, 1971) edited by Nigel Harris and John Palmer and with the current title in Cliff et al., *Party and Class* (London: Pluto, 1971). It argues passionately in favour of the need for a genuinely revolutionary socialist party in Britain against others who believe there is another alternative way to achieving real change. Transcribed by Einde O'Callaghan for the Marxists' Internet Archive, www.marxists.org/archive/hallas/works/1971/xx/party.htm

2   Desmond Morris, author of *The Naked Ape* (1967) and Richard Ardrey, author of *The Territorial Imperative* (1966), were popularisers of the idea that human society could be explained by innate behaviour, as with other species such as apes.

3   Daniel Cohn-Bendit was a prominent leader of the French student revolt in May 1968.

4   Daniel & Gabriel Cohn-Bendit, *Obsolete Communism: The Left-wing Alternative* (London: Andre Deutsch, 1968) p201.

5   The Narodniks were a 19th century Russian political movement, based among the intelligentsia, who believed the peasantry was the revolutionary class that would overthrow the monarchy and regarded the village commune as the embyro of socialism.

6   This figure and those following are taken from E H Carr, *The Bolshevik Revolution: 1917-1923*, Volume 2 (New York: Macmillan, 1951).

7   Victor Serge, *From Lenin to Stalin* (1937), www.marxists.org/archive/serge/index.htm

8   Nikita Khrushchev, *Speech to the 20th Congress of the Communist Party of the Soviet Union,* 24-25 February 1956, www.marxists.org/archive/khrushchev/1956/02/24.htm

9   Richard Hoggart was a British academic and writer. His book *The Uses of Literacy*, published in 1957, lamented the loss of an authentic working class popular culture in Britain and denounced the imposition of a mass culture through advertising, media and Americanisation.

10   Isaac Deutscher, *The Prophet Outcast* (London: Oxford University Press, 1970) p37.

11   Leon Trotsky, *From October to Brest-Litovsk* (1919) Ch 4, www.marxists.org/archive/trotsky/1918/hrr/ch01.htm.

Pluto Press

**Essays by Cliff, Hallas,
Harman and Trotsky**

Party and Class

Front cover of Party and Class, *Pluto Press Ltd for the International
Socialists, London, 1971. Duncan's essay "Towards a Revolutionary
Socialist Party" appeared here.*

The Decisive Settlement
Duncan Hallas

(*Socialist Worker Review*, October 1988)

*1688 marked an important turning point in the history of
Britain. The victory of William of Orange over James II in
what came to be known as the Glorious Revolution marked the
consolidation of bourgeois rule. Duncan Hallas looks back at
the events and the forces involved.*

On the 5th of November 1688 William of Orange landed
at Torbay, with a substantial army of Dutch, German,
Scandinavian and Scottish mercenaries. It was the beginning of
what Whig historians and indeed, until quite recent times, virtually
all bourgeois historians called the Glorious Revolution. This is the
same William who is portrayed throughout Northern Ireland, on
his horse, sword in hand, waving his hat at the Battle of the Boyne.

He became the symbol of the most backward, reactionary
attitudes. The very word Orangeism comes from his title. Yet if
you look realistically at events in 1688 you will find that this was
the decisive culmination of the English bourgeois revolution.

Even though there were much more dramatic events in an

earlier period, this was the decisive settlement. A settlement which lasted in form for 150 years and in practice for probably another fifty up to the 1880s. And that 150 years saw the establishment of maritime English supremacy around the world, the conquest of India, the conquest of North America, and the first British Empire.

But more than that, it was the period that saw the destruction of the English peasantry, to borrow Stalin's phrase, their liquidation as a class.

It also saw, and this is still more important, the world's first industrial revolution with all the rapid social transformations and upheaval that involved.

This was achieved by a ruling class whose framework and indeed whose personnel in family terms had been established in 1688.

But first it is necessary to look at the events of the preceding period, that is between 1640, the meeting of the Long Parliament, and 1660, the restoration of the Stuart monarchy.

Marx, writing about history, says that it is made by classes, consciously, but nevertheless with a false consciousness. In previous class societies the ideas in people's heads did indeed correspond to their class interests but they were expressed in veiled, concealed, ideological fashions. And in 17th century Britain the differing ideologies were expressed in religious terms. There were three main religious ideological forces in the country at the time.

First, there were the Roman Catholics or, to use the Protestant terminology of the day, the Papists. The Catholic Church was essentially an ideological representative of feudal or quasi feudal reaction.

There were bits of the church where this was not so, Ireland being one, but essentially in English and Scottish terms it represented the extreme right and the most backward sections of the land-owning classes on which the monarchy sought to rest.

Secondly, there were the Presbyterians and Calvinists. At that time Calvinism was the ideology of the relatively successful bourgeoisie. They were substantial merchants, including some very rich men, and a whole layer beneath them of "progressive" landlords, who were innovative, who invested to produce for a market, and who were essentially capital accumulation oriented.

The ideology of Calvinism had been adapted from its original form into ways which suited the needs of capital accumulation and which provided a justification for political action.

Then there was the Anabaptist tradition. This stood well to the left representing basically the aspirations of small property owners. We are so used to a society in which the vast majority are wage earners that we need to remind ourselves that at that time the majority, including many of the poorest, were small property owners.

Their aspirations differed considerably from that of the Presbyterians. They were called Independents. The categories were not rigid, many Independents were Calvinists as well, but events were to show that in the case of the Independents their ideal was a republic of small property owners. They represented the left in mass terms.

In addition to these three groups there was the forced compromise, "The Church of England as by law established", to give it its official title. The "as by law established" is the important thing. Before 1640 and again after 1660 there was no religious tolerance. Everyone was supposed to belong to the state church; indeed there was legislation on the statute book making failure to attend religious service on Sunday punishable by a fine of up to one shilling.

Why? Because ideas expressed in religious terms were the essential ideological arm of the government.

The Church of England was a battle ground precisely because it was the state church and different emphasis by different regimes led to different conflicts within it. It was not an homogeneous body, indeed it included near Papists on the one hand and people who were for all practical purposes dyed-in-the-wool Calvinists on the other, as well as a whole mass in between.

As the events of 1640 unfolded this then was the balance of forces. Because of a series of preceding events, the English bourgeoisie, in other words the House of Commons, dominated. Most of the members sitting in the House of Commons were medium-sized property owners, but they were market oriented, embryonic capitalists who leant towards Calvinism.

Essentially the monarchy represented a compromise that had been established much earlier, going right back to Henry VIII, between the old society and the new.

The monarchy had leaned on the bourgeoisie in the earlier period. Now the bourgeoisie had become strong enough to challenge it. Nevertheless, they did not start by saying "away with the monarchy". Rather their argument concerned the subject dearest of all to bourgeoisies everywhere, money!

In practice this meant that the House of Commons, in return for voting the King sums of money, wanted to effectively determine his policy. This led ultimately to the formation of two armed camps and civil war.

For the first years before that war the Presbyterian dominated leadership of the House of Commons was reluctant to press things to extremes. Therefore they fought in a very half hearted way.

This hesitation is expressed very well by an exchange between the general who the Presbyterian parliament had appointed as the supreme commander, the Earl of Manchester, and the man who was to replace him, Oliver Cromwell.

Manchester, when urged by the left to mount a resolute offensive to destroy the royal armies, said "though we are forced to fight against him, remember, in the eyes of God he is still our king". Cromwell's answer is beautifully brief, "if that be so my lord, we should never have taken up arms in the first place."

The conflict between these forces led to the effective dissolution of Presbyterian control. This happened because for reasons of military necessity they were compelled to consent to the formation of the New Model Army.

The New Model Army was made up entirely of relatively

poor men, in the main the small property owners. The army was, if you like, the political party of the Independents. It represented the most dynamic, the most forward looking people.

All sides were agreed that Charles had to go but what was to happen once he had gone? One side believed that young Charles, his son, would be King on their terms, whereas under pressure from the ranks the Independent leaders decided to make an issue of monarchy itself.

In Cromwell's immortal words "that man of blood Charles Stuart must die", Why? Mainly for ideological reasons.

The traditional notion was that the institution of the monarchy was divinely ordained and could not be altered. To break that view Charles was put on trial and had his head chopped off for treason.

No sooner was this done than new problems arose. The forces that had been relatively united in 1640 were much less so by 1644–5, and after 1649 they were profoundly divided. A coherent bourgeois force which could pull behind it the great majority did not emerge.

Consequently, a series of things occurred. The Long Parliament was purged. What was left was a parliament dominated by the Independents who had stayed. But they too proved too conservative and they also were dispersed. At the end of the day the regime was reduced to a military dictatorship through the generals.

The generals faced two problems, problems common to any bourgeois revolution. One was the process of establishing a regime, a set of institutions, a government and a legal system which facilitated the process of capital accumulation.

But, and this was the second problem, how could this be done without encouraging what the Royalist historian Clarendon called the "dirty people of no name" (meaning, not beggars, not proletarians but the mass of small property owners)?

We, with the benefit of hindsight, know what the fate of these people was to be. They were to be amongst the principle victims of the regime as it was subsequently established.

Cromwell had been reduced to military rule, his role becoming that of a sort of proto-Bonaparte.

As long as Cromwell lived he was able, in spite of everything, to enjoy a very broad layer of support. He was an extremely able man who managed to keep the regime going.

When he died it fell to pieces. The larger property owners, Presbyterians as well as Royalists, felt the need of a strong arm. So they brought back young Charles, who had been in exile in and around various European courts since 1648, who now became Charles II.

It was the Presbyterians who invited Charles back, as they thought, on their terms. In fact there was an enormous shift in the balance of forces. The army was on one pretext or another disbanded. Then there was the return of the Royalist exiles and the upsurge of the most backward elements in the country particularly in the North.

Consequently, just as the Cromwellian regime had proved to be unstable, so the restoration proved to be an unstable compromise. It lasted a surprisingly long time, until 1688, enjoying the grudging support of the majority of the big property owners until 1683.

Here we have an accident of history, the rule of the great-man theory. Of course these events have to be analysed in terms of social forces, but that does not mean that individuals in particular situations do not play a significant role and in certain circumstances, for a time, a decisive role. Such a man was Cromwell, such a man curiously enough, although he was, in terms of personal character and all else, the absolute opposite of Cromwell, was Charles II.

Charles II paradoxically, was the least enthusiastic of all the people on the Royalist side for the Royalist reaction. It was not that he didn't favour it, he did. But he wanted it slowly. He believed a new civil war and a new exile was to be avoided at all costs. The unstable compromise lasted as long as it did only because of this policy. Charles II may have been a very idle and frivolous man but at the same time he was very clever.

When he was succeeded by a more convinced monarchist, his brother James, the compromise fell to pieces very quickly. But why? As already stated the great problem with a bourgeois revolution is that you can overthrow the regime, but what then? You've got to have a stable ruling class and a stable state.

It is not to domestic forces but to foreign affairs that we must look to see how the problem was resolved. Although 1688 was made in a sense by the people who subsequently became the Whig oligarchy, their instrument was a foreigner and a foreign army. How was this possible?

To answer this it is necessary to look at these affairs in terms of four countries—the United Netherlands, France, Scotland and Ireland.

The Dutch were the commercial rivals of the English bourgeoisie. But, at the same time, United Netherlands was a barrier to the expansion of France. A series of wars took place between the two.

Furthermore, the crushing of the Dutch republic, if it could be achieved, represented two things which were not at all to the tastes of the capitalist landlords and the merchants in Britain.

First was the expansion of the power of France, which was the dominant power in Europe and clearly England's future rival. Secondly it would mean a victory, in religious terms and therefore in political terms, for the semi-feudal and quasi-feudal Catholic interests.

Consequently, the problem for the bourgeoisie was how to find a new Cromwell who would have some title of legitimacy, a very important consideration for quelling the masses. William of Orange became that man.

Again, the role of accident in history, or at least largely accident, played an important part. In the Netherlands, William was the equivalent of an American president—not an exact equivalent but he did not have an hereditary title, although the presidency so to speak had been in his family for some generations.

He was a Dutchman wholly committed to the struggle against France because the safety of the Dutch republic depended upon it. He was both able and flexible, and further-more he had married, for diplomatic reasons, Mary the elder daughter of James II. Finally he was a convinced Calvinist. Mary could claim, once Charles II was dead, to have a certain interest in the Stuart succession rights.

William was therefore an excellent candidate. The problem was how to get him on the throne. This involved uniting all the major sections of the big property owners, including those who had been Royalists.

Why? Because if they were divided and a new civil conflict were to emerge, the "mean and dirty people" might form a new model army again, and that they dreaded more than anything. Therefore, it involved conspiratorial connections by the Whig leaders with prominent Tory politicians (the term Whig and Tory had come into use by then), including those who had held office under Charles II.

Finally, it needed actions by the government to convince the property-owning classes as a whole that they were not safe under James's regime, that he would not accept the existing compromise, and in particular that he was determined to re-establish Popery, as they put it.

Indeed, he was determined to do so for reasons of ideology and interest. Absolute monarchy in France, absolute monarchy in Spain, these Catholic systems were the ones he aspired to.

In order to establish this he enforced measures against the Church of England and imposed Roman Catholics in important positions quite contrary to the law. At the same time he tried to raise an Irish army. For this he needed money, and therefore was compelled to trespass on what the bourgeoisie were most concerned about, the sacredness of property rights.

A prominent group, secretly and after many negotiations, invited William to come with an army. That army had to be composed of foreigners, and it had to be mercenary. It had to fight for pay and nothing else so that it could be paid off as soon as the battles finished.

When William launched his attack James had, on paper,

superior forces. Yet the whole thing ended without any fighting.

As William advanced, not very rapidly, in the direction of Oxford and the Thames Valley and then on into London, so James's forces, assembled to oppose, started to disintegrate.

Their officer corps, drawn from the propertied classes, shared the concerns of those classes. This can be illustrated by one well known example. John Churchill, founder of that family's fortune, had a very varied career, making his way by, as the historian Macaulay puts it, "a series of well timed treasons".

At this stage he was most important, first of all in convincing James that the army was thoroughly reliable and secondly that James was surrounded by traitors, therefore that he should follow Churchill's advice.

Churchill managed for a period of time to introduce complete confusion into the royal army until the scale of desertion became such that James was convinced it would be fatal to fight and so he fled, first to London and then ultimately over to Europe.

When James had fled, the Royalists controlling London sent a deputation to William at Oxford saying please come quickly. These were the people he was supposed to be fighting against. But again the coincidence of class interests, the need to establish a stable compromise mattered most to them.

Victory for William resulted in a number of important changes taking place. First, the monarchy, in the sense that James I and Charles I had understood monarchy, had gone. William owed his title to a vote in the House of Commons, that and the fact that they needed him.

In Macaulay's famous *History of England* there is a quote from the French ambassador to London saying "although the form of monarchy subsists, in truth this is a republic", and he was in essence right. He was much shrewder than some modern historians.

William's position in England was essentially not different from that in the Netherlands. He had to rule in collaboration with the existing ruling classes, he could not rule against them, he had no other base of support. In this peculiar way the bourgeoisie was established as the ruling class in a coherent sense. But the vast majority of MPs in the parliaments under William and right through to the first half of the nineteenth century were landowners.

Only a minority were merchants, bankers or traders. It's important to realise what that represented. As E P Thompson very forcefully and correctly argued about these landowners they were a land-owning class but in no sense a feudal land-owning class. Rather they were an anti-feudal, capitalist land-owning class.

Thompson asks how did the 18th century land-owning classes measure their worth with respect to one another? By their titles? No, although titles mattered. In fact by the size of their rent rolls.

In other words, in all essentials it was a thoroughly bourgeois regime, although the majority of people who ruled were not technically members of the bourgeoisie.

The second big change concerned the guarantee of property rights, the so-called Bill of Rights. That involved changing the judiciary, who until that time had been appointed by the king.

Thirdly there was the question of personal safety. In the whole period between 1640 and 1688 leading opposition people were apt to end up on the scaffold convicted of high treason.

This involved the automatic confiscation of all property so the families of those convicted lost as well. That had to be got rid of. The personal safety of the members of the ruling class had to be assured.

The fourth major change saw the domination of the rest of Britain by England and the establishment of the United Kingdom (although it did not become technically the UK until 1708) taking place at the expense of Scotland and Ireland.

Scotland was a very poor, backward and turbulent country. Its poverty can be measured as follows. In the last years of Charles II the crown's income from customs dues and customary taxes from England alone was one and a quarter million pounds.

From the entire kingdom of Scotland, which was legally

separate, £60,000. As one of their historians said it was ruled by an aristocracy which was "the poorest, the proudest, the most unscrupulous and the most mercenary in Europe". Consequently power in England meant domination of Scotland. Scotland was easy, it did not require thoroughgoing transformation. Money was sufficient and the Scottish aristocracy was bribed.

Ireland was different. James had tried to upset the settlement of Protestants in Ireland. Not because he loved the Irish—he was as bigoted and anti-Irish as any—but because the course of the reformation had left the mass of the peasantry in Ireland Catholic, and therefore potentially an army for counter-revolution which he had tried to create.

When he had fled from England, he ultimately made his way with a French fleet on to Ireland. There was a war for a period, the Battle of the Boyne in 1690 where he met king Billy on his horse. The outcome was the destruction of the old order in Ireland.

Of course, it had already been heavily eroded. The Elizabethan settlements and Cromwell's conquests had had their effect. Nevertheless the old order was still vital in 1688—now it was destroyed.

Finally, in terms of Europe, a regime was created which could be guaranteed to be anti-French.

Thus 1688 represented the final completion of the stabilisation of the English revolution and it represented it in the most conservative form possible, consistent with the establishment of a stable bourgeois administration.

Jack Robertson with Duncan in France in 1980.

We are not Parliamentary Roaders
Jack Robertson

My first tenuous connection to Duncan came through his
hometown of Manchester—though I was unaware of the
association at the time. After arriving there from Edinburgh
in the early 1970s, my first job was at Metro-Vicks, or The Big
House, the nickname given to the Metropolitan-Vickers factory in
Trafford Park. Then, the "park" was a vast industrial estate which
bordered the Manchester to Liverpool Ship Canal, Salford Docks
and Old Trafford. The industrial estate was so big it had its own
railway with freight carried by huge electric diesel engines. When
it was first built in the late 1890s by the American industrialist
George Westinghouse, it also had its own village, with streets set
out on a numerical grid—First Avenue, Second Avenue and so on.

Only later did I discover that Metro-Vicks was where
Duncan had served his apprenticeship. He started in the turbine
machine shop in January 1940 when he was 14 years old.
The next year, he took part in the historic apprentices' strikes
which began on the Clyde before spreading to other parts of the

Challenge, *weekly paper of the Young Communist League, 29 March 1941.*

country. Around this time, the factory employed about 16,000 workers. A couple of years earlier, the management entered into a joint venture with the aircraft company, A V Roe, or Avro, to assemble long-range aircraft at Trafford Park, notably Lancaster bombers. The first batch never got off the ground—they were destroyed by the Luftwaffe—but by the end of the war more than 1,000 had been built in Trafford Park, both at Metro-Vicks and at a specially constructed "shadow" factory on the Barton Dock Road formerly occupied by Ford.

By the end of the war, the workforce at Metros had peaked at nearer 30,000—many of these workers were women, employed as riveters, cabin outfitters and upholsterers. During the war, the Communist Party had a branch of around 100 members inside the factory. One of those was Hugh Scanlon, who—like many others—had joined the CP in 1937 at the time of the Spanish Civil War. The leader of the Transport Union,

*1983 pamphlet published by Edmund and Ruth Frow,
Working Class Movement Library.*

Jack Jones, was a CP fellow-traveller who actually went to Spain to fight against Franco's fascists in the International Brigades. Between the end of the Civil War in Spain, and the end of the Second World War, CP membership in Britain, on one estimate, had increased almost threefold, from around 17,500 to 45,000.[1]

Two of the most prominent members of the CP in Manchester in the 1930s were Ruth and Eddie Frow. At one stage or other, Eddie Frow worked at most of the major engineering works in the city—and was sacked from most of them too for his union activities. He eventually became District Secretary of the Amalgamated Engineering Union (AEU) in 1961. In March 1941, he represented the District Committee of the union at Tom Mann's funeral in Yorkshire. Ruth and Eddie's amazing collection of socialist books and pamphlets, which once lined the walls of every room at their house in Stretford, now form the basis of the Working Class Movement Library in Manchester. One of these pamphlets deals specifically with the struggles that went on at Metro-Vicks.

In her memoir after Eddie's death in 1997, Ruth Frow illustrates the type of activities CP members were expected to be involved with in the 1930s, with a quote from another of the CP's leading activists in Manchester, Jimmy Miller (better known by his stage name Ewan MacColl):

> The party was growing, slowly, but nevertheless it was growing. It had premises in Great Ducie Street, Manchester... We had one room on the top floor of a four-storey flight of rickety stairs, and in this room there was a duplicating machine, a rickety desk, a wastepaper basket and a typewriter... We were running factory papers, like the *Salford Docker*, for example, a duplicated news-sheet—one, two, three, four pages, sold outside the docks to blokes as they went in... But there'd be little satiric squibs, lampoons and verses and all the rest of it. These would deal with a little corner of the political picture.[2]

Hugh Scanlon eventually became plant convenor at The Big House and by 1947 had become Manchester Divisional Organiser in the engineering union. Although Hugh Scanlon left the Communist Party in 1954, he maintained contact with the impressive network of militants established by the CP in Manchester. It was from this base that Scanlon stood as a "Broad Left" candidate in the election for President of the AEU in 1968—and won.

In a book he wrote in 1959, *The Battle for Socialism*, the former *Daily Worker* journalist, Peter Fryer, wrote that: "In the 1930s and early 1940s, before the Revolutionary Communist Party was formed in 1944, several Trotskyist groups kept the Marxist tradition alive in Britain." By the time Peter Fryer wrote this book, he had resigned from the Communist Party after he had been sent to report on the Hungarian Revolution of 1956 and witnessed first-hand its suppression by Soviet tanks.

In Fryer's view, the great achievement of these tiny Trot-skyist organisations was that: "...in a period of reaction, under exceptionally difficult conditions, they brought the Marxist critique of Stalinist theory and practice and the Marxist alternative to Stalinism to the attention of enough working-class militants to ensure the movement's continuity." In the process, they were subjected to "a sustained campaign of slander and persecution without equal in the annals of the British working-class movement".[3]

One of the people who upheld this precarious tradition was Harry Ratner, a Jewish socialist who had first become active in revolutionary politics in London in 1936 at the age of 16. Describing the types of interventions he was then involved in, he later wrote:

> In addition to our Labour Party and trade union work and sales of literature at demonstrations and meetings of other organisations, we organised a series of meetings in the East End, just off the Whitechapel Road... The crowds we attracted were invariably hostile. Both the Fascists (Mosley's Blackshirts) and the Communist Party were very active in the area. One evening we would be attacked by the Fascists as "dirty reds" and told to "get back to Russia"; the next evening we would be attacked by Communist Party members as "bloody Fascists".[4]

A number of Trotskyist groupings attempted to oppose Stalin's encroaching influence on the party in Russia from 1928 onwards and, increasingly, internationally. In Britain, the first of these was the Balham Group, a small oppositionist group within the CPGB based in south London. It had about 12 members, which included names like Reg Groves, Hugo Dewar and Harry Wicks. In his 1973 memoir about the Balham Group, Reg Groves pays tribute to Duncan Hallas "for nudging me into the writing of these reminiscences".[5]

When the Second World War started, Harry Ratner's name didn't appear on any call-up lists—he had been living in France when the war started. If he'd kept quiet about it, he recalled, "it could be some time, if ever, before the conscription process caught up with me". Instead, he went to the local Labour Exchange and got himself put on the register, the logic being that:

We were not pacifists, and we rejected the option of registering as conscientious objectors as being an individualist and useless gesture. The imperialist war could only be transformed into social revolution by mass uprisings of workers and soldiers... the place of international socialists was in the factories and the armies, agitating and organising for this social revolution.[6]

Eventually, Ratner joined the Pioneer Corps and took part in the D-Day landings on the Normandy beaches in June 1944. It's unlikely they would have known each other at the time but this was also Duncan's first involvement in the war—he was 17 at the time. They both took part in the Battle for Caen, which, on the Allied side, consisted of three British and Canadian armoured divisions, 11 infantry divisions, five armoured brigades and three tank brigades. The German army, led by Rommel, consisted of seven infantry divisions, eight panzer divisions and three heavy tank battalions.

Duncan was always reluctant to talk much about this episode, playing down its significance, but Harry Ratner describes it in some detail: "After the initial success of the landings and the establishment of a bridgehead, the German resistance stiffened and it was not until 9 July, five weeks after the landings, that Caen was taken after prolonged and heavy fighting, and not until August that the Allied armies were able to break out of the bridgehead".[7] The number of Allied casualties between 6 June and 13 August 1944 has been estimated at 158,930.

Allied bombing turned much of the French countryside in and around Caen into a wasteland. The city and many of the surrounding towns and villages were destroyed, the University of Caen was razed to the ground and by the end of the battle, the civilian population had fallen from 60,000 to 17,000.

When Harry Ratner had the chance to visit Bayeux, the first sizeable French town liberated from the Germans, he found that:

In many areas and towns, the local Resistance had risen in advance of the arrival of the Allied armies, defeated the German forces, chased out the Vichy collaborationist officials, and seized all official buildings. Local "Liberation Committees" representing the various Resistance organisations had seized power and were arresting collaborators, disarming the Vichy militia and police, and organising food supplies etc.[8]

The French President, De Gaulle, was alarmed at this development of power from below: "It was too reminiscent of the 'dual power' that had sprung up in Russia and Germany after the First World War when soviets and councils of workers and soldiers had disputed power with the official state machine".[9] Within the Liberation Committees, the Communist Party had emerged from the war with the most prestige—their members had been the most active force in the Resistance and had suffered the highest casualties.

However, instead of encouraging development of the workers' committees, the leaders of the CP in France followed the policy laid down by the Kremlin, which meant that, in Harry Ratner's word, they used their prestige "to defuse the situation and to prop up de Gaulle's authority". All over France, they persuaded the local Resistance committees to accept the authority of "delegates" and "prefects" appointed by de Gaulle.

When it was founded, in the summer of 1920, the Communist Party of Great Britain (CPGB) had regarded itself as a revolutionary party, inspired by the 1917 October Revolution. As a revolutionary party, the CP specifically rejected reformism and the parliamentary road to socialism. By 1925, everyone who was worth anything in the British revolutionary movement had joined the Communist Party of Great Britain.

Writing about the origins of the CPGB on the 50th anniversary of the first major test of its revolutionary credentials—the General Strike of 1926—Duncan noted that, outside of its ranks "...were large numbers of class-conscious workers, many of them in the Minority Movement and (after 1925) the National Left-Wing Movement. But the CP was the motor and guiding force of these considerable movements. And they were considerable".[10]

By March 1926:

...the Minority Movement was able to claim the support of trade union bodies representing 957,000 workers. The Left-Wing Movement (operating inside the Labour Party) included some 50 constituency and borough Labour Parties who were refusing to operate the ban on Communists forced through the 1925 Labour Party conference by the right wing. The *Sunday Worker*, a "non-party" paper standing "for the side of the workers in the class struggle", which acted as spokesman for both movements, had "a stable circulation of 85,000 copies a week" and an occasional sale of nearly 100,000 by early 1926. Its editor was, of course, a leading CP member acting under party discipline.[11]

There could be no question of the importance of the role played by the CP during the General Strike: "What it did, or failed to do, mattered. It influenced the course of events. It was a real factor in the situation", the party members played a role which was "out of all proportion to their numbers". It was also the case that: "Any revolutionary who criticises the political line of the party in that crisis must first pay tribute to the integrity and steadiness under fire of the CP rank and file and leadership alike, in the face of a selective but nevertheless brutal repression such as few of us, in the revolutionary movement today, have yet had to face":[12]

There were 9,000 arrests all told. Over 13 percent were CP members (24 percent of the CP membership) as compared with an arrest rate of 0.2 percent for TUC affiliated trade unionists as a whole (4,365,619 affiliated members in 1926). Not many of the convicted CP members were likely to get work again for many a year. Moreover, the entire top leadership of the CP had already been arrested, tried for sedition and sentenced to six- or 12-months imprisonment in October 1925.[13]

According to the CP's official historian, James Klugman, these arrests were "...perhaps the greatest compliment that capitalism could have paid to the role of the Communist Party in preparing the working class for the coming general strike". This assessment was shared by Duncan: "The ruling class feared the CPGB in 1925-26".[14]

Despite this magnificent record, the political direction taken by the CPGB had nevertheless contributed to the defeat of 1926—"the shattering defeat", as Duncan called it—and it did so, not only because it failed to fight hard against widespread illusions in the TUC's "left wing", it had enthusiastically promoted those illusions. In the USSR, the Left Opposition to Stalin—the faction within the leadership led by Trotsky, which first emerged during 1923 when Lenin was critically ill—had argued this at the time. The lessons of this defeat are as relevant today as when they were first made, as Duncan wrote in 1976:

On this 50th anniversary of the British general strike the most important thing for revolutionaries to do in the midst of all the celebratory sentimentalism and sogginess, is to look critically, yet again, at the whole problem of the relationship of left reformists and centrists to the revolutionary movement and the nature of the trade union bureaucracy in times of crisis.[15]

In his book *The Comintern*, Duncan explains that the Communist International, which arose out of the Russian Revolution of October 1917, was not an optional extra but an essential, indispensable part of the revolution. He quotes Lenin, who had said in January 1918 that: "We have never harboured the illusion that the forces of the proletariat and the revolutionary people of one country, however heroic and however organised and disciplined they might be, could overthrow international imperialism. That can be done only by the joint efforts of the workers of the world".[16]

The idea of creating a genuinely revolutionary party in Britain at the end of the First World War was no pipe dream. As Duncan wrote later, it was a time of:

> ...massive working class radicalisation all over Europe. The Tsar had been overthrown the year before and the Bolsheviks were in power in Russia; the German Kaiser was forced to flee mutinous soldiers and armed workers that November and a supposedly "Red" government was installed in Germany. The Austrian Empire fell to pieces and a socialist workers' militia controlled Vienna. In Britain itself, the growth of working-class consciousness was dramatically shown by the explosion of trade union membership from 4 million members in TUC-affiliated unions in 1913 to 8 million in 1919.[17]

Furthermore:

> 1919 was to see a massive and most militant wave of strikes and the beginning of the Irish war of independence. The Labour leaders could feel the coming storm. They had rivals, revolutionaries in the working-class movement, few in number but not without influence and soon to join together to form the Communist Party.[18]

By the time of the General Strike, the Comintern had turned into a tool of Kremlin foreign policy. The real turning point had been the events of 1923. That crucial year had seen "...the defeat of the German October, the beginning of the Russian bureaucracy's growth to self-consciousness, the emergence of the Left opposition and the violent bureaucratic reaction to it".[19]

Until 1924, the central thrust of the strategy of the British Communist Party was united front work in the unions. Under the increasing influence of Stalin, the focus on the Minority Movement—and therefore on the rank-and-file in the workplace—switched decisively, and rightwards, to a reliance on the bureaucracy of the TUC. In April 1925, the formation of an Anglo-Soviet Trade Union Committee was announced. The sixth plenum of the Comintern executive, in March 1926, declared that its aim was to demonstrate, "...the practical possibility of creating a unified International, and of a common struggle of workers of different political tendencies against reaction, fascism, and the capitalist offensive".[20]

As Duncan explains: "What it in fact demonstrated was that the temporarily dominant left-reformist bureaucrats on the British TUC General Council found it useful to acquire some 'left' cover, protection from Communist Party criticism, at practically no cost." In practice, what this meant was that:

In the period from July 1925 to May 1926, the British government was coldly and carefully preparing to break the power of the miners' union. In this same period, the left trade union leaders, heroes of the Anglo-Soviet Trade Union Committee, bemused their followers with their leftist rhetoric, made *no* preparations for the inevitable conflict with the government, and covered up for the right. Within two months of the sixth plenum...they had joined with the right to sell out the General Strike.[21]

The thinking behind the government's approach was that, whereas the Communist Party in Britain was relatively weak, the TUC was a real power. Following this logic, the role of the CP was to encourage the TUC and not antagonise it with "premature" criticism. Duncan points out that the disastrous upshot was that:

> During the nine-month "truce" between government and unions leading up to May 1926, it was essential for the Communist Party to criticise, constantly, concretely, and clearly, the inactivity of the left trade union leaders in the face of government preparations for a showdown, to warn of impending disaster, to exert all of its efforts to develop rank-and-file preparation *independently* of the union bureaucracies, "left" as well as right. Instead it helped to strengthen illusions in the lefts, those "friends of the USSR", and to help them to keep control over the trade union movement—a position summed up by the notorious slogan put forward by the Communist Party: 'All Power to the General Council'. It was the General Council of traitors, as was soon to be proved.[22]

When Harry Ratner returned from the war and arrived in Manchester after being demobbed in 1946, he started work at the Metro-Vicks factory within a week. He joined forces with Don Ellis, a comrade from the "minority faction" within the RCP in London which was in favour of "entry" into the Labour Party—which by then had about 1 million members. Ellis was a skilled toolmaker. Previously, Ratner had never been inside a factory of any sort.

Their intention was to build a group of like-minded socialists inside Manchester's heavy engineering industry. They were joined soon after by several other comrades who were supporters of the RCP "majority"—including Duncan Hallas. Ratner was no great fan of Duncan's Trotskyism; on the key issues, their views were at opposite ends of the spectrum. Nevertheless, they were active during the same period and their experiences overlap more than once. In his book,

Reluctant Revolutionary, Ratner dryly notes: "Duncan Hallas later became one of the leading comrades in the 'state caps' faction that became the International Socialists and then the Socialist Workers Party".[23]

By the spring of 1947, the RCP branch in Manchester had about a dozen members. Its first public activity:

> ...was selling the *Socialist Appeal* outside factories and bus depots and holding street corner meetings. We started by holding meetings on a piece of ground oppo- site the Salford Central Mission, because it was near Salford docks and because we found that several AEU and other union branches held their meetings in the Central Mission on Sunday mornings. We would set up a platform, and while the other two or three comrades stood around displaying *Socialist Appeal*, one of us would climb onto the platform and start speaking in an attempt to draw a crowd.[24]

For their first attempt to hold an indoor public meeting, they booked the Houldsworth Hall on Deansgate and fly-posted outside Metro-Vicks and all over Trafford Park. It was not a great success. Nobody but their own members turned up, plus a handful of members from the Manchester branch of the Socialist Party of Great Britain out on a recce.

During 1946-47, the RCP was in decline. According to Ratner, the workers who were at all politically conscious "were pinning their hopes on the newly elected Labour government in which they had confidence. Those that were becoming disillu- sioned were not turning to the RCP". The RCP was divided into two mutually hostile organised factions: those who favoured trying to build a nucleus of a revolutionary party inside the Labour Party, and those who wanted to build outside.

They were also divided on the economic perspectives for the coming period:

The majority held the view that we were entering a period of economic boom; the destruction of capital during the war and the shortage of consumer goods had created a market for both capital and consumer goods. The minority clung to the orthodox position outlined by Trotsky before the war that it would herald a new phase of crisis in the system. Against mounting evidence to the contrary, they continued to deny there was a boom and argued that: "Large-scale industrial and political struggles and the radicalisation of large layers of the working class were imminent.[25]

Harry Ratner recalls that, when Tony Cliff came to the Manchester branch in support of the majority's economic perspectives, "I was the minority spokesman. I blush with shame, even now, at the nonsense I must have talked... Looking back, it is difficult to credit we could have been so blind to reality".[26]

In June 1949, a new organisation called the Socialist Fellowship was launched at the Labour Party Conference by a number of Labour Left figures and members of Gerry Healy's "Club" (see John Rudge's article for details). The monthly newspaper *Socialist Outlook*, produced by the Club, became its effective mouthpiece. When the Korean War broke out in June 1950, the editorial line of *Socialist Outlook* was: "We are against all imperialist intervention in Korea. We are for unification of that country and its freedom from imperialist domination. While the armies of the North fight for those aims, we consider they deserve the support of the world working class".[27]

At the time of the Korean crisis, a number of left Labour MPs within Socialist Fellowship—including such names as Fenner Brockway and Bessie Braddock—supported the war and resigned from the Fellowship. During the same period, Tony Cliff was successfully pulling together a group of comrades who argued that the Soviet Union was a "state capitalist" society. One immediate consequence of this analysis was that the "state caps" objected to any attempt to defend the Soviet Union and support North Korea. In their view, "...the Korean War was a struggle between Russian imperialism on the one hand and American imperialism on the other".[28]

As a result, the "state cap" group were expelled from the Club together with any other opposition to Healy's control. The Socialist Review Group was duly formed at the end of August 1950. The first article in the very first issue of *Socialist Review* (Vol. 1 No. 1 November 1950) was written by R Tennant (one of Cliff's most common pseudonyms at this time). The introduction to the article, which was about American imperialism and Russian imperialism, reads:

> The war in Korea serves the Great Powers as a rehearsal for their intended struggle for the redivision of the globe. The fate of the Korean people is a grave warning to all humanity what sufferings the march of aggressive imperialist powers will entail.

In words that sound uncannily resonant today, the final paragraph of the article reads:

> In their mad rush for profit, for wealth, the two gigantic imperialist powers are threatening the existence of world civilization, are threatening humanity with the terrible suffering of atomic war. The interests of the working class, of humanity, demand that neither of the imperialist world powers be supported, but that both be struggled against. The battle-cry of the real, genuine socialists today must be: Neither Washington nor Moscow, but International Socialism.[29]

It was also at about this time that Chanie Rosenberg met Duncan for the first time. In the obituary she wrote for Duncan in *Socialist Review*, Chanie recalls:

Tony Cliff and I and our one-year-old baby went to Manchester with the aim of building a Socialist Review Group in the town, and stayed with Duncan in his tiny room, which contained a single bed and chest of drawers. Out went the contents of a drawer to accommodate the baby, the bed was given to us, and Duncan slept on the hard floor with a thin blanket. Whatever comforts there were—food, a hot water bottle—were piled on us. He was totally self-effacing. After giving us all he had, he started on the politics and organisation we had come to discuss.[30]

In August 1950 while all this was going on, Duncan married Irene Gosling. He was registered on the marriage certificate as being a "Technician in a Medical Laboratory" (which one is not known) while Irene's occupation appears as "typist" at a film company. Here we enter into the realm of speculation, but since there was only one established film company outside London at the time, this must mean that she worked at the Dickenson Road studios of Mancunian Films, which specialised in making "Northern" comedies, often starring a young George Formby. (The studios were based in a former Wesleyan church in Rush-olme, which happened to be just round the corner from where I lived in the 1970s, in Rusholme Grove. The premises were taken over by the BBC and were the location for the first ever broadcast of Top of the Pops and for The Rolling Stones first ever TV appearance, in 1964).

It was also at about this time that Duncan wrote one of his most influential articles as his contribution to an early debate in the Socialist Review Group. During the course of the article, which is actually a debate about the Stalinist parties, he wrote:

> The leadership of, say, the British Labour Party (BLP) is not proletarian. It consists of trade union functionaries, lawyers, clergymen, doctors, profes-sional "liberal" politicians, company directors, ex-civil

servants, ex-university teachers, scions of the nobility, etc. It is formed of *various sections of the middle classes*, including an important (but numerically declining) group from the bureaucracy of the TUs. It is *a petty-bourgeois* leadership in ideology as well as in composition. The (real) programme of the party is neo-liberalist class collaboration and pro-imperialism. It is diametrically opposed to the struggle for the unity and emancipation of the workers in Britain or anywhere else. It is a petty-bourgeois programme—and a very reactionary one at that. Finally, the internal regime of the party is not democratic. The democratic façade conceals the dictatorship of the parliamentary leadership and the TUC bosses. All these facts are well known and beyond dispute.[31]

The crucial point Duncan was arguing was that:

The only meaningful definition of a workers' party is in terms of its composition. A party which bases itself mainly upon the working class is a workers' party. The nature of its leadership and programme has nothing to do with the question. Naturally, such a party cannot have *any* programme. It cannot have the programme (openly) of the Economic League or Hitler. Naturally also, such a party, with a petty-bourgeois leadership, must play a dual role corresponding to the conflict of interests between the leadership and the membership. All this is obvious. The reason we (as revolutionaries) are concerned with the question at all is because, in order to win the working class, it is necessary to approach such parties in a certain way. That is to apply the united front tactic to them in order to win the proletarian rank and file from the bourgeois ideologies of the leadership. No one has yet shown any other way of doing this.[32]

In his *Socialist Worker* pamphlet *The Labour Party—Myth and Reality*, Duncan explains how the famous Clause Four and shibboleth of the Labour Left had first been introduced. Among those who led the transformation of the Labour Party from a pressure group dependent on the Liberals—as had been the case since 1900—were Arthur Henderson (secretary of the party from 1912 to 1934), the Fabians Sidney and Beatrice Webb, and the "extreme moderate" Ramsay MacDonald.

Henderson was shrewd enough to realise that a respectable, constitutional party, appealing to working people was necessary to head off dangerous, revolutionary forces. He was:

> ...far-sighted enough to see, immediately after the Russian February revolution in 1917, that "some sort of socialist faith was the necessary basis for the consolidation of the Labour Party into an effective national force". Hence the wording of Clause Four: "To secure for the workers by hand or brain the full fruits of their industry, and the most equitable distribution thereof that may be possible on the basis of the common ownership of the means of production and the best obtainable system of popular administration and control of each industry and service.[33]

Henderson was quite willing to co-operate with left wingers, on one condition—that they accept that the party "must operate *solely* by means of Parliamentary Democracy":

> This was the really important issue. Socialist rhetoric was now in order. Indeed, it was necessary. The lefts who really believed in the rhetoric had a vital role to play here. But the party must be bound hand and foot to the institutions of the capitalist state... Thus the Labour Party was born... It was a product of the class struggle, but it was also (consciously and deliberately

as far as its leaders were concerned) an anti-revolutionary party.[34]

After going to Edinburgh University as a mature student and then taking on full-time employment as a teacher, Duncan's political activities went off the radar for a period. As John Rudge notes elsewhere in this tribute, the first time that Duncan came to the attention of the wider IS membership was when he attended the organisation's conferences in late 1968: "These were important conferences, for IS membership had been increasing rapidly and the organisation needed to accelerate the trend already started of transforming itself from a propaganda group into an action orientated, interventionist one".[35]

By this time, Duncan had become one of the leading activists in the Wandsworth Teachers' Association and, along with Chanie Rosenberg, was one of three members of the Teachers' Rank and File group who had been elected to the Inner London Teachers' Association. As Chanie recalled: "When the rank and file decided to call for pay strikes in 1969, Duncan took over the leadership of the movement and led a terrific, tireless struggle to get the vote for strike action".[36]

Most of the other 24 members of the Inner London Teachers' Association, apart from six CP members, were headteachers and all of them were vehement opponents of strikes. Duncan "was a magnificent debater, and coolly, in a restrained, teacherly manner, thoroughly outwitted all the heads in both knowledge and arguing ability time after time".[37]

The more interventionist approach that began to be adopted by the IS at this time is clear from one of the earliest articles Duncan wrote for *Socialist Worker* on 8 May 1969. This is his analysis of Harold Wilson's Labour government:

Why did they do it? We have a Labour government, and the Labour Party is supposed to be the working men's party, the trade union party. And now they are whipping up a real hysteria against the unions, against stewards, against strikers, against the very people who have been the backbone of the Labour movement. Politics is about power. Socialist politics is about workers' power.

These are the facts that the Labour Party, including even the best and most sincere of the Labour "lefts", has been dodging for years.

In a capitalist society most of the power is in the hands of the big business bosses. It has to be taken from them. They can't be talked or tricked into giving it up. And this can only be done by a working class organised and conscious of its position in society and determined to liberate itself, and the rest of the people, by taking power—the power to decide about everything that affects their lives—into their own hands. To educate, agitate and organise for workers' power—for that's what socialism means in the first instance—is a tough job.

How much easier to concentrate on building an electoral machine, to win a parliamentary majority. Instead of telling workers to get off their knees, to learn to think and fight, you can use the prejudices created by the capitalist brainwashing machine...

You can win friends and influence voters and when you win a general election you can, you hope, introduce all sorts of reforms which will somehow change the system. Well, it has been tried. We are now in our fourth year of the current instalment. The bosses are richer and more powerful than ever. We are no nearer a democratic, humane, classless society than we were under Macmillan or Home.[38]

The weekly bulletin of the left wing in the Labour Party, *Tribune*, had hailed Wilson's election victory in 1966 with the headline 'Socialism is Right Back on the Agenda!'. What was really on the agenda, Duncan wrote later, was "...a government which deliberately doubled unemployment (from around 300,000 to

600,000) by deflationary economic policies, which introduced a racist immigration law, which slavishly supported the USA's genocidal war in Vietnam and *every* twist and turn of US foreign policy, which made more cuts in social services than the previous Tory governments and, to cap it all, tried to introduce anti-union legislation" (Barbara Castle's *In Place of Strife*). All in all, "Everything the Labour left claimed to stand for was trampled in the mud by the 1964-70 Labour government. It was, by *any* standards, a mean, nasty and thoroughly reactionary government".[39]

During the debates that took place inside IS at the end of the 1960s and into the 1970s, Duncan's role alongside Cliff was crucial. In the collective tribute to Duncan published in *Socialist Review*, Ian Birchall wrote:

> If Cliff's analysis and drive were crucial, Duncan provided an ideal counterpart to him. Cliff often "bent the stick" (overstated the point in order to convince comrades of the importance of a new strategy); on occasion Duncan would gently but firmly bend it back again... He had a long practical acquaintance with the British trade union movement and understood its peculiar strengths and weaknesses. For those of us who had come to revolutionary politics in the 1960s, he provided a fascinating link with the early years of Trotskyism.[40]

When I joined the IS in Manchester in 1972, the branch was pretty grim. We met downstairs at the Milton Hall in Deansgate and, for a period, seemed to be engaged in constant faction fights. However, this all began to change very rapidly, mainly because of the fantastic eruption of workers' struggles that took place in the early 1970s. The occupation of the Upper Clyde Shipyards was already underway, printworkers on Fleet Street had taken unofficial strike action to free the Pentonville Five—the London dockers who had been jailed for their defiance of Ted Heath's Industrial Relations Act—and the miners had just defeated a Tory government after solidarity action by car workers in Birmingham had forced the police to close the gates at the Saltley coking depot. In Manchester, more than 30 of the major engineering factories had been occupied in support of a claim for shorter hours and higher pay.

During this period of upturn in struggle, the IS grew exponentially. In Manchester, this meant that we had members in a lot of important workplaces—not just in factories but increasingly in white-collar occupations such as education, the NHS and the civil service. We could hold well-attended public meetings—often at the Houldsworth Hall—and very often the keynote speaker would be Duncan Hallas.

In one of his most influential articles "Towards a Revolutionary Socialist Party" (first published in the 1971 book *Party and Class*), Duncan wrote that: "The events of the last 40 years largely isolated the revolutionary socialist tradition from the working class of the West. The first problem is to reintegrate them." This was not so much a task of building an entirely new, organised layer of thousands of workers with a shared consciousness of socialism and how to achieve it, it was a tradition that needed to be re-created:

> For such a layer existed in the twenties in Britain and internationally. Its disintegration, initially by Stalinism and then by the complex interactions of Stalinism, Fascism and neo-reformism, reduced the authentic socialist tradition in the advanced capitalist countries to the status of a fringe belief. As it emerges from that status, old disputes take on new life. The nature of the socialist organisation is again an issue.[41]

The basis for the beginnings of a revolutionary party, Duncan argued, existed primarily "...amongst those industrial militants who used to look to the Communist Party, amongst increasing numbers of radicalised young workers and students and amongst the revolutionary groups". The latter, he added, "are an important but difficult problem".

Why was this the case? Because: "The root cause of the sort of sectarianism that has plagued the British left is the isolation of socialists from effective and influential participation in mass struggles".[42]

In conditions where workers were once more on the move in large numbers:

> The isolation is rapidly diminishing but its negative effects—the exacerbation of secondary differences, the transformation of tactical differences into matters of principle, the semi-religious fanaticism which can give a group considerable survival power in adverse conditions at the cost of stunting its potentiality for real development, the theoretical conservatism and blindness to unwelcome aspects of reality—all these persist.[43]

The other urgent task, of attempting to build an effective rank-and-file movement, also faced important obstacles, the most important of which was that: "There is a clear discrepancy between the state of morale and the organisational readiness for battle in both the capitalist camp and the working-class camp." This was the assessment made by Tony Cliff in his 1975 book, *The Crisis: Social Contract or Socialism*, published for *Socialist Worker* by Pluto Press.

On the one hand, Cliff argued, "The ruling class is suffering from a loss of nerve but has a relatively strong, centralised organisation inherited from the past." On the other, "Amongst workers, the position is precisely the opposite: the state of morale and confidence is excellent, but the level of organisation, its structure and staffing, are really appalling. That too is an inheritance from the past".[44]

This weakness was already apparent when the Confederation of Shipbuilding and Engineering Unions (CSEU), which represented around 2 million workers, submitted a major wage claim to the Engineering Employers Federation (EEF) in 1971. This was the first real test nationally of the new president of the

AUEW, Hugh Scanlon. He had been elected three years earlier, heavily reliant on the Broad Left electoral machine in the industry, which in turn was an amalgam of Communist Party and Labour Left shop stewards and convenors.

Once again, what happened next starkly demonstrated what happens when too much reliance is placed on "left-wing" union leaders. When the talks eventually collapsed in 1972, the miners' strike was already causing massive problems for the employers and the Tory government of Ted Heath. The leaders of the engineering unions, which included CP members like Ken Gill of AUEW TASS, could have gained an astonishing victory if they had called a national strike and joined forces with the miners.

Instead, Scanlon argued that negotiations should take place only on a plant-by-plant basis. Even worse, when the Sheffield District of the AUEW announced their intention to organise a city-wide strike of all their 45,000 members and to stay out until the EEF conceded their claim in full, Scanlon and the AUEW Executive instructed the district to abandon its proposals on the grounds that they were unconstitutional and contrary to the union rule that required a district ballot before a district strike. Many of the CSEU factories in Sheffield were led by Communist Party convenors whose factories were in the heart of the Yorkshire coalfield, where Arthur Scargill had just been elected President of the Yorkshire National Union of Mineworkers (NUM).

In the one area of the country where a large-scale battle was organised in support of the claim—Scanlon's home territory of Manchester—more than 30 different factories had either gone on strike or had been occupied. Scanlon's first visit to the area took place six weeks after these strikes started. Then, his advice to a specially convened, district-wide shop-stewards meeting was that settlements could be negotiated which excluded a reduction in hours. The eventual settlement, reached six months after the miners' historic victory at Saltley, was at a level only slightly above what the shipbuilding employers had agreed with the same unions three months earlier.

The assessment of the deal in *The Economist* was "positively triumphalist": "The employers resisted by adopting trade union tactics; a £2 million strike fund, daily briefings to keep wavering employers in line and even expulsion from the bosses' club, the EEF." (Six were actually booted out, including some of the largest engineering firms in the country: GEC, the second biggest; Hawker Siddeley, the fourth; GKN, Ferranti and British Steel).[45]

In their book on the strike wave of 1972, *Glorious Summer*, Ralph Darlington and Dave Lyddon write:

> The Broad Left and CP politics of the local officials meant that they were not prepared to further challenge the national union's left-wing leadership over the conduct of the dispute. The leading Broad Left stewards were also more oriented on union structures than on shop-floor organisation and were unable, and unwilling, to challenge the district officials. [John] Tocher admitted that "there was a lot of disillusionment after the sit-ins... People had sacrificed a lot, many of them got nothing".[46]

When Heath's Tory government was finally booted out in 1974, the newly elected Labour government under first Harold Wilson and then Jim Callaghan, with Denis Healey as Chancellor of the Exchequer, moved under ruling-class pressure to introduce a stringent monetary policy. This helped to push unemployment to a new post-war record of 1,635,000. The two people who were enlisted by the government to ensure that their drastic assault on working-class living standards—through the wage controls introduced under the Social Contract—were Hugh Scanlon of the AUEW and Jack Jones of the TGWU. They were the most "left-wing" officials of the day and leaders of the two biggest unions, regularly tagged by the Tory press as the "Terrible Twins" of the TUC.

Scanlon and Jones effectively acted as go-betweens for Labour, ferrying the government's demands back and forth to Congress House. At the same time, the electoral machine which

Baron Scanlon of Davyhulme, The Charter, *March 1979.*

had conveyed them to high office now switched to reverse and became a conduit through which the government's demands were communicated down to the network of local officials, factory convenors and shop stewards which had got them elected in the first place—up to and including recommending that their members cross picket lines when strikes took place against wage restraint.

In 1979, Scanlon was made a Life Peer and took the title Baron Scanlon of Davyhulme (his home address) in the County of Greater Manchester. He was said to have taken up golf. I remember going to a gathering held at Manchester Town Hall to celebrate the retirement of the AUEW Divisional Organiser and former Chairman of the Communist Party, John Tocher, at which Scanlon was one of the guest speakers. Virtually the entire audience consisted of left-wing CSEU convenors and shop stewards and here, on his home patch, he told them, only half-jokingly: "Every time I turn over a sod, I think of you lot."

As Duncan later explained: "The Labour government's "Social Contract"—a deal between government, employers and unions which thousands of workers knew as the Social

Con-Trick—was carried through with the indispensable aid of the trade union leaders, including those of the left such as Hugh Scanlon of the engineers, Jack Jones of the transport workers, and Lawrence Daly of the miners' union. As professional intermediaries between workers and employers, trade union officials stand at the heart of reformism".[47]

The result of the Social Contract was that it:

> Achieved for the capitalist class what no Tory government has achieved within living memory. Average real earnings of working people were *cut*. Under a Labour government and with the full agreement of the trade union leaders, average real earnings *fell* by 2 percent in 1975-6 and by 4 percent in 1976-7. No previous Tory government had managed to cut real earnings for employed workers since 1945—and *neither did the Tories under Margaret Thatcher* in the six years 1979-85. The government of Ted Heath had fallen in its attempt to do so. So, here was Labour acting as an alternative government, succeeding for British capitalism where its own parties had failed.[48]

By the time I was encouraged to come to London in 1977 (for reasons which are not entirely clear), the effects of the Social Contract were already all too evident. (As usual, Cliff was the first to see what was coming—his book on the dangers it posed was written by November 1974, only nine months after the Labour government was elected). Until that point, I'd been working in Manchester engineering factories since 1972—the first, for just a few months, was Metro-Vicks; then a foundry and workshop called Knowsley Engineering, directly behind the Old Trafford football ground; and finally at Massey Ferguson on Barton Dock Road.

My time at Knowsley engineering was a real education: I was elected plant convenor mainly as a result of organising a successful campaign to have decent toilets installed. Shortly

"Our Norman" - a regular cartoon in Socialist Worker
by Phil Evans.

afterwards, I was called upon to get everybody out in support of a national one-day strike, called by Hugh Scanlon, in protest at Ted Heath's Industrial Relations Act. Most entertaining of all was that, when the government was forced to introduce a three-day week because of the power shortage brought on by the 1972 miners' strike, it also made the big mistake of introducing inflation-linked pay rises which were triggered monthly by the Office of National Statistics (ONS) inflation figures. These were announced on a Friday morning and we would all gather round the radio, like the shop steward Arnold in the Phil Evans cartoons, to hear how much it had gone up by this time (it always had)—and then work out how much of a pay rise we'd all got.

Eventually, the management sacked me and marched me off the premises on a Friday afternoon when they were able to provide evidence (from experts at the photocopying company,

Xerox) that I had produced a scurrilous factory bulletin called *Knowsley Knews* on their own office machine. Fortunately, thanks to the intervention of our IS district organiser, Pete Robinson, I mounted a lone picket on the following Monday, then dashed inside the works and called a mass meeting demanding support against such blatant victimisation. They kept me on in the end thanks to the assistance of the AUEW Divisional Organiser, John Tocher. He told the company, in no uncertain terms, that this was the Manchester district of the union, and it did not accept its convenors being dismissed. Characteristically, though, he also insisted that I stand for re-election—which I did and lost.

Not long after that, I left and got a job at the Massey Ferguson works on Barton Dock Road. This was the one which had first been built by the government as a "shadow factory" to produce aircraft engines during the war, under Ford management. Later, it was taken over by Platt Brothers which made machinery for the textile industry. Until I read his memoir, I had no idea that Harry Ratner and a few of his comrades had worked at Platt's and led one of the first ever strikes over redundancies there.

Unlike Metro-Vickers and other older established factories, the Barton Dock Road plant mainly employed semi-skilled machinists. Skilled "setters" looked after each section in the machine shop and set up the machines. Eventually, I became shop steward in the machine shop (where a nephew of Hugh Scanlon, Eddie Scanlon, worked at the same time), then secretary of the Joint Shop Stewards Committee and editor of a semi-official, combine-wide bulletin which covered Massey Ferguson plants in Coventry (where another IS member, Roger Kline, was a leading steward), Kilmarnock, Knowsley in Liverpool (where another IS member, Ray Long, worked) and the Perkins Engines sister plant in Peterborough.

In Manchester, the only other IS member at Massey's was Stevie Taylor. He was the convenor at the Massey Ferguson parts department, also on the Barton Dock Road. We did, however, have regular meetings at the Trafford Hotel which drew in workers from other factories on the Trafford Park estate, and occasionally we would get guest speakers along, among them Tony Cliff, Harry McShane and Duncan Hallas.

On arrival in London, my primary job was the production of the rank and file paper for the engineering industry, *Engineers Charter*. I worked in the Industrial Department alongside Steve Jefferys and John Deason at the time of the Grunwick Strike, the firefighters' dispute and the Right to Work Campaign. It was a tumultuous period. When the IS head office at Cottons Gardens was fire-bombed by the National Front, we had to move our regular Central Committee meetings from Shoreditch and from then on met in Cliff and Chanie's front room in Hackney.

What struck me most from these meetings was the extraordinary rapport between Cliff, Duncan and Chanie—and the enthusiasm with which they all approached the issues of the day. What I didn't fully appreciate at the time was that this had developed from such a long association, and all the political ups and downs they had gone through together.

Cliff's ear was almost permanently glued to the radio for the latest news. Writing about him shortly after his death in April 2000, Duncan said that, "Cliff's importance to the movement consists of two elements. First of all was his consistency. Once he had broken with Stalinism, he never wavered." The second attribute was that: "Cliff had an absolutely unerring sense when something was going wrong...he sensed before anyone else the need for change".[49]

By the second half of 1977, Cliff's political antennae were telling him that all was not well inside the working-class movement. Strikes were taking place, but they were going on for much longer than had been the case in 1972. With a few notable exceptions, nowhere near as much solidarity action was being taken by other workers; the negative influence of the trade union bureaucracy had become much more important; and more often than not these disputes ended in defeat. Again, there were exceptions, such as the Gardners' factory occupation in Manchester or the 1979 campaign by the engineering unions. But whereas the general pattern of the early 1970s had been "victories punctuated by defeats", now it was more often "defeats punctuated by catastrophes"—the eventual sacking of Derek Robinson[50] at British Leyland being the prime example.

At the beginning of the discussion over the balance of class forces, which became known as the "downturn" debate, Cliff was in a minority of one. Duncan was one of the first to share Cliff's general assessment, but with caveats. Interviewed for *Socialist Review* in May 1980, Duncan said, "We had this discussion in the SWP about the balance of class forces—the whole upturn or downturn argument. It was necessary and important to come to a realistic appreciation of the situation and that meant recognising the *reality* of the downturn".[51]

However, it was also the case that, "We should not suppose that this *general* appreciation, which is undoubtedly correct in my opinion, enables us to predict very specifically." To give one specific example: "Some of us were very sceptical about the prospect of last year's engineering strike taking place at all—I certainly was. Well, we were wrong".[52]

For many people in the organisation, what made the "downturn" argument difficult to come to terms with was that, away from the industrial struggle, things did not appear to be going badly at all. Most of the rank-and-file groups seemed to be in a healthy state and, not least, the debate took place against a backdrop of the inspirational victory against the National Front at Lewisham, the successful launch of the Anti Nazi League and the phenomenal success of Rock Against Racism.

Ultimately, though, the massive demoralisation which the Labour government had created among its working-class supporters, in terms of wage cuts and unemployment, led to its defeat in the general election of 1979 and Margaret Thatcher's victory, which plagues us all to this day.

Following the subsequent defeat of the year-long Miners' Strike of 1984-85, Duncan wrote that: "Thatcherism did not start with Thatcher, but with the policies of Callaghan and Healey. It is a response to the needs of British capitalism in this period of capitalist crisis. In office, the Labour Party has always served the needs of the capitalist system".[53] Furthermore:

> It is clear from the record that the election of a Labour government in no way guarantees benefits for the working class, let alone advances towards socialism. The working class may have won benefits when Labour governments were in office: the welfare state set up in the years after 1945 is probably the best example. But the Labour government of 1974-79 was just as willing to cut back that welfare state, when the needs of British capitalism demanded this, as its predecessor had been to set it up. A Labour government committed to working *within* the capitalist system is dependent on the willingness, or unwillingness, of the capitalist class to make concessions.[54]

The real reason the welfare state and the gains of 1945-51 had been introduced was not the result of the election of a Labour government; it was because of the mass radicalisation that followed the Second World War. "The capitalist class made these concessions, not because Mr Attlee had been elected prime minister, *but because they feared the strength and militancy of the working class*".[55] He used a lot of italics in his writings did Duncan, very reminiscent of the way he would emphasise a point in one of his talks by suddenly, and often alarmingly, raising his voice from a whisper to a crescendo.

To sum up, to the end of his days, Duncan never altered his view that: "The key to working-class advance lies not with the election of Labour governments, nor with a Labour Party tied to the apron strings of parliamentary electoralism. It lies in the strength and activity of the working class itself."

Nothing that has happened since, either during the Tony Blair or Gordon Brown years, or now with the leadership of the Labour Party in the hands of Keir Starmer, can be said to have changed that analysis. When Jeremy Corbyn unexpectedly became party leader—mainly because Blair and Brown had been so dreadful—the entire Parliamentary Labour Party pulled every trick in the book to undermine his credibility and damage his reputation, even to the extent of ensuring that he would never win a general election.

Duncan was no longer with us to witness the Corbyn phenomenon, but he did see what happened immediately after Labour's electoral defeat in 1979: "From the 1979 conference through the 1980 conference and the January 1981 special conference at Wembley, the left, though suffering some defeats, was able to score a series of victories on both policy and organisation".[56] In itself, he wrote:

> ...this is unremarkable. The same thing happened after the electoral defeat of 1970, culminating in the adoption of "Labour's Programme 1973", with its famous promise of "a fundamental and irreversible shift in the distribution of both wealth and power in favour of the working class" (the wording of which was written by Tony Benn).[57]

Nevertheless, there had been substantial changes, a very important one being:

> There is a *movement* associated with the name of Tony Benn, a movement going far beyond the ranks of the regular attenders at Labour Party ward and constituency meetings. Benn's campaign for the deputy leadership produced big and enthusiastic meetings at a series of union conferences... and he can still pull much bigger crowds than all the right-wing MPs put together.[58]

Ultimately, "the forward march of Bennery" was halted when Healey won the deputy leadership election, by a whisker, at the

October 1981 Labour Party conference and by the successes of the right in the elections for Labour's National Executive. The immediate upshot of this was that, despite these defeats, "Benn remains a focus of a very much bigger Labour Party left than has existed since the early fifties".[59]

On the other hand, it had also become increasingly clear that the left was in retreat and that the extent of the swing to the left was extremely narrow: "It has been a swing among activists (including a lot of union activists), not among the masses." The results of consultation exercises carried out by the TGWU and NUPE on the 1981 deputy leadership election "...was profoundly revealing. It showed big support for Healey who could scarcely even get a reasonable minority amongst the activists at the time".[60]

The reason for this state of affairs, Duncan wrote, was clear enough: "It is the profound downturn in the industrial struggle in the last few years... The activists moved left, seeking a 'political solution' in the Labour Party to their industrial weakness. But the mass of workers do not move left in such circumstances. Their radicalisation is *always* associated with a rising level of direct action".[61]

There was no doubt in Duncan's mind that the politics of the Bennite left were reformist politics. "All the genuine spokesmen and women of the Labour Left stand, thus far, on the common ground of electoralism and parliamentary politics." They can, and do, talk about and even encourage extra-parliamentary mobilisations. "However, the extra-parliamentary activity envisaged is directed towards what happens *inside* parliament".[62]

Benn made this quite explicit when he spoke at a major rally on "The Crisis and Future of the Left" held at Central Hall, Westminster, on 17 March 1980. The ticket-only event, which was organised by the Labour Co-ordinating Committee, was dubbed the "Debate of the Decade" and attracted a full house of 2,600 with queues forming outside. The keynote speakers were Tony Benn, Paul Foot, Tariq Ali, Stuart Holland, Hilary Wainwright and Audrey Wise MP.

In his speech, Tony Benn asserted that:

The radicalisation of the main body of the labour movement, the genuine restatement of the socialist case,
the debate on democracy in the Labour Party today is
sharper and more real than it has ever been. That is the
case for democratic socialism. I can only lay one claim
for it and that is that the British Labour Party is the
instrument of the British working-class movement and
nobody here can deny it whatever view they may take.[63]

Duncan was not invited onto the platform for this debate,
but he did speak from the floor. During his allotted two minutes,
he said:

Comrades, two minutes, two points. Tony Benn said at
one point that I could just hear above the hecklers, "If
the Labour Party fails then certain consequences may
follow". What did he mean *if* the Labour Party fails?
We're not talking here, comrades, about some hypothesis, some untried experiment, some new movement of
which we have no experience. For God's sake we have
had seven Labour governments, five of them, well four-
and-a-half anyway, with a majority in parliament and
indeed Brother Benn was a cabinet minister in two of
them over a considerable number of years.[64]

Expanding on this point, Duncan said:

Now, if you take the view that the Labour Party is a
socialist party—you know, the 1945 manifesto said
the Labour Party is a socialist party and proud of it—
from that point of view of course we have to say that
the Labour Party is an abysmal failure, because we're
talking about a record of seventy years".[65]

On the other hand:

...from another point of view and a more important point of view—and that's what really ought to concern us tonight—the Labour Party has been a roaring success. It has been a roaring success in terms of the ideas of those who have always been its central leaders, from the sanctified Keir Hardie down to the next one... a party of reform within capitalism using socialist rhetoric to conceal policies of reforming capitalism. A party attempting to solve the problems of working people, yes attempting to do, but always subordinated to the central priorities of capitalism.[66]

At the end of his two minutes, Duncan concluded with this flourish:

Now, and this is my final point, you know we are asked to believe in miracles, we are asked to believe that an institution which throughout its entire history, although admittedly with internal conflict, has governed this country over a great many years and has preserved and sometimes strengthened British capitalism— we're asked to believe that this can become a socialist organisation. My God, comrades, maybe the SWP has a hell of a hard struggle ahead of them. I don't doubt it. But at least that's the struggle of the road to a fundamental transformation of society. Their road is the road of another attempt to shore up capitalism.[67]

Notes

1   Andrew Thorpe, "The Membership of the Communist Party of Great Britain 1920-1945" in *Historical Journal* 43:3 (2000) pp777-800. The figures Thorpe quotes are January 1939—17,539 members, March 1945—45,435 members.

2   Ruth Frow, *Eddie Frow—The Making of an Activist*, (Manchester: Working-Class Movement Library, 1999) p.51.

3   Peter Fryer, *The Battle for Socialism* (London: Socialist Labour League, 1959) pp42-43.

4   Harry Ratner, *Reluctant Revolutionary: Memoirs of a Trotskyist, 1936-1960* (London: Socialist Platform. 1994) p.120

5   Reg Groves, *The Balham Group: How British Trotskyism Began* (London: Pluto Press. 1973) p7.

6   Ratner, *Reluctant Revolutionary*, pp24-43.

7   Ratner, *Reluctant Revolutionary*, p79.

8   Ratner, *Reluctant Revolutionary*, p81.

9   Ratner, *Reluctant Revolutionary*, p81.

10 Duncan Hallas, "The Communist Party and the General Strike", *International Socialism*, 1: 88 (May 1976), pp.16-24

11 Hallas, "The Communist Party and the General Strike", p17.

12 Hallas, "The Communist Party and the General Strike", p17.

13 Hallas, "The Communist Party and the General Strike", p17.

14 Hallas, "The Communist Party and the General Strike", p17.

15 Hallas, "The Communist Party and the General Strike", p17.

16 Duncan Hallas, *The Comintern* (London: Bookmarks. 1985). Republished by Haymarket Books, 2008, p7. www.marxists.org/archive/hallas/works/1985/comintern/

17 Duncan Hallas, *The Labour Party: Myth and Reality* (London: Socialist Workers Party, 1981). Republished in September 1985. www.marxists.org/archive/hallas/works/1981/02/labour.html

18 Hallas, *The Labour Party Myth and Reality*, p10.

19 Hallas, *The Comintern*, pp164-165

20 Hallas, *The Comintern*, p116.

21 Hallas, *The Comintern*, p116.

22 Hallas, *The Comintern*, p117.

23 Ratner, *Reluctant Revolutionary*, p120.

24 Ratner, *Reluctant Revolutionary*, p120.

25 Ratner, *Reluctant Revolutionary*, p122.

26 Ratner, *Reluctant Revolutionary*, p123.

27 Ratner, *Reluctant Revolutionary*, p139.

28 R Tennant (aka Tony Cliff), "The Struggle of the Powers", *Socialist Review*, Vol 1, No 1 (November 1950). www.marxists.org/archive/cliff/works/1950/11/powers.html

29 Tennant (Cliff) "The Struggle of the Powers".

30 Chanie Rosenberg, Frank Henderson & Ian Birchall, "Duncan Hallas—An Agitator of the Best Kind", *Socialist Review 268* (November 2002). https://socialistworker.co.uk/socialist-review-archive/duncan-hallas-agitator-best-kind/

31 Duncan Hallas, "The Stalinist Parties" (1951), included in Duncan Hallas (ed) *The Fourth International, Stalinism & the Origins of the International Socialists* (London: Pluto, 1971) pp65-75. www.marxists.org/archive/hallas/works/1951/xx/stalparty.htm

32 Hallas, "The Stalinist Parties".

33 Hallas, *The Labour Party: Myth and Reality*, p9.

34 Hallas, *The Labour Party: Myth and Reality*, p10.

35 John Rudge, "Duncan Hallas: A Life on the Frontline" in this volume.

36 Rosenberg, Henderson & Birchall, "Duncan Hallas—An Agitator of the Best Kind".

37 Rosenberg, Henderson & Birchall, "Duncan Hallas—An Agitator of the Best Kind".

38 Duncan Hallas, "Workers' Power—The Only Alternative to the Labour/Tory Run-around", *Socialist Worker*. May 1969, www.marxists.org/archive/hallas/works/1969/05/wpower.htm

39 Hallas, *The Labour Party: Myth and Reality*.

40 Rosenberg, Henderson & Birchall, "Duncan Hallas: An Agitator of the Best Kind".

41 Duncan Hallas, "Towards a

Revolutionary Socialist Party", in *Party and Class* (London: Pluto, 1971) p9.

42   Hallas, "Towards a Revolutionary Socialist Party", p24.

43   Hallas, "Towards a Revolutionary Socialist Party", p25.

44   Tony Cliff, *The Crisis—Social Contract or Socialism* (London: Pluto, 1975) p131.

45   Ralph Darlington & Dave Lyddon, *Glorious Summer—Class Struggle in Britain 1972* (London: Bookmarks. 2001) p.132

46   Darlington & Lyddon, *Glorious Summer*, p.134

47   Hallas, *The Labour Party: Myth and Reality*, p27.

48   Hallas, *The Labour Party: Myth and Reality*, p28.

49   Duncan Hallas, 'Tony Cliff', *Socialist Review* 241 (May 2000), www.marxists. org/archive/hallas/works/2000/05/ cliff.htm

50   Derek Robinson was a CP member and union convenor at the British Leyland Longbridge plant. He was sacked by British Leyland management in 1979.

51   "Where do we go from here? An interview with Duncan Hallas", *Socialist Review* (April/May 1980), www.marxists.org/archive/hallas/ works/1980/04/whereto.htm

52   "Where do we go from here? An interview with Duncan Hallas"

53   Hallas, *The Labour Party: Myth and Reality*, p34.

54   Hallas, *The Labour Party: Myth and Reality*, p35.

55   Hallas, *The Labour Party: Myth and Reality*, p35.

56   Duncan Hallas, "Revolutionaries and the Labour Party", *International Socialism* 2:16 (Spring 1982) pp.1-35

57   Hallas, "Revolutionaries and the Labour Party", p27.

58   Hallas, "Revolutionaries and the Labour Party", p28.

59   Hallas, "Revolutionaries and the Labour Party", p28.

60   Hallas, "Revolutionaries and the Labour Party", p32.

61   Hallas, "Revolutionaries and the Labour Party", p32.

62   Hallas,"Revolutionaries and the Labour Party", p28.

63   Peter Hain (ed) *The Crisis and Future of the Left* (Full transcript of the "Debate of the Decade")(London: Pluto Press, 1980) Tony Benn speech, p.53

64   Duncan Hallas intervention from the floor, in Hain, *The Crisis and Future of the Left*, p.63

65   Hain, *The Crisis and Future of the Left*, p.63

66   Hain, *The Crisis and Future of the Left*, p.63

67   Hain, *The Crisis and Future of the Left*, p.63

In the Beginning...
Duncan Hallas

(*Socialist Review*, February 1984)[1]

Following the antics of the TUC of late, many socialists are looking to the election of left leaders to solve the problem. Duncan Hallas looks at the history of the bureaucracy and the role of its left wing.

When Marx died in 1883 the total number of trade unionists in Britain was well below a million. A considerable proportion of them were organised in small, often localised, craft societies and membership fluctuated markedly with the trade cycle. Collective bargaining, where it took place at all, was typically local, firm by firm, and sometimes, literally "piece by piece", as in the boilermaking trades.

The union officialdom was not conspicuous, not an influential social layer, and had little *national* presence or cohesion (although the TUC had existed since 1868). When Engels died, twelve years later, the situation had changed somewhat as a result of the mass strikes of the late eighties and the rise of the "New Unionism", the organisation of the unskilled. By 1892 there were about one and a half million trade unionists, many in quite big unions, and although the numbers fell off for a while they were climbing towards two million by the end of the century.

Neither Marx nor Engels, therefore, had much experience of *stable, mass* working class organisation. Neither seriously discussed, a few casual comments aside, the question of the social role of the labour bureaucracy.

Understandably enough. They were concerned with the enormous transformation from the mass struggle and semi-revolutionary atmosphere of the early decades of the century to the conservative, "respectable" (and weak) trade societies of the 50s, 60s and 70s. Of course the contrast can be overstated but it is real enough.

For Marx, it was due above all to the fact that Britain, the heartland of the new industrial capitalist order, was still the "workshop of the world". In the 1880s, the little town of Burnley, up on the Pennine slopes, produced about 80 percent of the *world* output of machine made carpets. And much later, in 1913, 40 percent of the total new *world* tonnage of steam ships was built in British yards, 25 percent of it on the Clyde alone.

So Marx's comment that Britain had produced not only a bourgeoisie but also a bourgeois aristocracy and bourgeoisified (to use a later term) proletariat, had a real, material basis. He was right to stress that, the *main* fact, which determined the immediate prospects for revolutionaries; equally right in predicting that this state of affairs must pass away. But the very concentration on these brute facts blinded Marx and Engels to the problem of the labour bureaucracy, even in the eighties.

Lenin too. Taking up and vastly developing Marx's insight into the reality and consequences of uneven development, he produced a theory of imperialism (1916), the operative content of which, in this context, was that "a whole layer of working men", not only in Britain but in all the ten industrialised countries, had been "bought off"—the famous theory of the "labour aristocracy".

Lenin himself thought of this as very much a minority—a fifth, a quarter at most. But he thought that this layer was decisive in making opportunism and reformism dominant in the workers' movement.

He was both right and wrong about this. Right in that the German pipefitter or the British boilermaker was objectively an "aristocrat" in relation to "his own" working class, let alone those of the Third World (in 1914 the rates of the British Engineering Union (ASE) for fitters and turners were exactly double the labourer's rates). Wrong in thinking that this layer of skilled workers was therefore irrevocably conservatised.

In the event, the mass strikes of 1917-18 in Austria-Hungary, Germany and Britain, which shook the imperialist powers to the foundations, were, in the main, led by "labour aristocrats". He was wrong too, in the belief that "the most exploited and oppressed" would always be the most rebellious.

Naturally, the opposite is not true either.

Marx, because he had never seen a developed Labour movement, Lenin, because such a thing did not exist in Russia, laid too little emphasis on the problem of the labour bureaucracy.

It was, in fact, the pro-imperialist English Fabians who first pinpointed the problem. The Webbs' *History of Trade Unionism* (first edition, 1894) pointed to an important change in the, still very weak, British trade unions in the last half of the nineteenth century:

> During these years we watch a shifting of leadership from the casual enthusiast and irresponsible agitator to a class of permanent salaried officers expressly chosen out of the rank and file of trade unionists for their superior business capacity.

The Fabian couple naturally approved of this change but it never occurred to them to doubt that what they called "this Civil Service of the Trade Union world" was essentially conservative. They wrote:

Whilst the points at issue no longer affect his own earnings or conditions of employment, any disputes between his members and their employers increase his work and add to his worry. The former vivid sense of the privations and subjections of the artisan life gradually fades from his mind: and he comes more and more to regard all complaints as perverse and unreasonable...

Unconsciously biased by distaste for the hard and unthankful work that a strike entails, he finds himself in small sympathy with the men's demands, and eventually arranges a compromise on terms distasteful to a large section of his members.

The Webbs also noted how "insidiously, silently, unknown even to himself the official insensibly adopts more and more of the vices of his middle class neighbours".[2]

Now note that all this was written about the British, the first institutionalised labour movement, when it was still dominated by craft societies, which, typically, had a rather low ratio of officials to members and in which the election, and regular re-election, of *all* officials was still the norm.

Spontaneous

In fact it was a bit out of date by the time it was published. With the rise of the "New Unionism" from 1889, and still more, in the years of the "great revolt" of 1909-1914, union membership rose from 1,530,000 (1894) to 4,145,000 (1914) and the numbers of full-time officials rose much more than proportionately. And, typically, the officials of the new unions were appointed, not elected.

From this time on the role of this new social layer has been crucial in the class struggle.

It expanded rapidly as union membership shot up during and immediately after the First World War (reaching nearly eight and a half million at its peak in 1918). Moreover, when the decline set in, in the early twenties, the officialdom did not shrink. Hinton and Hyman make the point that "while union membership fell drastically during the 1920s, the number, of full-time officials appears actually to have increased".[3]

The influence of the bureaucracy was, of course, enormously enhanced by the growth of national negotiations and often very detailed national agreements, especially after 1914. Agreements which the bureaucracies fought to enforce on unwilling sections of the membership at the cost, often, of fighting against "unofficial" action.

Even before 1914 this was apparent. "Practically every one of the great strikes from 1911 to 1914 was begun as an unofficial, spontaneous movement of the workers, spreading rapidly," wrote the Communist Party historian, Ralph Fox.[4]

Only then did the reformist trade union bureaucrats lend the strike the official support of the union, while their swift acceptance in every case of the "mediation" of the Liberal government doomed the strike to semi-failure.

It is something of a simplification but it will stand as an indication of the dual nature of trade unionism and the trade union bureaucracies under capitalism: on the one hand, a weapon of sections of workers against their bosses, on the other hand, a means of social control over workers in struggle by the bureaucracies in the interests, objectively, of the boss class.

This duality is *always* present, is inherent in the very nature of trade unionism, but, of course, the different elements are not always of the same weight. The balance of class forces, the moods of the working class, the actual course of class struggle have profound and usually determining effects on the outcome.

The really spectacular, open sell-out is the exception, not the rule. The labour bureaucracy is not all-powerful, far from it, and its normal rule is one of "balancing", of seeking a deal within the framework of capitalism, more or less favourable to the workers concerned according to the circumstances.

There have been periods, e.g. from 1940 to the middle fifties, when the bureaucracies have opposed practically all strikes. There have been periods, e.g. from the late sixties till very recently, when they have led a good many strikes—or misled them, but at any rate called them.

Nor is it the case that the officials *usually* want to lose disputes. The National Graphical Association (NGA) leadership did not, does not, *want* to lose to Eddie Shah. They wanted, and want, a compromise without risking a general confrontation with the print bosses. In the given circumstances this is a self-defeating policy but that is a different matter.

The officials, as a social layer, are rooted in working-class organisation. Without it they are non-existent. They seek, typically, to defend it in their own fashion—class-collaborationist, sectional and so on—but to defend it. Nor are the officials invariably forced into action by an insurgent membership. They often are, but Arthur Scargill today has pushed hard for the overtime ban which sections of the workforce are less than enthusiastic about.

The matter, then, is more complicated than a simple "the officials always sell out" position suggests. What is true is that they have a built-in tendency to limit struggles and to class-collaboration—as a group, that is. What then, of the role of left officials? Undoubtedly there is a very real difference between Arthur Scargill and Frank Chapple and it is nonsense to suppose that this makes no difference to what their organisations actually do.

The question is, given the general nature of the bureaucracy, how can its conservative influence be most effectively countered? It is a very live issue. The Broad Left Organising Committee, which is calling a conference in March, puts the weight of its activity on electing left officials. The Socialist Workers Party has always put the emphasis on seeking to strengthen rank and file organisation. Both trends have a quite long history.

Writing of the pre-1914 syndicalists, Bob Holton noted:

> With hindsight the most striking point about syndi-calist industrial strategy was the belief that trade union reconstruction and dual unionism were the only

options available. There was, as yet, no conception of independent workplace organisation as a third alternative. Unlike the wartime shop stewards and workers' committee movement, the pre-war syndicalists failed to grasp the potential importance of this form of organisation, either as a means of moving from amalgamation *propaganda* to all-grades workshop *action* (on the railways—DH), or as a way of building a counterweight to trade union officialdom.[5]

Most of them believed in amalgamation to form industrial unions (organisations of everybody in the industry) as the means to overcome craft sectionalism, which they saw as the main problem. Union structure, rather than the conservatism of the officials, was the syndicalist target, indeed conservatism was seen as a consequence of the craft structure.

It is easy now to see the fallacy. The great syndicalist organisational success, the amalgamation which created the National Union of Railwaymen (NUR), with its model "industrial" structure, did not lead to a fighting union. The "non-sectionalist" officialdom proved as class collaborationist as its sectionalist predecessors.

Questions of union organisation are sometimes extremely important. Sectionalism is a curse. But class collaboration has deeper roots. It is organic to the labour bureaucracy as a social layer, whether craft, industrial or general.

The shop stewards and workers committee movement of the war years did indeed make a great advance. It was forced on them by the active collaboration of practically the entire officialdom with the government and the employers. The famous statement of the Manchester conference in 1916, "We will support the officials just so long as they rightly represent the workers but will act independently immediately they misrepresent them", is still today an excellent guideline.[6]

The shop stewards and workers committee movement itself did not survive very long. The 1922 lock-out in the engineering trades, where its main forces were, finished it off. But out of it came an important section of the cadre of the Communist Party.

They carried over into it important elements of a critical understanding of the role of labour bureaucracies and an emphasis on rank and file organisation. Moreover, the CP's attempt to establish a rank and file oriented industrial movement from 1924 on coincided with (and to a limited extent caused) the first period in which a group of left officials played a leading role in the TUC.

These officials, or some of them, had a considerable reputation for militancy and class consciousness. A J Cook, elected general secretary of the Miners' Federation early in 1924, had been prominent in the bitter Cambrian strike in 1910 and had become one of the leading left wingers in South Wales.

George Hicks, who had been a leading militant in the building trades in London and conspicuous for attempts at amalgamation, was now general secretary of the AUBTW (bricklayers). Alf Purcell of the furniture trades had a long history of involvement in socialist causes in Salford. Alonzo Swales of the Amalgamated Engineering Union (AEU) had been prominent in the amalgamation movement and was reputed to be a reliable ally of the CP.

All these men (except Cook, who favoured biblical rhetoric) spoke the language of Marxism. Cook and Purcell had joined the CP at its foundation or soon after. Significantly, both had left as the party began to exert some discipline on party union officials.

Nonetheless, it was an impressive looking crop of lefts, certainly nothing quite like it had been seen before and, in the crucial years from 1924 to 1926, Cook, Hicks, Purcell and Swales played a leading role in the TUC, whose general secretary Bromley and his deputy Citrine were also reckoned as adhering to the left.

This leftish leadership was confronted by the ruling class offensive of 1925-26, which aimed, first of all, to break the power of the Miners' Federation, then the biggest union, as a means of bringing the rest to heel.

It responded, at first, with apparent vigour. The mine owners' ultimatum of June 1925, demanding pay cuts and increased hours, was met by the decision of a conference of executives to call for a total embargo on the movement of coal.

The government backed down to gain time. The mine owners withdrew their ultimatum and were awarded a subsidy for nine months to enable a Royal Commission to report. A temporary victory had been gained without a shot being fired.

Of course, the struggle had merely been postponed. The government set out to prepare systematically for the inevitable confrontation. The TUC, including its left wing leaders, talked left and did nothing at all. A combination of militant rhetoric (the September 1925 TUC was, in words, the most radical ever) and practical passivity prepared the way for the sell-out of May 1926.

The effect of the left leaders was twofold. They raised expectations and so, to some degree, willingness to fight and at the same time disarmed criticism and spread illusions. As Page Arnot, the first CP historian of the general strike, wrote in 1926:

> Knowledge of the existence of this left wing was at once a stimulant and a narcotic for the masses. It gave them a rallying ground, lent confidence to their leftward mood; but then it put vigilance to sleep and led to overtrustfulness.[7]

When the general strike was actually called, the lefts collapsed completely and, with the exception of Cook, joined the right in the catastrophic sell-out of 12 May when the strike was ignominiously called off.

It was not a matter, as it might appear in retrospect, of a conscious conspiracy to sell out. There were real conflicts between the left and the right-wing bureaucrats but they were conflicts within the framework of trade union assumptions. The lefts, no less than the right, shrank from a showdown with the capitalist state.

Trotsky accurately described them a few months before the general strike:

> The left faction of the General Council is distinguished by its complete ideological shapelessness and is therefore incapable of organisationally assuming the leadership of the trade union movement.[8]

Some of the lefts were intoxicated by their own rhetoric; all hoped and believed, or half-believed, that bluff and deception would shatter the walls of the capitalist Jericho. Sober calculation, realism and ruthless determination—all qualities displayed by the bourgeois leadership—were completely absent. And so, in the time of crisis, the left leaders proved worse than useless. They betrayed their own past as well as the working class and yet, at the same time, they were true to themselves. Left officials they had been, officials they remained.

Ultimatum

The great crisis of the middle twenties led to a shattering defeat for the working class and a prolonged period of right wing dominance in the unions. Not until some 40 years later, in the late sixties, did a new group of lefts, the Scanlon-Jones leaderships, become temporarily dominant in the TUC. The outcome was a less spectacular but no less real betrayal—the Social Contract and its result, the weakened and rightward moving TUC of today.

The point, for revolutionary socialists, is that the betrayals were not primarily the consequence of individual lack of moral fibre. They were a function of the very nature of labour bureaucracies of whatever political complexions and *therefore* of the necessity to build independently of the officialdom, without any ultra-left ignoring of the (real but limited) struggle in the union machines.

Trotsky's brilliant criticism of the British CP's policy in 1925-26 with its slogan "All Power to the General Council" was not centred on the fact that the party supported the left officials against the right (it had to), but on its *reliance* on electing left officials at the expense of its own struggle for leadership through rank and file organisations. His summary of the outcome is very pertinent to the attitude revolutionaries must have to the Broad Left Organising Committee and similar operations.

> (They were) actually subordinating the Communist Party to the Minority Movement... The masses knew as the leaders of this movement only Purcell, Hicks and Cook, whom, moreover, Moscow vouched for. These "left" friends, in a serious test, shamefully betrayed the proletariat. The revolutionary workers were thrown into confusion, sank into apathy and naturally extended their disappointment to the Communist Party itself, which has only been the passive part of this whole mechanism of perfidy and betrayal.[9]

It is very tempting, when shopfloor activity is hard, as it is today, to see the election of left officials as a short cut. We must remember where it is a short cut to.

Notes

1   From *Socialist Review,* 62 (February 1984) pp12-14. Transcribed by Einde O'Callaghan for the Marxists' Internet Archive.

2   Sidney & Beatrice Webb, *History of Trade Unionism* (London: Longmans, Green & Co, 1920) www.gutenberg. org/files/66887/66887-h/66887-h. htm

3   *Trade Unions and Revolution*, p18. This little pamphlet is factually valuable but marred politically by a too propagandist approach - D H.

4   Ralph Fox, *The Class Struggle in Britain 1880-1914*, quoted by Brian Pearce in "Some Past Rank and File Movements" in *Labour Review,* Vol. 4 No. 1, (April-May 1959) pp13-24. www.marxists.org/archive/ pearce/1959/04/rankandfile.htm

5   Bob Holton, *British Syndicalism 1900-1914* (London: Pluto Press, 1976) p205.

6   This is, in fact, a quote from a bulletin issued by the Clyde Workers' Committee from 1915. Clyde Workers' Committee, *To All Clyde Workers* (1915) www.marxists.org/archive/ gallacher/1915/clyde-committee.htm

7   Robert Page Arnot, *The General Strike* (1926) quoted in Joseph Redman (Brian Pearce) "British Communist History" in *Labour Review*, Vol 2: No 4 (July–August 1957) pp106–110. www.marxists.org/archive/ pearce/1957/07/commhist.html

8   Leon Trotsky, *Writings on Britain, Volume 2: Problems of the British Revolution*, Ch I, www.marxists.org/ archive/trotsky/britain/probs/ch01. htm

9   Leon Trotsky, *Writings On Britain*, Ch 14, www.marxists.org/archive/ trotsky/works/britain/ch13.htm

In a Class of Our Own
Duncan Hallas

(*Socialist Worker*, 22 November 1975)

A comrade from Scotland asks: "The working class are supposed to be the agent for building socialism but who are the working class?

"In the case of miners, dockers, engineers and railwaymen it is obvious that they are part of the working class but what about the large numbers of white-collar workers in teaching, clerical, administrative, management and supervisory jobs?

"Do they produce surplus value or do they live off surplus value? In other words are they part of the proletariat or are they petty-bourgeois?"

For Marxists, a worker is someone who does not own means of production and so is forced to sell his labour power to someone (nowadays, some institution) who does, a capitalist, in order to earn a living. A worker is a wage earner, wholly or mainly dependent on wages for his livelihood.

On this basis, clerks and teachers are workers and so, to a large extent, are most supervising personnel below the level at which shareholding—a share is a certificate entitling you to a part of the surplus value produced by the workers—becomes important. Workers and their families are the overwhelming majority of the population in Britain.

But, of course, that does not end the matter. It is quite clear that a town clerk on £12,000 a year or a headteacher on £6,000, even if they own nothing beyond personal possessions, are in a very different position from a council dustman or the lady who cleans the floors.

The difference is not only a matter of money, of job security, big pensions and so on. It is also the fact that the typical high-salaried individual is part of a *chain of command* for a capitalist (or state-capitalist) enterprise or for the capitalist state. This is not true in all cases; some highly-paid people are technical specialists, but these, too, tend to adopt the outlook of the top brass whose material conditions they share to some extent.

The really important thing is that the line between working class and "petty-bourgeois" cannot, under modern conditions, be drawn *simply* by reference to the *source* of income, since the great bulk of employed people are wage or salaried earners, proletarians on a strict definition. The petty-bourgeoisie of the last century, shopkeepers, artisans, independent professional people etc still exists, but is now much less important than the salaried people.

The line is drawn in the course of political struggle. The lower ranks of the salaried hierarchies can be drawn into the working class movement, even the middle ranks can under favourable circumstances. The extraordinarily rapid growth of white-collar trade unionism is an aspect of this struggle, although only an aspect.

But before developing this point it is necessary to dispose of a red-herring: the distinction between productive and non-productive work. Not that this distinction is unimportant in some connections. It is, but it is not decisive in *this* connection.

Marx called "productive work" that work on which surplus value was realised, and which therefore contributed *directly* to the accumulation of capital. Non-productive work was that which did not.

The distinction has nothing whatever to do with usefulness. Some absolutely essential jobs—not least the reproduction of the workforce itself—are "unproductive" from this point of view. Some "productive" work is downright harmful—the manufacture of heroin for instance.

Marx made the distinction because it was useful for the job he had in hand, the analysis of "the economic law of motion" of capitalist society. To focus on capital accumulation was essential for this purpose.

But "productive" and "non-productive" are not at all the same thing as manual and white-collar. There are productive white-collar workers (Marx himself included managers in this category) and there are non-productive manual workers.

The definition of productive work, made for the purpose of economic analysis, has no relevance to the question of "who are the working class".

To return to the political problem: how can sections of the "intermediate" layers of society—both the salaried and the "old" petty-bourgeoisie—be pulled to the side of socialism?

These social groups can play no *independent* political role in society.

But that does not mean that they are politically unimportant. Far from it. Normally they are, in large part, an essential prop for the ruling class and a broad political base on which conservatism rests.

But under conditions of acute social crisis these layers move—either left or right, to socialism or to fascism. "For the social crisis to bring about the proletarian revolution," wrote Trotsky in connection with Germany in 1930, "it is necessary that, besides other conditions, a decisive shift of the petty-bourgeois classes occurs in the direction of the proletariat...

"When revolutionary hope embraces the whole proletarian mass, it inevitably pulls behind it on the road of revolution considerable and growing sections of the petty-bourgeoisie."

The opposite can happen and did in Germany. If there is no revolutionary lead, then "the petty-bourgeoisie swings in the direction of the most extreme reaction with such force that it draws behind it many sections of the proletariat". It provides the mass base for fascism.

The outcome depends, first and foremost, on the struggle for revolutionary politics inside the working class.

Stalinism, the United Front and the International Socialist Tradition
Dave Sherry

Duncan Hallas had a huge bearing on my political development, as he did upon thousands of my generation and many others before and since. Those who knew and worked alongside Duncan will fondly remember him as an inspirational speaker, a prolific and talented writer and an outstanding teacher of Marxist ideas. He was what Gramsci called an "organic intellectual"—more than a theoretician and frankly dismissive of what he called "Academic Marxism". In 1983 Duncan flew to the United States to do a speaking tour marking the centenary of Marx's death. To coincide with his visit, *Socialist Worker* in the US carried an article he wrote on Marx's legacy:

> The incredible richness of Marx's thought nowadays supports a whole industry—a growth industry until very recently—of commentaries on commentaries on

Marx and so on, ad infinitum. The people who make a living out of this—and not a bad living either—are not Marxists, although most of them think they are. Why not? Because as Marx wrote as a young man, "the philosophers have only interpreted the world in various ways. The point, however, is to change it". To be a Marxist, you have to be a fighter in the cause of the working class, nationally and internationally, as Marx himself was.[1]

Duncan was certainly a fighter in the cause of the working class. From the moment he joined the tiny Trotskyist movement as a teenage engineering apprentice, he was an active, conscious participant in the class struggle. He was an enthusiastic paper seller—from the *Socialist Appeal* in 1943 right through to *Socialist Worker* from the time it first appeared in 1968.

As a schoolteacher in the late 1960s he was a key figure in Wandsworth NUT and helped build the militant teachers' rank and file movement in London. According to fellow teacher Chanie Rosenberg, "Duncan played a crucial role in a movement that changed teachers' attitudes from being 'ragged-trousered educationalists', who needed two jobs to keep their heads above water, to being organised trade unionists and an integral part of the working class".[2]

James Connolly, the subject of one of Duncan's best talks at the SWP Skegness event in 1981, wrote, "The only true prophets are those who carve out the future".[3] All his adult life Duncan strove not to just comment or analyse but to shape the world he lived in.

Year after year, until forced to retire due to ill health in 1995, he would fill the big meeting halls at the SWP's annual Marxism event and its Skegness rallies, speaking on or debating a multitude of topics—Historical Materialism, the Origins of Humanity, the Trade Union Bureaucracy, the General Strike, Marx and the National Question, the Russian Revolution, the Spanish Civil War, the Communist International, the Labour

Party, Trotsky's Marxism, the Rise of Stalinism, Fighting Fascism, the French Revolution and so on.

For decades, like Tony Cliff, but in a different fashion, he was a major public face of both the International Socialists and then the Socialist Workers Party, travelling the country week after week, speaking at local branch meetings. He was a prolific and engaging writer, contributing regularly to *Socialist Worker* and all of the party's publications. For a time, he was the National Secretary of the IS and later the editor of *International Socialism*.

In his obituary for Duncan in 2002 Paul Foot wrote:

> I got to know Duncan more intimately when I was working on *Socialist Worker* and he would appear on Monday mornings to write the leaders. He would grab himself a disgusting coffee, light up an infernal cigarette, bark out testy comments about the state of the world, and then, grabbing a biro, would scribble out in longhand an impeccable editorial. He was the most coherent socialist I ever knew, whether he was writing or speaking.[4]

He was a skilful debater and polemicist and when controversy raged or a formal debate with other organisations and individuals was needed Duncan stepped up. A recently digitalised tape recording of his debate on the 50th anniversary of the Spanish Civil War with leading Communist Party member Monty Johnstone is a fine example of how he would start by addressing the strength of his opponent's argument before demolishing it.[5] He travelled abroad to speak at events of sister organisations in the International Socialist Tendency and people all over the world remember him, not least the groups of workers and activists in South Africa, where he did a popular speaking tour before the fall of apartheid.

At a time when most of the left worldwide still had illusions in Stalin's Russia, Duncan was one of a tiny minority who insisted that revolutionary socialism was equally opposed to the barbarism of the Western empires and the barbarism of the

Stalinist regimes. As a teenager he became increasingly aware of the deadening influence of Stalinism on the labour movement both locally and internationally—a block to revolution and the opposite of everything Marx stood for, discrediting both in the eyes of most working people.

He'd maintain that position from 1943, when he joined the Workers International League, one of the more outgoing of the early Trotskyist grouplets,[6] then the Revolutionary Communist Party (RCP) and then the Socialist Review Group (SRG), right up to and beyond the collapse of Stalinism and the USSR itself in 1991. By then, of course, the numbers of adherents and supporters of the theory of bureaucratic state capitalism had increased considerably, but that was thanks to a few individuals like Duncan, one of the tiny handful of members of the British section of the Fourth International, who supported Tony Cliff when he first developed the theory in 1947-8 and who helped form the Socialist Review Group alongside him in 1950.

In rejecting Stalinism, Duncan never made what he called "the no less dangerous mistake of Stalinophobia".[7] And that was important, because it set the tone for the United Front method of looking outward and working both *with and against* the Communist Parties—something unique to our tradition that continues to be applied to other areas of our work today. As John Rudge notes in his contribution to this collection, "The Stalinist Parties", written by Duncan in 1951, can rightly be considered as one of the founding texts of the IS Tradition."

In the foreword to a book on the Russian Revolution I wrote five years ago, I acknowledged "owing a great deal to Tony Cliff, Duncan Hallas, Paul Foot, Chris Harman and Harry McShane— five remarkable socialists who enlivened the international socialist tradition for me and thousands like me in the early 1970s and for many others before and since. The five would have had a lot to say had they been around for the centenary of 1917. I was fortunate enough to have been around when they did have their say".[8] I could never have written such a book without drawing heavily on Duncan's enormous contribution to defending and developing the revolutionary socialist tradition over a period of 60 years, or without his advice and encouragement over the long period I got to know him.

On most of the many occasions he came to speak in Glasgow and Central Scotland between 1975 and his retirement in 1995, he stayed with me; something I relished and miss even now. On every occasion, bar none, his routine was to deliver a talk that made people glad they had come to hear him, then head for the pub so he could meet and talk with the members and non-members, who loved him all the more for it. I was fortunate because I learnt so much just listening to him and asking questions, mostly about politics but lots of other things too. Like Engels, Duncan had enormous intellectual breadth and a range of knowledge covering the natural sciences and the whole of human history, yet he was genuinely modest, loath to talk about himself or his exploits.

On the rare occasions he did it was fascinating. I remember an instance when he came to Glasgow for a few days to speak at local SWP branch meetings and at lunchtime Socialist Worker Student Society (SWSS) meetings. In the morning as he was leaving to catch his train back to London, I noticed he'd left an elaborate looking shaving brush in my bathroom and I handed it to him. "It was originally Donald Dewar's," he told me. "I 'acquired' it after he'd left it behind in the washroom of the debating chamber at Glasgow University. I debated with him there and I also debated with another character you'll know of—Nicholas Fairbairn QC."

Dewar became a lawyer and a prominent right-wing Labour politician, defeating the SNP at a key Glasgow parliamentary by-election in 1978. Later as Blair's man in Scotland, he led the referendum campaign for a devolved parliament, serving as its inaugural First Minister in 1999. Fairbairn became a prominent Scottish Tory QC and MP. In any debate my money would have been on Duncan knocking spots off the pair of them.

On another occasion, during the 1984 miners' strike, he came to Glasgow to do a series of meetings. One was in

Sauchie, a small mining town near Stirling, where there was an SWP branch with a group of young SWP miners who played a leading role in the strike. It was an excellent meeting, held in the local public hall. As we arrived outside the venue before the meeting Duncan said, "Davey, you know I tutored in this hall a few times for the NCLC (National Council of Labour Colleges) over 30 years ago."

Hallas, McShane and the Right to Work campaign

Harry McShane recalled attending a number of NCLC talks given by Duncan in the 1950s during his stay in Scotland. Like Duncan, Harry was a lifelong revolutionary. Breaking from the CP in 1953 after being a member for more than 30 years took considerable courage. At the age of 61 it would have been easier to take a back seat and retire. Instead, he returned to work in a Govan shipyard and embarked upon a political re-assessment. As Paul Foot wrote in McShane's obituary, "Harry identified Russia as state capitalist and the communists as the unwitting stooges of another imperial power".[9]

Paul would often speak of how Harry helped convince him about Marxism and revolutionary politics after he moved to Glasgow to work as a columnist on the *Scottish Daily Record* in 1960. From 1960-62, Harry was on the editorial board for nine of the early issues of *International Socialism* when it was the quarterly journal of the Socialist Review Group (the SRG). In 1961 the SRG launched a new monthly paper aimed specifically at trade union activists. It was edited from London and was originally entitled *Industrial Worker* but was soon renamed *Labour Worker*. In 1962 the SRG became the International Socialists and according to Ian Birchall, "*Labour Worker* was not a great success; a meeting in December 1962 was told that the members took no interest in it. In May 1963 the paper was transferred to Glasgow, where Foot became editor. The editorial board included Harry McShane, although he was not a member of the IS group".[10] Foot wrote:

When I first met Harry in 1961 he was 70 but full of the joys of life and hopes of a better world. He was still a revolutionary socialist but scarred from his bitter experience with the Communist Party and wary of joining another organisation. But when in 1963 we set up the first fledgling organisation of the International Socialists in the Horseshoe Bar near Glasgow Central Station, Harry never missed a meeting.[11]

He was a revolutionary for nearly 80 years. When he was 93 he spoke at the *Socialist Worker* Marx Centenary Rally in Glasgow, alongside Tony Cliff and Paul Foot. I was present on a number of occasions when Duncan Hallas and Harry spoke together at political meetings. One of them was in 1978, when along with a few other SWP central committee members they came to a special meeting of the Glasgow District Committee of the SWP in 1978 to try and talk some of us out of what was an ultra-left position in the run-up to the first Scottish Devolution referendum. Another was three years earlier in November 1975. In the summer of that year I had become the IS full-time organiser for the West of Scotland and already under the Labour government unemployment had doubled. Duncan, as editor of *International Socialism*, had written the "Notes of the Month" for its November issue, pointing out the source of the problem:

> Two milestones on the gallop to the right by the "official leadership" of the British working class movement; the 107th Trade Union Congress voted by 6.9 million to 3.4 million to support the "voluntary" £6 wage-cutting policy; the Labour Party conference voted overwhelmingly in the same sense and rejected outright all demands to reflate the economy. It is ironic to recall, so short are "official" memories, that the Social Contract Incomes Policy and its £6 successor were originally sold as an alternative to mass unemployment. Not so

GLASGOW
SOCIALIST WORKER RALLY
"Fight for the Right to Work
No Return to the Thirties"
Speakers:—DUNCAN HALLAS
(I.S. Central Committee)
HARRY McSHANE
(Sec. Unemployed Workers Movement in the Thirties)
Chairman:—GEORGE KELLY
E.T.U. Convenor—Central Electrical Workshops

On Sunday 23rd November in the Glasgow City
Halls (Lesser Hall) Albion St., from 7 — 9.30 p.m.
Donation Ticket 10p   All welcome

*Leaflet for a Glasgow meeting with Duncan
Hallas and Harry McShane, 1975.*

very long ago Len Murray, Jack Jones, Denis Healey and Harold Wilson were proclaiming wage restraint as the way to avoid unemployment. Not any more. Now we have both wage-cutting "wage restraint" policies *and* one and a quarter million unemployed...

The first requirement, as Trotsky once wrote, is to look reality in the face. And the reality is that a very right-wing Labour government has the active support of the bulk of the trade union machines and the acquiescence of the rest in its reactionary policies.[12]

By the end of the year the official government figure would soar to over 1.4 million and continue rising. In 1975 IS nationally had been discussing the idea of launching a new rank and file initiative—the Right to Work Campaign (RTWC)—associated with the National Rank and File Movement. The plan was for a first Right to Work March early in 1976 that would involve the unemployed and draw in wider forces to resist unemployment, including hopefully the Communist Party and its Liaison Committee for the Defence of Trade Unions.

The RTWC was able to draw upon the ideas and inspiration of the National Unemployed Workers Movement that Harry McShane and Wal Hannington had helped to build and lead during the 1930s. Harry—who was 87 at the time—was delighted to be involved and willing to do all he could to help. John Deason convinced him to write the introduction for the first national RTWC pamphlet that the campaign produced.

Consequently in November 1975 we managed to build a big Glasgow *Socialist Worker* Rally in the City Halls on the slogan "Fight for the Right to Work—No Return to the Thirties", with Harry McShane and Duncan as the main speakers. The combination worked well. Both were on song and won the audience to the Right to Work initiative. At the end of the meeting we recruited to the IS a number of young unemployed workers, a couple of students and a key British Leyland engineering shop steward, who worked at the Albion truck plant, where we already had a few members and a good *Socialist Worker* sale. Our new member stayed after the meeting to speak with Harry and Duncan and he was suitably impressed. A few weeks later he was instrumental in convincing his shop stewards committee to sponsor unemployed youth on the first RTW march from Manchester to London in February/March 1976, setting an example for the rest of the district.

In an article entitled "On the United Front Tactic", written at the end of December 1975, Duncan argued how it was essential in the fight against unemployment at the time:

It is not a trick. The limited aims involved in a united front—for example the right to work—are aims that are sincerely supported by the revolutionary organisation. Neither is it simply a propaganda operation. Its aim is, above all, to generate united action around partial and immediate demands, to raise the confidence and combativity of the working class.

The Tribunites claim to stand for full employment. So does the Communist Party. So do we. Ken Gill and Eric Heffer are on record in favour of it. So, for that matter, have been Jack Jones and Michael Foot in the recent past. Practically all unions have "deplored" rising unemployment. Therefore this is an issue around

Harry McShane on the Right to Work march in 1976.

which we as revolutionaries can and must try to force the widest possible united action alongside everyone in the working class movement who takes the demand seriously...

At the same time, we are not organisational sectarians. If useful initiatives arise independently... we will support them with vigour, whilst trying all the time to achieve one united campaign... The relevance and possibilities of united front work at the present time are not confined to the right to work. But the whole situation makes it central, the key field on which attempts at unity in action must be concentrated.[13]

Right to Work marches were meat and drink to Harry. He began organising the unemployed alongside John Maclean at the end of the First World War and it became his main task over the next 20 years. In 1922, during a spell in prison for fighting the eviction of an unemployed family, Harry joined the Communist Party. The 1932 Hunger March from Glasgow to Westminster began with the Scottish contingent, led by McShane. On arrival they had to fight through police lines to get into the rally in Hyde Park. Three days later they had to battle the police again in order to present their petition to parliament.

Harry sent off the first RTW march from Manchester in February 1976 with a magnificent speech, bettered only when he spoke to over 6,000 people at the final rally in the Albert Hall on 20 March. The theme of his speeches was a simple one— governments and politicians solve nothing. The ebb and flow of the capitalist tide sweeps over all governments and their plans. Only the workers in action could do anything to roll it back!

Joining the International Socialists—Duncan's influence

I joined the IS at the start of 1973, finally convinced after reading a series of articles on Stalinism, the Soviet Union and the Communist Party that Duncan Hallas had written for *Socialist Worker* and for *International Socialism* in late 1972. The Communist Party and the nature of Russia were perplexing me at the time but Duncan's articles gave me confidence and clarity about exactly what the IS stood for. My subsequent experience was that when it came to explaining complex issues to an audience—big or small—there was no one better than Duncan.

I had first encountered IS and *Socialist Worker* earlier in 1971 at the start of the Upper Clyde Shipbuilders (UCS) campaign. I started buying the paper from a young primary school teacher I knew, Ruth Smith, who was an IS member. I was convinced into taking a few extra copies every week to sell to friends and workmates as a result of her getting me along to my first IS meeting in 1972—a wonderful if scary Glasgow rally called in the immediate aftermath of Bloody Sunday in Derry. Bernadette Devlin (now McAliskey) delivered one of the best speeches I have ever heard to a packed audience of many hundreds. Harry McShane spoke warmly from the floor in support of her and in a few sentences convinced me of the importance of James Connolly's Marxism for understanding the Irish struggle and for building working class unity around it.

The Glasgow meeting was part of a nationwide tour in response to Bloody Sunday organised by the IS. At a number of these meetings Duncan Hallas spoke alongside Bernadette on behalf of IS but on this occasion it was Steve Jefferys and Frank Drain, a young Irish building worker living in Scotland. Duncan was an obvious candidate to be at the forefront of this tour. He had an abiding interest in Ireland and wrote and spoke expertly on its history and current politics.

Earlier in 1969 Bernadette had been elected to Westminster as the independent socialist MP for Mid Ulster. That same year she had addressed a mass picket for equal pay and union recognition involving hundreds of striking women workers at Better Sound Recordings (BSR)'s East Kilbride factory, near Glasgow. BSR had just sacked their Irish workforce in Derry. So even before Bloody Sunday, Bernadette—a real firebrand—was already of some renown around Glasgow.

Her response to Bloody Sunday was bold—crossing the floor of the House of Commons to confront the Tory front bench and punch the Home Secretary, Reginald Maudling. Her audacity enraged the establishment but exposed the Tory cabinet's collusion over the atrocity in Derry, the assassination of 13 unarmed civilians on a peaceful protest march, ordered from the very top and carried out by a small hand-picked squad of British paratroopers.

Bernadette's appearance was big news in Glasgow, which explains why there was a bomb scare at the Woodside Halls during the meeting and why busloads of irate Orangemen and women descended on the venue to hurl abuse and to try to halt it. They didn't succeed—fortunately the organisers had prior warning and so too did the police. The event was well stewarded by the Glasgow IS and access to the hall was by ticket only. It was an inspiring event and one of the reasons I eventually joined the IS. But I didn't join until the end of the year.

I was 14 when Harold Wilson's minority Labour government

was elected in 1964. I had grown up in a Labour household and after 13 years of Tory rule, I naïvely thought we'd get socialism. My father's response was quite the opposite: "Wilson? He's no socialist, he's a Daz salesman!" Nonetheless I joined the Labour Party Young Socialists (LPYS) after Labour was re-elected with a big majority in 1966. But the LPYS was moribund in Bellshill where I lived—one of the safest Labour seats in the UK.

The best account of that 1964-70 Labour government is provided in Duncan's pamphlet, *The Labour Party: Myth and Reality,* first published in 1981. By 1969 I was thoroughly disillusioned with Labour and looking for change elsewhere— especially after the events of 1968 and Wilson's refusal to condemn the US bombing in Vietnam. The 1970 general election was the first time under-21s got to vote. So I voted Labour to keep out the Tories but Heath won. By now I was convinced parliament was a dead end.

Thereafter things hotted up. I was 20 when I left Art School in 1970, hoping to get a job in local government. But rising unemployment and a freeze on council posts scuppered that, so for a while I worked as a labourer in the local steelworks in Coatbridge, making pipelines for the North Sea. On my second day at work I was involved in a *wildcat* strike. An immediate mass walkout, combined with effective picketing of every shift changeover, halted all production. The worker who had been sent home and docked a day's wages for a minor offence was reinstated by the following morning—with no loss of pay for him or those who struck in support. All this was done without recourse to the officials of the steelworkers' union BISAKTA.

In spring 1971 I got a job in Glasgow Corporation and joined the Local Government workers' branch of NALGO. I was soon part of a campaign initiated by some CP branch activists to set up proper departmental shop stewards organisation across every Glasgow Corporation department.

Heath's new Tory government was well to the right of anything since the 1930s. Initially successful, it used the threat of unemployment and the spinelessness of the union leaders to inflict defeats on the power workers and the postal workers. Its panoply of anti-union laws came into force in June that year, raising the stakes. Two weeks later the Tories announced that UCS, the consortium owning four of Glasgow's five shipyards was to be deliberately starved of government funds and allowed to go bust. Here was a "lame duck" the Tories could exploit for their purposes. Six thousand of the 8,500 workers were to be sacked and 30,000 more ancillary jobs on Clydeside would go too. Unemployment on the Clyde was already 40 percent up on the previous year.

The Tories were stunned by the anger and militancy of the response. Mass meetings in every yard voted to occupy if sackings went ahead, defying the Industrial Relations Act. A hundred thousand workers took part in a one-day strike and there was a huge march through Glasgow. But the action at UCS was never as militant as the first signs indicated. Jimmy Reid and all the key stewards were CP members and while strong on rhetoric, accepted the party's gradualist approach of downplaying militancy to court "public opinion". Under their control, the occupation became a "work-in" whereby workers continued to work with supervisors in charge, ensuring orders were completed and ships handed over to the government liquidator.

The campaign was more a Scottish popular front than a confrontation with the Tories. Nonetheless the refusal to accept redundancies shook the government and galvanised other workers. UCS signalled that sackings and closures were not inevitable and the work-in became a symbol of resistance. Jimmy Airlie told the *BBC TV News* cameras: "The only way we'll be beaten is if we're starved into submission. It's the responsibility of the labour movement to see that does not happen because it's not only our fight, it's the fight of every man and woman in this country—the fight for the right to work".[14]

The response was even more dramatic than Airlie's appeal— 1,300 shop stewards from Scotland and the North of England met in Glasgow to endorse the work-in and called on workers everywhere to give financial support. It also unanimously backed

Jimmy Reid's call for another strike in defiance of the law and a demonstration through Glasgow. On 18 August 200,000 Scottish workers struck and there was another huge march through the city with representatives from every workplace in the West of Scotland and big delegations from England. Thousands of workplaces organised weekly levies. Money and messages of support flooded in from all over the world.

Overnight Jimmy Reid became a working class hero. CP members active in my union branch were trying to recruit me and while I agreed with some of what they said—especially against the right wing—I wouldn't join them. One of my mum's uncles had joined the CP during the war but having read George Orwell and well aware of the Gulags, I was hostile to the idea that Russia was socialist. *Socialist Worker's* critique of the CP strategy at UCS and its argument for nationalisation under workers' control made sense as the work-in dragged on throughout 1972. Without realising it I was moving closer to IS and that's when I read Duncan's articles on Russia. They convinced me about the theory of State Capitalism and the importance of the paper's masthead slogan—*Neither Washington nor Moscow, but International Socialism.*

At the same time, *International Socialism* issue 53 appeared with a timely article on the impact of UCS and the lessons of the sit-ins and occupations so I bought a copy. But the most impressive article in it was its editorial, "The Decline of Reformism". At the time I didn't realise that Duncan, who was then the editor, had written it. One thing I did know was that it slaughtered the Communist Party's *British Road to Socialism* and its strategy of snuggling up to and relying on the left union leaders to defeat Heath's anti-union laws. And it did so by contrasting the Communist Party approach with the direct action of the rank and file—the mass strikes against the jailing of five Pentonville Dockers. I quote some excerpts from it below:

> Nothing in recent years has conspired to expose with
> such clarity the role and function of the trade union

leadership as the Industrial Relations Act... The trade union bureaucracy does not operate at the outer limits of the system, beyond which point capitalism cannot concede but remain capitalism; not at all. It operates within an inner perimeter whose limits are the well-being and profitability of the system... For all of them the idea of consciously leading the movement into conflict with the system is anathema. For the right wing the attitude flows from its basic conviction, for the left it is supposedly because "the members are too backward, not ready", etc... Yet fundamentally they perform the same function and role: they are an estate within capitalism, locked into capitalist norms and objectives...

If the struggle depended on such forces the prospect would be bleak indeed. While the so-called left wing was conspicuous by its silence, while the right attempted to retard the movement, first the dockers, then the printers, then tens of thousands of other workers demanded to be heard... Five dockers (it could easily have been five printers, five building workers or any five workers) asserted the independent, separate interest of the working class. Their response to the government's assault was simple and direct, because they represent workers directly, because they embodied direct power, because at certain decisive moments in history, to compromise is to accept defeat. In a few short eventful days, the government, the courts, the trade union bureaucracy were confronted. The emperor was not only naked but obviously ill equipped.

The trade union leadership are unwilling and incapable of leading the sort of struggle that will defeat the Act and the government. For them the rules of the struggle must always leave the contestants alive and able again to fight another day. For victory, another quite different force is required; a party able, willing and anxious to offer real leadership to win battles of the class but seeing those battles as an integral part in the strategy that will win the war for the final elimination of capitalism.[15]

Immediately after reading this, it struck me that here was a much bigger, more generalised and far more important version of what I had been part of at the Coatbridge steelworks a year earlier—a demonstration of workers' power! Not too long after reading it and Duncan's *Socialist Worker* articles on Russia, I was asked by Murray Armstrong, the secretary of the Glasgow IS, to join—and I did.

Fascism, Stalinism and the United Front

In the early 1970s the Nazi National Front (NF) began organising a series of street marches and meetings across Britain to exploit the first real economic crisis since the Second World War for their own sinister ends. This ominous threat—targeting immigrant communities—grew to the point where, in electoral terms, it became greater than that mounted by Oswald Mosley's British Union of Fascists (BUF).[16] In response, the Anti Nazi League (ANL) was launched in 1977. The ANL and the mass movement it generated is one of the great achievements of the revolutionary left in post-war Britain.

An important factor in the success of the ANL was the reputation of the SWP (and its predecessor the IS) in fighting the fascists over the five-year period beforehand. It had long been established in the IS that opposition to fascism had to involve physical confrontation and a No platform/No free speech for Nazis approach. Why? Because their real aim was to use the democratic process in order to destroy it—in particular all forms of working-class organisation, including the trade unions—as Mussolini had done in 1921 and Hitler did in 1933.

The IS had taken that approach from the late 1960s onwards. In 1969, as editor of *International Socialism* at the time, Chris Harman devoted a specially expanded double issue of the publication to encompass much of Trotsky's key writings on Germany—his attempt to arouse the working class and its large but Stalinist-dominated German Communist Party to the dangers that threatened it. Titled *Trotsky: Fascism, Stalinism and the United Front 1930-34,* this publication helped educate and train a new generation of revolutionaries on the whys and hows of combatting fascism.

Duncan Hallas also played an important role both in terms of the theory and the practicalities of combatting fascism. He personified Lenin's notion that the party has to act as the memory of the class. His popular pamphlet *The Meaning of Marxism* was written for its new members and the growing readership of *Socialist Worker.* It was written as a guide to action, with an important lesson from Germany in the 1930s that was crucial to the fight against the National Front in the 1970s:

> The Great Depression was undermining the parliamentary capitalist republic. Unemployment reached six million. The Nazi Party was growing by leaps and bounds. At the election of 1930 Hitler got nearly six and a half million votes. They were the votes of the middle classes, the rural population and some unorganised workers. The organised workers held fast for the traditional workers' parties. Six million plus votes went to the Social Democrats and over four and a half million to the Communists. The growing menace of fascism was obvious. So was the need for the working class movement to unite and smash it!
>
> Unfortunately the leadership of the [Communist] International, by this time completely subservient to Stalin, thought otherwise. Following his victory over the remaining opposition in the Russian Communist Party in 1928-29, Stalin swung the Comintern round to a policy of insane ultra-leftism. The centrepiece of this "Third Period" policy was the theory of "social fascism". The social democratic party—and by extension the unions that it controlled—were described as "fascist

organisations". According to Stalin himself, "fascism is the military organisation of the bourgeoisie, which leans upon social democracy for active support. So social democracy, objectively speaking, is the moderate wing of fascism." So there could be no question of using the discontent of the social democratic rank and file to force their party to join a united front against fascism. Nor was the victory of Hitler itself to be feared. "We are not afraid of the fascist gentlemen," said the Communist leader in the Reichstag, "they will shoot their bolt quicker than any other government."

In 1932 Hitler's vote rose to nearly 14 million. Still the main enemy for the Communist Party was social democracy. In 1933 Hitler became Chancellor of Germany. Even then the CP clung to its absurd line: "The talk of the German Communists being defeated and politically dead," said the official Comintern journal in April, "is the gossip of philistines, of idiotic and ignorant people". By this time most of the party's activists were in concentration camps or in hiding.[17]

Socialist Worker between 1973 and 1976 is full of reports from around the UK of how the IS with others confronted the Nazis and tried to break up their meetings and marches. In 1974 the NF announced it would march through the streets of Leicester on Saturday 24 August. Two months earlier they had held a rally at Conway Hall in Red Lion Square in London. There was a big march and counter-protest outside, which the International Socialists and the International Marxist Group (IMG) had organised. The riot police—the Special Patrol Group (SPG)—attacked the demonstration and killed Kevin Gately, a student from Warwick University. The following Saturday there was a big protest march against his killing.

The NF march that was to follow in August had initially been planned for Manchester but they switched it to Leicester. Perhaps they were worried about the strength of anti-fascist

*Some of the 2,500 IS marchers listen to Duncan Hallas, of the IS executive, speaking in Spinney Hill Park (*Socialist Worker *389, 31 August 1974).*

forces in Manchester, but they announced the switch because of the Imperial Typewriters dispute—an important and bitter strike there led by new Asian activists who were taking on a vicious multinational employer, the racism of the local trade union organisation, as well as attacks by the police and the NF. As a deliberate provocation the Nazis announced they intended to congregate outside the factory before marching through the immigrant areas of Leicester.

The International Socialists, the IMG and others called a counter-march to confront the NF. However the local Labour Party, the Communist Party, the churches and some of the unions called a separate march that was going to assemble a long way from the NF meeting point at Imperial Typewriters and march in the opposite direction.

On the day 1,300 police were mobilised to protect fewer than 800 NF supporters. Even the police estimated there were 5,000 opposing the NF, while Leicester Radio put the figure at 6,000.

Everyone agreed that the IS contingent was more than half the demonstration, having mobilised its members from as far away as Southampton and Dundee. I was on the Glasgow IS coach that travelled to Leicester, packed full, including a big contingent from the Glasgow Indian Workers' Association with their banner, as well as delegations of trade unionists and students.

On the day a crowd of 2,500 gathered in Leicester's Spinney Hill Park for the IS pre-march rally. Duncan Hallas spoke powerfully for the IS. He began by addressing the opposing argument. "Was it really permissible for democrats and socialists to deny free speech to the fascists?" By the time he'd finished he'd proved beyond doubt that free speech for Nazis means crushing the freedom of those they harassed. He ended by reminding us we were in Leicester to confront them and harry them, and while other forces "had marched off in the wrong direction away from confrontation", our much larger mobilisation had "achieved an important victory even before it set off". The NF's intention to assemble at Imperial Typewriters and then intimidate the immigrant areas "had been thwarted by our magnificent counter demonstration. But remember this, comrades," warned Duncan, who'd fought the Nazis in 1944, "fascism and racism are not defeated by one glorious demonstration."

So our march moved off through the immigrant areas and past Imperial Typewriters, while the NF were corralled into a tiny recreation ground and a 200-yard march at the other end of town. When the marchers arrived back in Spinney Hill Park, they were joined by another large group of IS members who'd gone to hound and disrupt what must have been a demoralised bunch of Nazis and their supporters.

Dealing with the Communist Party, the trade union leaders and Labour's social con-trick

In autumn 1974 Jimmy McCallum, a leading IS member in Glasgow, encouraged me to attend a special IS national cadre school at Cottons Gardens in East London. A small group of comrades from around the country spent an intensive weekend in a series of group discussions led off by Tony Cliff, Duncan Hallas, Nigel Harris and others on the politics of IS and the current state of the class struggle under the new Labour government. All the speakers were impressive, Duncan especially so, because of his unique delivery, his ability to generalise and his vast experience of the movement past and present.

The school coincided with a West of Scotland-wide unofficial strike wave against the Social Contract—an education in itself. By the end of October 60,000 Scottish workers had been involved in bitter, mainly unofficial disputes for a £10 increase. The strikes involved bus workers, lorry drivers, schoolteachers, distillery workers, council dustmen, council electricians, council sewage workers, car workers, Hoover and Rolls Royce workers, as well as many light engineering and assembly plants where a majority were low-paid women. Even Ladbrokes betting shop staff struck. But national and local full-timers fought hard to push their members back to work.

In October Jack Jones, leader of the Transport and General Workers' Union (TGWU), addressing a special meeting of Scottish TGWU shop stewards in Motherwell, lectured them on the virtues of the Social Contract. The SMT bus workers were so angry they occupied the TGWU Glasgow office and sent pickets to Transport House, the union's London HQ, demanding it ditch "the social con-trick".

Invariably in these disputes prominent CP members, including the secretary of Glasgow Trades Council and the TGWU regional official, would intervene to urge moderation, compromise or surrender. During the binworkers' strike they told the strikers to get back to work and negotiate. When the Labour council brought in the army to break the strike, the council electricians who maintained the depots and incinerators walked out to join the pickets and called for a strike of all council workers. The leading electricians' shop stewards were active IS members.

Glasgow Trades Council could have waged a campaign against the use of troops by mobilising the whole movement: it was national news. Instead it condemned the Glasgow IS for issuing a leaflet calling on the troops not to cross the picket lines, and organised a local, token demonstration that kept well away from the rubbish dumps and incinerators, where the troops were working. The West of Scotland Shop Stewards body that had been so instrumental in mobilising the huge demonstrations in support of UCS in 1971 was never convened.

After the Glasgow Trades Council's token march the TGWU officials instructed the strike committee to call a mass meeting and accept a return to work, despite the fact that the dispute was of tremendous national significance. There was a big fight over this at the Glasgow Trades Council meeting—then a large representative body, which held monthly meetings of 200-300 elected delegates. The IS had about 30 delegates. Harry McShane was also a delegate and the old head of our IS trades council caucus. The IS had an influence and made an impact but we were too small to defeat the CP.

In the end the movement that had grown in the Scottish strikes faded. Although many won increases, the Social Contract survived its first serious test. Faced with their Battle of Saltley Gate, the leaders of Glasgow Trades Council marched their troops in the opposite direction, away from battle. What could have been a successful campaign against wage controls was never developed because the main organisation capable of giving it direction failed to do so. Of course individual CP members played a positive role in many of the struggles and a couple of them joined the IS, but as a political force the CP failed because it looked to friends in high places, insisting the Social Contract would be headed off by left officials and politicians; and at trade union conferences rather than by mass action.

During this strike wave the emergence of a real rank and file movement was within reach. At one point, five strike committees were holding five separate meetings in five separate rooms in the same building—the Glasgow Trade Union Centre in Carlton Place. Had it been possible to unify the strikes, had the army strike-breaking been halted, then who knows the possibilities. Certainly, the Social Contract could have been defeated.

Unsurprisingly, this unofficial strike wave and the baleful role of the Communist Party was a big talking point at the IS cadre school I attended. During the lunch breaks Duncan would take a few of us to the nearby café to continue the discussion informally. His introduction to our session on the trade union bureaucracy was particularly impressive—using concrete examples like Glasgow to illuminate the role of the Communist Party leaders and left officials they courted. In doing so he provided us with a theoretical basis for understanding Stalinism and a context for working with and against the union leaders and the Communist Party, which was crucial, especially in places like Glasgow, where the CP was a major force.

Duncan had attended that year's Trades Union Congress at Brighton as *Socialist Worker's* reporter covering the debate around the Social Contract. His report is instructive about the manoeuvres at the highest level of the trade union bureaucracy and what was really at stake, and is a model of good socialist journalism:

> There was a near complete consensus behind something like the *Morning Star's* (the Communist Party's daily newspaper) view of world affairs. Or so it seemed. Even in the more sensitive field of domestic affairs some radical sounding propositions were adopted; for example, "nationalisation of the film industry without compensation and under workers' control" and not a voice raised against it!...
>
> It was all part of the Social Contract. This compact is between the trade union lefts, including especially the Communist Party and CP-influenced ones, and the right and the centre. It amounts to this; the "lefts" are allowed to get their resolutions through on all kinds of issues, excepting only the operative ones, the central issues of wages policy. In return the "lefts" refrain from carrying out any real fight against the General Council's right-wing policies in practice...
>
> It was an astounding piece of political chicanery. The great issue at Brighton was the determination of the General Council to enforce a wage restraint policy in a capitalist society racked by accelerating inflation; in other words, to enforce a cut in real wages. And the "left", instead of rallying all possible support against this

monstrous sell-out, accepted it in the interests of "unity".

The explanation is simple enough. On this issue the TUC leadership was deadly serious. All the friendliness and tolerance they found it convenient to extend to a licensed "left" would have disappeared had that "left" really exposed and denounced the Social Con-trick... The Communist Party reaped what they had sown. So Harold Wilson got what he wanted.

At the end of his report Duncan went on to draw the conclusion from the sell-out: the crying need for a genuine rank and file movement, something the IS was seeking to build:

From the first moment of Congress all efforts had been bent to setting the stage for this performance and the stage managers had a walk-over. "Unity" triumphed. The second National Rank and File Conference, which is now being prepared, will lack some of the smooth-ness and efficiency that the well-oiled TUC machine displayed at Brighton. It will lack all manner of things. But it will be devoted to serious debate on the best ways and means of defending working class interests. It will carry forward the work of developing a left in the work-places and in the trade union movement that does not believe in the "unity" of the lion and the lamb—a left that will not sell its principles for a mess of "left" reso-lutions and a seat on the General Council of the TUC.[18]

Duncan Hallas on the rise and fall of Stalinism

The "Soviet Union" collapsed over 30 years ago but the influence of Stalinism lingers on, casting a long shadow over the left in Britain and internationally. The USSR Ltd was ended in 1991. It was a strange paradox: the product of a revolution in 1917, led and supported by its working people, the first—and so far only—successful workers' revolution in history. Yet by the end of the 1920s revolutionary Russia had been isolated then turned on its head.

Under Stalin, Russia emerged as a Great Power. By the mid-1930s it had become one of the 20th century's bloodiest dictatorships. The regime continued to call itself socialist and communist but although it built statues to Marx and Lenin, it had become the opposite of socialism: a bureaucratic tyranny. The collapse and eventual disappearance of the soviets, along with the destruction of the social and cultural gains of 1917 meant the regime became increasingly undemocratic and repressive as Stalin sought to distort, then destroy the revolutionary Marxist tradition, both physically and politically, as the leading representative of the new ruling class in Russia.

This full-blooded counter-revolution swept away the remaining gains of the October revolution, persecuting and murdering thousands of Bolshevik revolutionaries. Many were tortured in secret police cells and herded to their deaths in freezing labour camps. Those purged as "fascists" and "traitors" made up about 90 percent of the leadership of the Bolshevik party and the soviet state during the 1917 Revolution and the Civil war of 1918-20.

Up to 20 million people passed through the "Gulags"—a network of forced labour camps across Stalin's Russia. By 1930 179,000 languished in them and at the time of Stalin's death in 1953 the figure had risen to nearly 2.5 million.[19] Stalin's counter-revolution destroyed the gains won by women and for LGBT+ rights in the wake of the October revolution. Increasingly the regime saw the family as the key institution in sustaining and reproducing its workforce. Homosexuality was recriminalised in 1934; abortion was banned again in 1936. "Soviet motherhood" was pushed and promoted as women in the Soviet Union—and later in its post-war satellites—faced subordination and the same double burden as women in Western capitalism.

When the group around Stalin finally took control at the end of the 1920s, they defended it by developing a military apparatus as powerful as that of any of their potential foes.

That was only possible by imitating Western military potential: and that meant building up heavy industry by squeezing the living standards of workers and peasants. A system of internal passports and labour books, introduced after 1930, further strengthened labour discipline.

In 1976 John Gollan, former General Secretary of the CPGB, wrote an article for *Marxism Today* to mark the 20th anniversary of Khrushchev's "secret speech" to the 20th Congress of the Russian Communist Party in 1956 which "exposed the crimes of the Stalin era". In response to Gollan's article, Duncan wrote a substantial critique for *International Socialism*. I quote excerpts from it here:

Stalin rose to a position of great power as the spokesman and guardian of the interests of his apparatus men, like the young Khrushchev... By 1928 the leading oppositionists and their followers had been thrown out of the party; many were in jail or in exile. The last remnants of inner party democracy had been destroyed. Gollan, though his subject is "Socialist Democracy", has no protest to make...

The first Five Year Plan was launched in 1928. Of it John Gollan writes, "a great socialist industry was created and collectivisation carried through... an historic achievement" though he adds, "but it was accompanied by gross errors of compulsion and coercion, condemned by Stalin himself in his speech *Dizzy with Success*, bringing even more acute strains".

A great industry was certainly created but a great *socialist* industry? If socialism, as Marx claimed, is the self-emancipation of the working class then the Five Year Plan marked the loss by the working class of whatever socialist elements remained in the USSR until then. The last vestiges of trade union rights disappeared. The Soviet trades unions discouraged strikes...behind them stood the political police.

Real wages fell rapidly... In agriculture the collectivisation by decree and "the liquidation of the Kulaks as a class" resulted in a catastrophic fall in output. The disastrous outcome sent a flood of starving ex-peasants into the towns...and its sinister by–product was the creation of a vast network of forced labour camps that were to persist on a *mass scale for more than 20 years*. Of course the horrors of the first Five Year Plan period have to be seen in context. The English and Scottish peasantry too, were "liquidated as a class" in their time and the casualties of the industrial revolution in Britain were certainly not lighter, proportionate to the population, than the USSR. But then, no one has ever pretended that early Victorian Britain was a socialist society.[20]

Once the Five Year Plan and its ruthless methods were adopted, it was logical to copy the West in other ways too by expanding the USSR's borders to grab further resources for accumulation; hence the division of Poland with Hitler in 1939, the invasion of Finland in 1940 and the division of Europe with Churchill and Roosevelt in 1944-45. The rapid build-up of Russian industrial and military power in the 1930s, triggered by the Five Year Plan, was great enough to smash the Nazi war machine between 1942 and 1945. Before he was murdered in 1940, Trotsky predicted that the Stalinist regime would not survive the war. On the contrary, because Russia was the decisive force in destroying the Nazi regime, it was able to expand west and create a buffer zone of client states—Poland, East Germany, Czechoslovakia, Hungary, Bulgaria and Romania—territories Stalin seized and forcibly remodelled into smaller lookalikes of his tyranny.

Towards the end of the war nuclear weapons were developed to fulfil the irrational needs of an irrational system. From the capitalist standpoint even the most horrific weapons of mass destruction are rational—a view shared by Stalin, his henchmen and their successors ever since. Bizarrely, some on the left, including leading communists, tried to argue that "Soviet" militarism—although there had been no soviets since the early 1920s—was different; that armed force was a neutral instrument and what mattered was which state wielded it. So the Western atom bomb was condemned and the "socialist" or "workers' bomb" celebrated.

According to Hallas, the industrial revolution of the Five Year Plan brought into being:

> ...a society in which the working class and the collectivised peasantry were—and are—deprived of all effective political and trade union rights. Events were soon to show that this was even true of the mass of the bureaucracy itself, economically privileged as it was and is. It brought into being a despotism ruled by a despot who "became ever more capricious, irritable and brutal"—Khrushchev's words not mine—and left a heritage of repression, which even now his successors cannot demolish (although they have modified it) for fear of the consequences. Their power and privileges are indissolubly connected with the exclusion from power of the workers.[21]

Khrushchev's secret speech reported that 98 of the 139 members of the party's Central Committee (CC) elected at the 17th Congress in 1934 were arrested and shot by 1938. The same fate befell not only the CC members but also the majority of the delegates to the 17th Congress. "How was it possible," asks Duncan, "for Stalin to order the execution of the majority of the Central Committee, nominally the ruling body between Congresses? Obviously because the totalitarian nature of the regime had, by the mid-1930s, reached the point at which, even the members of the highest party bodies were not only without power but even without personal security. 'L'Etat: c'est moi' ['The State: that is me'], Louis the Fourteenth was supposed to have said. Stalin could have said it with more truth".[22]

Apparently nothing made Khrushchev more indignant than Stalin's murder of senior members of his own faction: "It is not excluded that had Stalin remained at the helm for another few months, Comrades Molotov and Mikoyan would probably have not delivered any speeches at this Congress".[23] Evidently no one was safe—a terrible state of affairs for Khrushchev and the rest of the politburo. Their anxiety is clearly on display in Armando Ianucci's excellent 2017 film *The Death of Stalin,* which successfully combines realism with the darkest of black humour. The state funeral for Lenin in 1924, which was orchestrated by Stalin, went against Lenin's wishes. By contrast, Stalin's funeral was entirely in line with the personality cult that had characterised his near 30-year rule.

As Duncan shows, despite Khrushchev's claim to be a reformer, the collective leadership that took over after Stalin's death made only minor adjustments: "They resolved to ensure no new Stalin could get his boots on their necks and that their disputes be settled without shootings. This is the essence of the doctrine of 'collective leadership' as it is now understood in the Kremlin. Since Stalin's death in 1953 Malenkov and Molotov were 'peacefully deposed' by Khrushchev and Khrushchev was 'peacefully deposed' by Brezhnev and Kosygin".[24]

On the orders of Khrushchev, who denounced the personality cult of Stalin, the dictator's body was disinterred from Lenin's mausoleum in Red Square but Khrushchev's efforts to appear like an anti-authoritarian reformer don't stand up to scrutiny. It was he, after all, who put down the Hungarian workers' revolution of 1956 with a brutality he learned from Stalin and his chief executioner, Beria. Indeed, at a Politburo meeting after Stalin's death it seems that Khrushchev and his cronies murdered Beria. Duncan argued:

> The Brezhnev regime is still, in essence, Stalinist. Brezhnev's six-hour address to the current Congress typifies it. No delegate—a misleading term since there

are no genuine elections—will be so bold as to criticise any aspect of it. As in Stalin's day all power is at the top. The difference is that a small group instead of one man wields it. But the working class is still atomised, no labour movement is allowed to exist, let alone exercise power.[25]

This was written in 1976 and Duncan wasn't for a minute arguing the workers of Russia and the other state capitalist regimes would remain atomised and incapable of challenging their rulers forever. Like Tony Cliff he knew every cloud has a silver lining so he didn't just expose these authoritarian regimes as not socialist; he challenged the popular notion they were like George Orwell's *1984*—"big brother" states, so authoritarian that no opposition could challenge them. Instead he explained how state capitalism, like every other variant of capitalism, was creating its own gravedigger—a working class with the potential to shake society apart as shown by the uprisings and revolutions in East Germany in 1953, Hungary in 1956, Czechoslovakia in 1968, Poland in 1980, China in 1989 and eventually in Russia itself in 1992. In an earlier article, written in 1973, Duncan predicted this—not immediately, but in the not so distant future. Highlighting the tensions in the Russian economy, he showed how the intensity of capitalist competition would open up cracks in Brezhnev's regime leading to unrest inside the Russian empire. Subsequent events vindicated him.

In June 1973 a *Guardian* article reported: "Although Western businessmen have been turning their thoughts towards the USSR as a source for long term supplies of raw materials and energy, a growing number are also beginning to see the Soviet Union as a potentially valuable source of low cost labour".[26]

Duncan, shrewd editor that he was, picked up on this and in the next issue of *International Socialism* he used his "Notes of the Month" column to lay bare its consequences for the Brezhnev regime, just as the first real recession since the Second World War was beginning to hit the world economy hard:

Brezhnev's visit to Washington marks a further stage in the developing relations between the super-powers. Nixon and Brezhnev have a common interest in preserving the status quo on a world scale. Neither is able to dominate its "own bloc" to the degree that was possible at the height of the cold war... Both the pressures on the rulers of the USA and the USSR to co-operate and the possibilities of them doing so have increased...

Each partner has internal problems, which the other can help alleviate. In the case of the USA Nixon's need for foreign policy success to divert attention from Watergate is obvious but this is the least important factor. The long-term challenge of Europe and Japan to America's economic dominance gives the USSR—and also China—very great potential importance as a field for investment and a source of raw materials...

Brezhnev's problems are more urgent. The chronic weakness of Russian agriculture...ensures any natural disaster precipitates a food crisis. Russian grain production fell from 187 million tons in 1970 to 167 million in 1972. Only massive grain purchases—two thousand million dollars worth in 1972—staved off a catastrophe. Half of this huge total came from the USA...

That is the main business of Brezhnev's Washington visit. A trade agreement was signed last year... Brezhnev wants more. And as well as being able to offer raw materials he can offer what a former US state department official and former Treasury official are quoted in the *Guardian* as calling "dependable and inexpensive labour". In plain words low wages and no nonsense about trade union rights! USSR Ltd is a capitalist state with whom profitable business is possible...

But inevitably the effect of a significant increase in economic links with the USA—and Europe and Japan— must be to reduce the ability of the rulers of Russia to run the country as a single bureaucratic corporation...

Additional stress will be added to the already enormous stresses that exist under the surface of Brezhnev's despotic empire. One day, and it is perhaps not too distant, the resulting strain will be too great. The lid will blow off and the Russian and other working classes of the USSR will come back onto the political stage for the first time since the 1920s.[27]

And that's exactly what happened. Less than ten years later the writing was on the wall with the meteoric rise of the independent Polish trade union Solidarity in the early 1980s. The final demise of the Stalinist regimes came with the eastern European revolutions of 1989.

The ballast of the theory of state capitalism meant that the SWP and the International Socialist Tendency—unlike most of the left—was not blown off course in these turbulent times. We did not despair or collapse when the Russian Empire crumpled at its westernmost frontier in East Berlin and then unravelled eastwards from the Baltic States to the Caucasus. Nationalist movements exploded, protests spread like wildfire and two big miners' strikes shook Russia itself in 1989 and again in 1991 as Russian workers started to act independently "for the first time since the 1920s", just as Duncan had predicted in 1973. The Soviet Union officially dissolved in 1991. This was cause for celebration not despair. Huge workers' struggles had played a central role in sweeping away regimes that many on the old left defended as being "deformed" or "distorted" workers' states. Instead these were state capitalist dictatorships based on exploitation every bit as ruthless as their Western competitors.

CPGB on the road to ruin

It was not only the Russian Empire that dissolved in 1991, the Communist Party of Great Britain (CPGB) dissolved too. All of this fed the prevailing mood of "new realism" and the fashionable notion that class struggle and socialism were dead.

The CPGB was belatedly launched in 1920/21 out of the huge revolt that swept Europe in the wake of the Russian Revolution. The socialists who attended its founding meeting were confused on some issues but they were clear on the need to build a new party committed to the overthrow of capitalism and to workers' power. CPGB membership was around 5,000 in its early years but its activists were men and women who gained enormous influence and experience leading the big struggles of the previous decade. As James Hinton, the historian of *The First Shop Stewards' Movement*, wrote:

> Whatever distortions were later to be imposed on the British revolutionary movement by its subordination to the heirs of a degenerated Russian Revolution, the post war victory of soviet power over both syndicalism and parliamentarianism rested upon an authentic, if ambiguous experience of a section of the British working class movement during the war years.[28]

Stanley Baldwin's cabinet showed how much it feared the CPGB by jailing most of its leadership in the run-up to the 1926 General Strike and arresting hundreds of its ordinary members in the coalfields during it. While the majority of CP members fought to spread it, their leaders followed Moscow's orders, extolling the left TUC leaders who sold it out. The CPGB built up its trust in these left officials in the months before the strike and subordinated itself to them. The party slogan became "All Power to the TUC General Council"—not to the emerging Workers' Councils of action in Fife, South Wales and the Vale of Leven (the "little Moscows" as they were called). Thereby the independent movement of workers was subordinated to the needs of the Stalinist bureaucracy and its foreign policy interests. Thus, the CPGB leadership was unprepared for the sell-out by the left officials that defeated the strike, leaving the miners isolated. As Duncan argued:

Trotsky was savage in his criticism of the slogan "All Power to the General Council". This was not because the party supported the left officials against the right, which was essential, but because of its reliance on electing left officials at the expense of its own struggle for leadership through building rank and file organisation. Any revolutionary who criticises the line of the party in that crisis must first pay tribute to the integrity and steadfastness under fire of the CP rank and file and leadership alike, in the face of a selective but nonetheless brutal repression such as few of us, in the revolutionary movement of today, have yet to face.

But this record, magnificent as it is, does not exhaust the matter. Given its success in overcoming sectarianism and developing a broad class struggle movement, given the courage and determination of its members, the question remains: was the CP's political line correct? Trotsky and the Left Opposition in the USSR argued at the time that it was not; that, in spite of its splendid fighting spirit, the CPGB contributed to the shattering defeat of 1926; and that it did so, under the influence of the Comintern.

Its tragedy was that it was, understandably but fatally, involved in the political decay of the Communist International, in the advent of Stalinism. Its members played a heroic role in 1926. Its failure was a failure of political judgment, and for that failure the major responsibility lay with the leadership of the Communist International and Stalin's role in particular.[29]

For the next half century, whenever groups of workers learned the hard way just how treacherous Labour's leadership could be, it was often to the CPGB that they looked for an alternative. Yet, ever since the late 1920s the CPGB had been a contradiction. While its rank and file fought for workers' rights, its leaders identified with Stalin as he crushed workers' democracy. They defended his slogan "Socialism in one country", even though it rejected Lenin's insistence socialism could only be built if the Revolution spread. Soon after the East European revolutions, the collapse of the USSR and the dissolution of the Communist Party, one of its historians, who Duncan had debated with in Glasgow—Willie Thompson—wrote a book titled *The Good Old Cause: British Communism 1920-1991.* Duncan reviewed it in September 1992:

> The Communist Party is dead. Its Democratic Left successor recently reported less than 1,600 members (the CP claimed 7,600 in 1989), it has no perspective save "dialogue and realignment" and no future of any significance. It used to be a very different matter. It is impossible to understand the history of the left in Britain from the early 1920s onwards without understanding the CPGB's role and influence in various periods... Willie Thompson's interesting account is the only one to attempt to cover the party's whole history. However, his political approach is deeply ambivalent. His treatment of the 1920s is brief. Above all he fails to recognise its fundamental change of policy in 1929. The lunacies of "social fascism"—applied to the Labour Party and the now dominant union right; "left social fascism"—applied to the ILP and any left-winger unwilling to accept the new line; and the idea of an "ascending revolutionary wave" were disastrous— nowhere more so than in Germany where the CP unwittingly facilitated Hitler's rise to power.
>
> The Comintern parties were transformed by the imposition and implementation of the Third Period, just as the USSR was socially transformed by the First Five Year Plan with which it largely coincided. In Britain it required two congresses and a new leadership to enforce the new line. The new line also required a new membership "untainted" by recollections of past

experiences and past disputes. In 1927 the CP claimed 7,377 members. By 1930 it had fallen to 2,555—the majority of them new. The essential character of the CP had fundamentally changed. The left and often ultra left rhetoric remained—but it was to prove expendable with the next turn. This is not to idealise the pre–Stalinist party, which had plenty of faults. But it was still a genuine revolutionary party with a dedicated membership and, as Thompson freely concedes, "a significant presence in the diverse fields of struggle, assets which had considerable potential for growth". This was all lost.

After Hitler came to power in 1933 the ultra-left "social fascist" line was dropped for what became "popular fronts"—alliances not only with other working class organisations but also with sections of the Liberal and Tory parties. In full swing by 1935, this right turn took the CP to the right of the Labour Party leadership.

Certainly, the CP grew—a figure of around 18,000 members was claimed by 1939—but on what basis? The popular front line was essentially an attempt to build a block of working class and "progressive bourgeois" organisations to pressure the rulers of France, Britain, the US and lesser powers into a diplomatic and military alliance with the USSR against Germany, Italy and Japan. In Britain the centrepiece of this policy was the proposal of a Lib-Lab electoral pact with some seats allocated to the CP. This could only be achieved on the platform of the Liberal Party—as the right-wing leaders of the Labour Party gleefully pointed out.[30]

The Communist Party in France pioneered the popular front approach, insisting that only such a broad alliance could block the growth of fascism. It did so because the French alliance was central to Stalin's foreign policy and the popular front policy was rapidly adopted by the whole Comintern, especially where Stalinism had an influence, as in Spain. This meant subordinating class struggle and working class demands to maintain the class alliance with the supposedly "progressive bourgeoisie". Subsequent events in both France and Spain proved it a failure. Rather than combatting fascism, the popular front only served to confuse and disarm the working class, leading to terrible unnecessary defeats, where revolutionary opportunities were thrown away by the Stalinist leadership in the interests of Stalin's foreign policy. The outcome was Franco's 40-year regime in Spain, following the defeat of the republican forces in the Spanish Civil War, and a right-wing government in France that paved the way for a collaborationist Vichy regime compliant with the Nazi occupation after 1940.

Meantime the CPGB leadership went along with monstrous lies about the Moscow trials, denying or vigorously defending the horrors whereby those who had led the October Revolution were condemned to death as "fascist agents". Although some members left in disgust, others stayed because they could see no reason to believe what the millionaire press said about Russia when it lied so much about Britain. And the party still grew. How?

The world slump, mass unemployment, working class defeats and the threat of fascism led many to believe the Soviet Union offered the only bulwark against such threats. Indeed, the fascist threat produced a wave of middle class leftism, from which the party profited considerably. It was often communists who led the unemployed riots and marches of the early 1930s, the fight against Mosley and Franco in the mid-1930s and the rebuilding of workplace trade unionism in the late 1930s during re-armament. Until Hitler invaded Russia, the CPGB supported strikes during the early part of the war.

The build-up to the Second World War saw the CPGB first commit to fighting Nazi aggression. Then it did an about turn to denounce the war when the Hitler-Stalin pact was agreed. Finally, it reversed its position yet again to give uncritical support to Churchill's coalition and the war effort after Hitler invaded Russia. As Duncan Hallas put it: "The war, which on 21 June 1941 was an imperialist war in Britain and France, became a war for democracy on the 22nd".[31] With Russia now "our allies" in the fight against the Nazis, the CP grew to its peak membership of 56,000. At the end of the war it called for the continuation of the national coalition government under Churchill, completely misreading the mood for radical change, collective provision and a determination there would be no return to the 1930s—all of which gave Labour an unexpected landslide victory.

By the end of the war the CP was, according to Duncan Hallas, "in formal political terms, right-wing social democratic. Yet organisationally and ideologically it was Stalinist. With the onset of the Cold War it reverted to its Stalinist reflexes—strident defence of Stalin's regime and its satellites, combined with selective industrial militancy".[32]

Stalin had been behind its 1951 *British Road to Socialism*—a parliamentary approach hardly different to Labour's—which led it to concentrate on winning positions and influence in the leadership of the major unions at the expense of workplace struggle and the building of independent rank and file organisation.

When Harry McShane eventually broke from the CP in 1953, it was because of his faith in independent rank and file organisation, his opposition to the *British Road to Socialism* and a realisation that Communist Party members were being treated like a stage army and expected to uncritically agree with their leadership. "It was obvious Stalin was using the weakest Communist Party in Europe—the CPGB—to overturn policy throughout the European communist movement. Britain was the first country where the CP announced a parliamentary road to socialism—a complete nonsense. Working class power can't be won through a capitalist parliament. Workers' power is about workers controlling their own lives through their own organisations. It's a completely different state that the workers run themselves".[33]

According to Duncan, "There was a slow erosion, more important than the membership figures, of significant industrial cadre like Eric Heffer and Hughie Scanlon and various CP intellectuals. Then the contradictions between a left social democratic programme and the Stalinist heritage exploded in 1956 with Khrushchev's secret speech and the Hungarian Revolution in the same year, that shattered the Stalinist myth for many of its devotees".[34]

There had been revolts and uprisings against the state capitalist regimes Stalin installed in Eastern Europe: notably the East German uprising of 1953, and a workers' uprising in the Polish city of Poznan in 1956. The Hungarian Revolution that quickly followed it was different—it was initially successful. In 1956 Budapest and every major Hungarian town were in the hands of factory councils and local revolutionary committees. The British Communist Party, whose leadership saw the Hungarian uprising as CIA-inspired, sent *Daily Worker* journalist Peter Fryer to cover the events. Fryer's honest, accurate reporting contributed to dissent inside the British Communist Party and the creation of a new anti-Stalinist left. His report from Budapest highlighted:

> ...the striking resemblance of these committees to the workers', peasants' and soldiers' councils thrown up in Russia in the 1905 Revolution and in February 1917. They were at once organs of insurrection—the coming together of delegates elected in the factories, universities, mines and army units—and organs of popular self-government, which the armed people trusted.[35]

But in November that year, just as Britain, France and Israel launched their combined military attack on Egypt, Khrushchev's tanks swept into Budapest. The Russian forces faced bitter, armed resistance, which they eventually crushed by killing thousands and forcing 200,000 to flee across the border into Austria. Duncan noted:

> In Britain the party lost over 10,000 members—a substantial part of its working class cadre and union "influentials". The party survived 1956 but the

membership slumped. When the party made a limited recovery in the 1960s it was on a different basis. The activists became a smaller and smaller proportion of the membership and its ageing industrial base became more cautious and more conservative.[36]

Yet for all its many faults the CP still provided networks in industry around which the best militants could organise. It was these networks that took the initiative in fighting Labour and Tory attempts to impose anti-trade union laws in the 1960s and early 1970s. They led and kept control of the Upper Clyde Shipbuilders (UCS) work-in that helped turn the tide against Heath. But by then the party had long abandoned the revolutionary road it had set out upon in 1920. In 1968 the events in France, coupled with the Prague Spring, inspired many thousands of students and young workers to identify with new and genuinely revolutionary organisations, well to the left of the Communist Party. The CP opposed the Vietnam Solidarity Campaign, which mobilised tens of thousands of young people against the US war in Vietnam— one of the reasons I had for not joining it.

The CPGB's long drift rightwards accelerated in the 1980s when its magazine *Marxism Today* proclaimed Thatcherism unstoppable. It advised the Labour left to ditch Arthur Scargill and Tony Benn for Neil Kinnock; it advised Kinnock to do a deal with David Owen and the Social Democratic Party (the right-wing breakaway from Labour). By 1992 the Party was indeed over. Ending his book review of Willie Thompson's history of the CPGB, Duncan wrote, "Willie Thompson honestly and candidly charts the CP's sorry decline in the last half of his book and for that reason it can be recommended. Stalinism was a disaster not only in the USSR but internationally. The future of the left belongs to those who always rejected it".[37]

Hallas and the Comintern

From the mid-1920s, Russian foreign policy, increasingly under the control of Stalin and his supporters, blocked and hindered wider social change thus setting the bloody pattern of the 20th century and trapping the larger part of the international left, who identified more or less critically with Stalinist Russia, its Eastern European satellites and with its imitators in China and Cuba. As Duncan wrote in 1985:

> The small clique of bureaucrats who run the USSR, together with their allies, satellites and imitators, and even more so the ruling class of the USA, with their allies, satellites and ideologists, habitually refer to "the Soviets" doing this or that. There are no soviets in Russia and have been none since the 1920s. The "Supreme Soviet" and other bodies in the USSR that are given the name of soviet are in no way organs of workers' power as set up by the revolutionary workers in 1917. It suits the interests of the bureaucratic rulers of the USSR, however, to maintain the fiction—their claim to the inheritance of the workers' revolution of 1917 is used to validate their rule over the workers. It also suits the interests of the ruling classes of the West to identify soviets, workers' power, with their opposite—bureaucratic dictatorship *over* the working class.
>
> Of course, there was none of this in March 1919. The delegates meeting in Moscow (at the founding Congress of the Communist International or Comintern) had constituted the new International on the basis of uncompromising internationalism, a decisive and final split with the traitors of 1914, workers' power, workers' councils, the defence of the Russian Soviet Republic and the perspective of revolution in the near future in central and western Europe. The problem now was to create mass parties that could make all this reality.[38]

In 1985 Bookmarks published Duncan's book *The Comintern,* from which the foregoing quote is taken. The cover of the book is a striking drawing of the Tatlin Tower, intended as a monument to the Communist International. It was to have been twice the size of the Empire State Building in Manhattan. Designed by Vladimir Tatlin in revolutionary Moscow, sadly his monument never saw the light of day but fortunately for us Duncan's book did, thanks to Nigel Harris and Tony Cliff who persuaded him to write it.

Relatively short and concise for a book encompassing such an epic canvass, it is, in my view, Duncan's monument—a masterpiece that examines the actual history of the Third or Communist International from its founding conference in 1919 to its winding up under Stalin's orders in 1943. It is particularly good on the political conclusions to be drawn—both positive and negative—for those striving to build a better world today.

The Bolsheviks always insisted socialism could not be built in any single country, certainly not in backward, war-ravaged Russia. The essential precondition for ending class society required the pooled resources of a number of the more advanced capitalist states. Having led the October Revolution to success, they staked everything on international socialist revolution and looked in particular to the German working class. Lenin was clear: "It is not open to the slightest doubt that the final victory of our revolution, if it were to remain alone, if there were no revolutionary movement in other countries, would be hopeless. Our salvation from all these difficulties is an all European revolution".[39] Trotsky, speaking on behalf of the Soviet government in 1918, said, "If the peoples of Europe do not arise and crush imperialism, we shall be crushed".[40]

Because mass opposition to the war was already underway in Europe, the Bolsheviks were confident revolution would spread. Working class radicalisation under the conditions of war production was not confined to Tsarist Russia. Every major imperialist power passed through a similar experience. Despite the many difficulties, the Bolsheviks anticipated October would spark a wave of revolutions in the West; and it did. The abrupt end to the First World War proved their prognosis was sound. The most striking episode in the European crisis

The Comintern
(1985).

was not the Russian Revolution but a series of upheavals that engulfed the most industrially developed European power, Germany, from the revolution of November 1918 that toppled the Kaiser through to the Communist Party's abortive attempt to seize power five years later in October 1923.

The victorious powers were also affected. 1919 was the most dangerous year the British state had ever faced, while Italy saw two years of mass struggle culminating in the factory occupations and land seizures of 1920. But despite coming desperately close, with a whole series of revolts and workers' insurrections, the European insurgency was contained.

To triumph, the revolutionary crises that developed in a whole number of European states required, in advance, effective revolutionary organisations and a break with the unreliable reformist leaders. Only in Russia was this achieved. The defeat of the premature Berlin uprising and the murder of Rosa Luxemburg and Karl Liebknecht in early 1919 emphasised the need for an effective revolutionary international to replace a discredited social democracy. So the Third (or Communist) International was launched in March 1919 in the midst of the revolutionary wave at the end of the war. In his introduction to *The Comintern,* Duncan Hallas wrote:

The Communist International, which arose out of the Russian Revolution of October 1917, was not an optional extra but an essential, indispensable part of that revolution, which in turn was part of an international revolutionary upheaval. Conversely the events that were to follow ten years later—turning the Comintern into a tool of Russian foreign policy—was part of the strangling of workers' power inside the USSR by the rising bureaucracy under Stalin.

There is an enormous amount of literature on the Comintern. Some is Stalinist; more is social-democratic; and most is the output of various US universities, promoted by the CIA in the interests of US foreign policy—and doubtless much of this is CIA–financed too. This book aims to provide, from a revolutionary socialist point of view, an introduction to the Comintern, from its founding conference in 1919 to its winding up by Stalin in 1943.

In 1932 Trotsky, then a powerless and persecuted exile from the USSR, wrote a statement intended to serve as a political basis for an international left opposition to the Communist Parties under Stalin: "The International Left Opposition stands on the ground of the first four congresses of the Comintern. This does not mean that it bows before every letter of its decisions, many of which had a purely conjunctional character and have been contradicted by subsequent events. But all the essential principles remain even today the highest expression of proletarian strategy in the epoch of the general crisis of capitalism." The SWP stands on this ground, which is why the emphasis of this book is on the Comintern's revolutionary period, the period of the first four Congresses and immediately after.[41]

Though led disastrously by Stalin in the years following the defeat of the German Revolution and Lenin's death in

1924, there was a period when the Comintern made real progress. It helped turn revolutionaries in Western Europe and in the US to the construction of mass parties. In Britain it was instrumental in bringing together some of the competing factions of the revolutionary left, together with the leaders of the shop stewards and workers' committee movement, to form the CPGB in 1920-21. There were of course many bigger, more important achievements. Lenin's project of welding together the most militant, class conscious sections of the European and international working class into a current that could play a leading role in the class struggle, acting both with and against the reformist leaders but without becoming sectarian, was real and impressive. Six hundred delegates attended the Third Annual Congress of the Comintern, held in March 1921, and they came from 55 countries, including China, India, Palestine, the US and Australia. Its delegates represented millions of workers across the world.

The events that followed over the next 15 years, after the Third Congress in 1921—the turning of the Comintern into a tool of Russian foreign policy—was part of the strangling of workers' power inside Russia by the rising Stalinist bureaucracy. There is not space to cover every twist and turn so I will focus on just one of the many examples from Duncan's book to illustrate how Stalinism sought to destroy the revolutionary Marxist tradition both physically and politically: the Chinese Revolution of 1925-27.

1923 was a crucial year for the Comintern and for revolutionary Russia.

Lenin was no longer the man at the wheel. His health had given way in 1921 and recovery was never more than partial. In May 1922 he suffered a paralysing stroke that temporarily deprived him of speech. Two more strokes followed in December that year. A fourth, in March 1923, ended his political life, though he did not die physically until January 1924.[42]

The defeat of the German Revolution in 1923—a combination of inexperience and misjudgement on the part of the leadership of the German CP and weaknesses in the Comintern leadership, because Trotsky was no longer able to exert the same influence he had enjoyed previously with Lenin's support—meant that by 1924 Russia was left isolated and exhausted and Lenin was dead. In his *Lessons of October* written in 1924 Trotsky wrote, "In the latter part of last year, we witnessed in Germany a classic demonstration of how it was possible to miss a perfectly exceptional revolutionary situation of world-historic importance".[43]

Yet despite the German defeat, the stabilisation of Western capitalism was at best precarious and temporary. In virtually every European state the workers' movement at some point over the next dozen or so years would seriously threaten the social order. In addition a Chinese workers' revolution appeared on the horizon. China, the vast, populous landmass bordering Russia, was a semi-colony partitioned between Britain, France, the US and Japan. The Chinese Communist Party (CCP) was founded in 1921 against the backdrop of anti-imperialist struggle and working class militancy. By 1925 it was the effective leadership of the growing Chinese labour movement.

On 30 May 1925, the British-controlled Shanghai police fired on a demonstration, killing 12 people. The effect was swift and tumultuous. Shanghai, the great foreign stronghold with its Western banks and mills and its exclusive foreign zones, was paralysed by a general strike involving 400,000 workers. At Hankow on 11 June, British soldiers fired on a demonstration, killing eight and wounding 12. On 23 June a demonstration of students, workers and military cadets paraded in Canton. British and French machine gunners opened fire on the march; 52 students and workers were killed and 117 wounded.

> A boycott of British goods and a general strike was immediately declared. Hong Kong, the fortress of Britain in China was totally immobilised. Not a

wheel turned, not a bale of cargo moved. Not a ship left anchor. This explosion was led by rebels, young nationalists—and the Chinese Communist Party that grew massively out of it. Soon it had 30,000 members, compared with less than a thousand in 1924, and the overwhelming majority were workers in the coastal cities. The Chinese working class was new but already large; about 3.5 million workers in the modern mainly foreign-owned industrial sector and 11 million in small enterprises, mainly Chinese-owned. Before the movement that followed the 30 May, the unions, new and in many cases led by the Communists, counted their members in thousands. But by the end of 1925, they had three million members.

All of this was highly disconcerting for the Kuomintang leaders, now dominated by Chiang Kai-shek. They were nationalists and knew that without mass popular support they could not hope to break the power of the imperialists and their warlord protégés. So they had to support the protest movement after 30 May. But they were bourgeois nationalists, with innumerable family ties among merchants, capitalists and landowners—groups which, in China, were closely intertwined. Workers' power and peasant revolt was as frightening to them as to the foreign bosses of the Jardine Matheson, Shanghai and Hong Kong bank. So the Kuomintang sought to use, control and then destroy the mass movement—a difficult operation that was impossible without two conditions: first the fast-growing CP must be subordinated to the Kuomintang; secondly the Kuomintang needed the continued supply of Russian guns and Russian military expertise, which alone could make possible the expansion of a reliable "professional" army, for use against workers, peasants and warlords alike.[44]

The Bukharin-Stalin leadership of the Comintern guaranteed both. When Chiang Kai–shek launched his first military coup in Canton in March 1926 and imprisoned local Communist Party leaders and strike committee activists, the Chinese CP was ordered by the Comintern to submit. In January, the Russian CP had declared, "To our party has fallen the proud and historic task of leading the first victorious, proletarian revolution in the world. We are convinced that the Kuomintang will succeed in playing the same role in the East".[45]

"Thus," writes Duncan, "the Chinese CP was subordinated to the Chinese bourgeoisie in the interests of the foreign policy pursued by the Russian bureaucracy. Stalin's emissary in China, Borodin, declared, 'the present period is one in which the communists should do coolie service for the Kuomintang'".[46] Trotsky, still a member of the politburo but effectively isolated and excluded from influence, attacked the Stalin clique that promoted an alliance between the Chinese CP and the Kuomintang (KMT), the party of China's bourgeois nationalists.

Recalling the fight over "permanent revolution" in Petrograd in April 1917, Trotsky wrote, "The new and absolutely false theory promulgated by Stalin about the 'immanent revolutionary spirit' of the colonial bourgeoisie is, in substance, a translation of Menshevism into the language of Chinese politics".[47] Trotsky's warnings were ignored. Chiang Kai-shek, leader of the Kuomintang and Stalin's supposed ally, turned his forces on the Communist-led workers' movement and butchered it. Chiang now wanted to reassure the imperialist powers, whose troops still held the foreign concessions in China, that the Kuomintang was "safe". The Communist Party, the unions and all traces of workers' organisation in Shanghai were completely eliminated.

There was one final urban spasm. An attempted coup was launched in Canton, where the Chinese CP still had a substantial underground organisation. It was timed to coincide with the 14th Congress of the Russian CP in December 1927, where the opposition inside Russia was to be finally proscribed. Its aim was to give Stalin and Bukharin a "victory" to celebrate and Stalin's emissary, Heinz Neumann, led it. Without political preparation, without genuine mass support, it was crushed within days. Another massacre of workers followed. The Chinese CP's last working class support was wiped out. This then was the final fruit of the period of Bukharin's leadership of the Comintern.[48]

Subordinating anti-colonial struggles to the needs of Russian foreign policy and exporting "Menshevism into Chinese politics", as Trotsky had warned against at the time, would become the hallmark of Stalinist influence on anti-colonial struggles for decades to come. For China the consequence was disastrous: imperialist domination of the country was given a further 20-year lease of life. Strangely, instead of exposing Stalinism, such defeats strengthened his hold and the lie of socialism in one country. International defeats made it harder for Trotsky's internationalism to win an audience inside beleaguered Russia and easier for the Stalinist bureaucracy to strengthen its grip.

The end of the Comintern
In August 1939, Stalin reversed his foreign policy. "Despairing of an effective military alliance with Britain and France, he made a pact with Hitler on 23 August—the partition of Poland between Germany and the USSR, the absorption of the Baltic states of Estonia, Latvia and Lithuania by the USSR, and a pledge of Russian neutrality in the coming war. The war started a week later. The German army invaded Poland on 1 September. By 3 September Germany was at war with Britain and France but Stalin stood by his pact with the Nazis. On 17 September the Russian army crossed the border into Poland to seize Stalin's share of the booty".[49]

The Comintern Centre did not immediately react to this new situation. Duncan Hallas wrote:

Presumably, it had not been told what to say. At any rate the British and French CPs did not immediately change course... The French Communist deputies voted for the war with more enthusiasm than those of most other parties, while British CP leader Harry Pollitt rushed out a pamphlet *How to Win the War*. But this was not at all what was wanted. Moscow decreed that the "anti-fascist alliance" was now out and another somersault was imposed on the Comintern parties.[50]

Early in November 1939 the Comintern Executive declared:

The ruling circles of England, France and Germany are waging a war for world supremacy. This war is the continuation of many years of imperialist strife in the camp of capitalism. Three of the richest states—England, France and the USA—hold sway over the most important routes and markets... They want to divide anew, to their own advantage, the sources of raw materials, food, gold reserves and the masses of people in the colonies. Such is the real meaning of this war, which is an unjust, reactionary and imperialist war... The working class cannot support such a war against Germany.[51]

The Comintern had been arguing the exact opposite of this since 1935.

Yet less than two years later, events forced Stalin into yet another U-turn in foreign policy, when Hitler invaded Russia. The Comintern again fell obediently into line, without any explanation for the change, calling for "the mobilisation of every force of the nations embattled against Hitler in a life and death struggle".

After June 1941 the Comintern would cease to have any significance for Stalin. By then it had served its purpose.

Churchill and Roosevelt, representing the ruling classes of the West, now Stalin's allies, did not like anything that might remind their workers of the revolutionary years—even if only in name. In May 1943 the Executive Committee of the Comintern called for its dissolution. In June it announced that this had been "unanimously agreed" by its various sections. On 8 June 1943 the Comintern was formally liquidated... Formal liquidation had come long after its death as a revolutionary international. The liquidation of its leading personnel had also come earlier. The Bolshevik Party, the driving force of the Comintern in its early years, had a central committee of 24 members in 1917. Of these, seven died before Stalin established his dictatorship and two, Stalin himself and Alexandra Kollontai,[52] were still alive in 1943. All the other fifteen were murdered, with or without trial, by the Stalinist regime. They included all the Bolshevik representatives on the Comintern executive in the early years: Bukharin, Radek, Trotsky and Zinoviev—the only exception is Lenin.[53]

In 1943 the Comintern was officially buried and after 1944 Stalin's empire was massively expanded on the basis of military conquest and on agreements with the Western powers—notably Roosevelt and Churchill. As Duncan explains in the final chapter of his book:

There were, in fact, three separate and related developments. First, most of Eastern Europe was conquered by the armies of the USSR and incorporated in its "sphere of influence" in the post-war carve-up of central Europe. Then, in 1947–8, these were transformed from the top down into more or less close replicas of Stalin's Russia. Second, the communist parties in the West pursued, until the outbreak of the Cold War in 1947, policies of class collaboration which were, if it were possible, to the right even of the People's Front period. They grew massively and were represented in the governments of

France, Italy, Belgium, Denmark and a number of other countries, including Batista's Cuba.

Third, in Albania and Yugoslavia in 1944, in China in 1948–9 and later in Vietnam and Cuba, regimes essentially similar to that of the USSR were established by military means, by the conquest of weak native bourgeois regimes—which had been essentially puppets of foreign powers—by peasant armies led by intellectuals. These three processes were not clearly distinguished by the groups, which made up the Fourth International.

A contributory factor to this disorientation was Trotsky's refusal to accept that a counter-revolution had taken place in the USSR and his insistence that the USSR was still some form of workers' state, however distorted. This meant that during the Cold War, when Stalinism was putting forward a view of the world divided into two opposing camps, socialism versus imperialism, the Fourth International groups were drawn into a similar worldview—of workers' states versus imperialism. This led most of them into a position of "critical support" for Stalinism and, since it now seemed that a "workers' state" could be created by means other than working-class revolution, to the adoption in varying degrees of political ideas which looked to some agency other than the working class for the achievement of socialism. Thus they came, in practice, to jettison much of the core of the communist tradition, the tradition of the revolutionary Comintern which Trotsky himself had fought and died to uphold.

For that tradition is concerned with socialism as the self-emancipation of the working class. Its essentials are uncompromising internationalism, unconditional support for workers' struggles against every ruling class, the goal of a workers' state based on workers' councils as the agency of the transition to socialism, and unequivocal rejection of all suggestions that any other class, alliance of classes, political grouping or party can substitute for the working class in bringing socialism.[54]

Throughout Duncan's life, Stalinism cast an enormous shadow over the socialist movement, both in terms of discrediting genuine socialism on an international scale and in distorting the politics of those who looked to the leadership of the CP at a local level. In response to this, Duncan played a huge role in rescuing the genuine revolutionary tradition, demonstrating the gulf separating the idealism and principles of the early years of the Bolshevik revolution from what followed under Stalin. In doing so, he helped restore both the spirit and practical method of the united front, thus encouraging revolutionaries to engage in common struggle with workers who were influenced by reformism, while remaining independently critical of the politics of the reformist leadership, including that of the CP. Duncan embodied a living revolutionary tradition, linking the earliest Trotskyist organisations in Britain to new generations of revolutionaries who emerged in the 1960s and 1970s striving to understand *both* the crimes and failures of Western capitalism *and* the bankruptcy and tyranny of Stalinism. Above all, he sought to link that theoretical understanding to a practical strategy to deal with the challenges of the present, to create a revolutionary organisation that could influence political struggle and working class battles in the present and in the future.

I'll end by quoting Duncan's last few sentences from his book on the Comintern:

> The world working class is bigger than ever before. The difficulties facing us are immense of course. But they are capable of solution. Workers' revolution and workers' power are not utopias. They are the only way forward for humanity.[55]

Notes

1   Duncan Hallas, 'The Legacy of Marx', *Socialist Worker (US)*, (March 1983).

2   Chanie Rosenberg in "Duncan Hallas—An agitator of the best kind", *Socialist Review* 268 (November 2002), p20.

3   James Connolly, *The Reconquest of Ireland*, Ch 8. www.marxists.org/archive//connolly/1915/rcoi/chapo8.htm

4   Paul Foot, *Socialist Worker* (28 September 2002).

5   The debate is available at https://mrc-catalogue.warwick.ac.uk/records/BOO/7/5/19

6   For a detailed account about why the WIL was more outgoing see Hallas, "The Sad Fate of British Trotskyism", *Socialist Worker Review* 91, (October 1986) p21.

7   Duncan Hallas, *The Fourth International, Stalinism and the Origins of the International Socialists: Some Documents* (November 1971) p75.

8   Dave Sherry, *Russia 1917: Workers' Revolution and the Festival of the Oppressed*, (London: Bookmarks, 2017) p10.

9   Paul Foot, "Harry McShane obituary", *Socialist Worker* (April 1988).

10 Ian Birchall, *Tony Cliff: A Marxist for His Time*, (London: Bookmarks, 2011) p221.

11 Paul Foot, *Socialist Worker* (April 1988).

12 Duncan Hallas, "Notes of the Month", *International Socialism* 83 (November 1975) p3-4.

13 Duncan Hallas, "On the United Front Tactic", *International Socialism* 85 (January 1976) p8.

14 BBC TV, *6 O'Clock News* (August 2, 1971).

15 Duncan Hallas, *International Socialism* 53, (October/December 1972) p3.

16 See "The ANL and its lessons today—Interview with Paul Holborow", *International Socialism* 163, (Summer 2019) p66.

17 Duncan Hallas, *The Meaning of Marxism*, (London: Pluto Press, 1971) p38-39.

18 Duncan Hallas, "All those in favour of cutting wages, please show", *Socialist Worker* 391 (14 September 1974) p12.

19 Figures from the official records of the NKVD, quoted in Tomas Tengely-Evans, *The Shadow of Stalinism*, (London: SW pamphlet, January 2022)

20 Duncan Hallas, *Communism and Stalinism: On John Gollan's 'Social Democracy; Some Problems'*, *International Socialism* 1: 87, (March/April 1976), p25, 27 & 28.

21 Hallas, *Communism and Stalinism*, p29.

22 Hallas, *Communism and Stalinism*, p29.

23 Hallas quoting Khrushchev, *Communism and Stalinism*, p29.

24 Hallas, *Communism and Stalinism*, p29.

25 Hallas, *Communism and Stalinism*, p29.

26 Cited by Duncan Hallas, 'Notes of the Month', *International Socialism* 1: 60 (July 1973), pp1-2.

27 Duncan Hallas, "Notes of the Month", *International Socialism* 1: 60 (July 1973) pp1-2.

28 James Hinton, *The First Shop Stewards Movement,* (London: George Allen & Unwin, 1973) p17.

29 Duncan Hallas, "The Communist Party and the General Strike", *International Socialism* 88 (May 1976), pp17-24.

30 Duncan Hallas, "The Road to Ruin", *Socialist Review* 156 (September 1992) p29.

31 Duncan Hallas, "The Road to Ruin", p29.

32 Hallas, "The Road to Ruin", p29.

33 Harry McShane & Joan Smith, *No Mean Fighter* (London: Pluto Press, 1977), p245.

34 Hallas, "The Road to Ruin", p29.

35 Peter Fryer, *The Hungarian Tragedy* (London: Index Books, 1956) p46.

36 Hallas, "The Road to Ruin", p29.

37 Hallas, "The Road to Ruin", p29.

38 Duncan Hallas, *The Comintern* (London: Bookmarks, 1985) p25.

39 Lenin, quoted in EH Carr, *The Bolshevik Revolution, Vol 3*, (London: Pelican, 1983), p63.

40 Quoted in EH Carr, *The Bolshevik Revolution, Vol 3*, p17.

41 Hallas, *The Comintern*, p8-9.

42 Hallas, *The Comintern*, p84.

43 Leon Trotsky, *Lessons of October*, (1924), quoted in Hallas, *The Comintern*, p89. The full text is available at www.marxists.org/archive/trotsky/1924/lessons/index.htm

44 Hallas, *The Comintern*, p19-20.

45 Nigel Harris, *The Mandate of Heaven* (London: IS Books 1978) p9.

46 Tilak, *The Rise and Fall of the Comintern* (Bombay: Sparks Syndicate, 1947) p33 quoted in Hallas, *The Comintern*, p120.

47 Leon Trotsky, *On China* (New York: Pathfinder, 1976) p297.

48 Hallas, *The Comintern*, p122.

49 Hallas, *The Comintern*, p155-156.

50 Hallas, *The Comintern*, p120.

51 Hallas, *The Comintern*, p157.

52 It is worth noting that part of the reason that Kollontai survived was her capitulation to Stalinism. She rewrote her 1919 account of the meeting which planned the October insurrection, the original of which mentioned Trotsky and not Stalin. In her 1937 version Trotsky becomes "Judas-Trotsky, an infamous traitor and future Gestapo agent" and Stalin plays the star role. See Paul Ginsborg, *Family Politics Domestic Devastation and Survival 1900-1950* (New Haven, CT: Yale University Press, 2014) p398.

53 Hallas, *The Comintern*, p157-8.

54 Hallas, *The Comintern*, p165-6

55 Hallas, *The Comintern*, p167.

Britain's Oldest Colony:
A History of Famine, Brutality...
and Heroism
Duncan Hallas
(*Socialist Worker*, 21 August 1969)

The embattled workers of the Bogside and Belfast are following in the long tradition of struggle against imperialism and its reactionary Green and Orange Tory friends.

Ireland has a special place in the story of capitalism in Britain. It was the first British colony—just ahead of Jamaica—and for more than three centuries the exploitation of the people of Ireland was a big source of income for the rulers of this country.

For practical purposes Ireland was conquered in the 17th century, though the country had been an English dependency in name from a much earlier period. The effect of the conquest was well described by a left-wing historian in the 1930s:

Ireland now became, what it has since of necessity remained, a source of cheap food and raw materials for

England. At first cattle were reared, and by 1660 some 500,000 head were being exported annually to England.

When these exports were found to be causing a fall in agricultural prices and rents, an Act was passed in 1666 forbidding the export of cattle, meat or dairy products. This Act crippled the Irish cattle industry and when cattle began to be replaced by sheep a further Act forbade both the export of wool to any other country and the export of anything but the raw wool to England. Later still, the Irish cloth industry was deliberately destroyed when it became a dangerous competitor.

The most important Irish export, however, soon became human beings—cheap labour for the developing industries of Britain, and later, the USA.

A comparatively small group of English landowners got hold of most of the land in Ireland, leaving the mass of the Irish people as tenants with no security whatever. Merciless rack renting reduced the people to a state of poverty unknown in any other part of Europe. Every year thousands and tens of thousands were forced to emigrate by the threat of starvation.

That was before the Great Hunger, the famine of 1845-49. The famine was man-made. There was food enough in Ireland to feed the population—if they had had the money to buy it.

At this time the country was still a major exporter of wheat—and wheat exports continued throughout the famine. The potato crop first failed in 1845.

In that year 515 people were officially recorded as dying of starvation and 3,250,000 quarters of wheat were exported. By 1847, when 21,770 deaths by starvation were recorded, wheat exports were still over 2 million quarters and even in 1848. when nearly 300,000 died of hunger 1,828,132 quarters of grain were sent out of Irish ports.

This was the decisive turning point in 19th century Irish history. On the eve of the famine the population was estimated at over six million—slightly greater than it is today. As a direct consequence of the famine over a million Irish men, women and children died, a quarter of a million emigrated to England and Scotland and over a million left for the USA.

Reservoir

Post-famine Ireland was a ruined country.

Except for the North East corner, where the linen Industry had survived and expanded and shipbuilding was soon to develop, the whole country became simply a vast reservoir of surplus labour, barely kept alive by subsistence agriculture and available when required by the expanding industries of Britain and North America.

Even the export of wheat soon ceased to be important as a result of the adoption of free trade by the British government. Russia and the USA replaced Ireland as the principal sources of wheat imports to Britain. Not until the 1950s was there any significant growth of industry outside the six counties.

The first modern revolutionary movement in Ireland, the United Irishmen, was founded in Belfast in 1791. The great French Revolution aroused more popular enthusiasm in Ireland than perhaps in any other country in Europe.

At first the United Irishmen (UI) was an open political organisation agitating for universal suffrage but it was soon driven underground. The UI adopted the demand for a national convention and an Irish Republic on the French model.

This was high treason to the government of King George and the society began to prepare for an armed rising. For a time the United Irishmen succeeded in breaking down the hostility between Catholics and Protestants and combining both against the English ruling class and its Irish supporters.

In 1798 the United Irishmen were forced into a premature rising which was most savagely repressed.

This rising and its defeat had a big influence on the subsequent development of the national movement. The actual rebels had been mostly peasants and they had shown very little respect to the property rights of the small but influential minority of wealthy Irish.

This, together with the Jacobin ideas of Wolfe Tone and his friends, made a lasting impression. The Irish middle class learned its lesson. In future it was to fight on two fronts, against the English ascendancy but still more against the Irish people. Green Toryism was born.

From now on the British government could count on an ally in Ireland. An unreliable ally and one that would exploit every weakness to gain concessions for itself but an ally nonetheless.

The aim of the middle class was reform within the system, privilege for themselves. Their method, peaceful agitation directed at the British parliament, their instrument to control the peasants—90 per cent of the people—the Roman Catholic Church.

The chief spokesman of the Irish middle class in the first half of the last century, Daniel O'Connell, the so-called "Liberator", chose to fight on the issue of Catholic emancipation, that is the removal of the legal discrimination that existed against Catholics as such.

O'Connell was successful in terms of his own aims. Catholic emancipation was achieved. Middle-class Irish Catholics got a modest share of privilege, the peasants got the famine!

The long-term effects of O'Connellism were even more pernicious. Religious sectarianism had been declining in Ireland for a century. By reviving it, by concentrating on the religious issue, O'Connell and his followers helped to revive the waning sectarianism of the North East.

Tradition

The "official" church-supported nationalist movement continued in the O'Connell tradition right down to 1914, when the nationalist parliamentary leader, John Redmond, called on Irishmen to enlist in the British Army to fight for "King and Country".

There was another tradition, the tradition of 1798, carried forward by the Irish Republican Brotherhood, the Fenians and, in a different way, the Irish Land League. Men like John Mitchell and James Fintan Lalor kept alive the message of Wolfe Tone—"I appeal to that large and respectable class of the community—the men of no property".

The political wing of Fenianism was unable, in spite of heroic efforts, to break the hold of middle-class nationalists and the church on the peasantry.

This lack of a massive popular base forced the Fenians into the blind alley of sporadic acts of terrorism, an experience and a method repeated by the IRA in the 1920s and 30s.

The agrarian counterpart of Fenianism, the Land League, was more successful. The League got mass peasant support for its tactics of resisting rent increases and evictions by means of the boycott.

It was also helped by the declining importance of Irish land-ownership as a source of income to the British ruling class and the very real fear of the British Liberals and Tories that peasant resistance could give the Fenians substantial popular support.

In the event successive British governments introduced legislation to give the peasants land bit by bit (with "adequate" compensation to the landowners), a course of action they would never have adopted but for the threat of revolution.

By the first decade of the present century it looked as though the Irish question could be solved by a compromise between the British ruling class and the Irish middle-class nationalists. "Home Rule", which would have kept Ireland under effective Westminster control, whilst turning over the job of running the country to the "respectable" nationalists, was the order of the day.

A Home Rule Bill was actually introduced by the British Liberal Government just before the 1914-18 war. Two factors wrecked this unholy alliance, the Orange Tories who had been built up to create a "minority problem" in the interests of British ascendancy and, more important, the heroic sacrifice of the heirs of Fenianism and the pioneers of the revolutionary socialist movement in Ireland.

At Easter 1916, at the height of the World War, a few hundred armed men marched out to challenge the whole force of the British Empire. The men who seized the GPO in Dublin for the then non-existent Republic of Ireland were not supported by the great majority of working people in the city, let alone the country. The rising was soon crushed—though 22,000 British troops had to be employed—and most of the leaders executed.

Yet Connolly, Pearse and the others changed the course of Irish history. In spite of the lack of mass participation they had correctly judged the balance of forces.

Swung

It was one of those few moments when a handful of militants can decisively alter the course of events.

Lenin wrote soon afterwards, "Anyone who calls this a putsch is incapable of understanding what a real revolution is like".[1]

The rising and its aftermath completely discredited the parliamentary nationalists. It swung the majority of the Irish people behind the lower middle-class nationalist party Sinn Féin.

The Tan War followed and by 1920, both the British government and the majority of the Sinn Féin leadership were ready for a compromise—partition.

The economic basis of Northern Irish separation was the development of the shipbuilding and allied industries of Belfast. A "native" capitalist class, whose interests required the British and imperial markets, became the leading force in the area.

Due to the O'Connellite character of the national movement, it was possible for this class to gain the solid support of practically the whole Protestant population for the archaic ideology of Orangeism.

"Home rule means Rome rule", "Remember the Boyne", "No Surrender" and the rest of the irrelevant clap-trap became and remained the sum and substance of the political thinking of a high proportion of the Protestant working class in the North.

This made them clay in the hands of the Orange bosses who had, and have, close links with the British Tories. Carson and Smith, the Ulster Tory leaders were violently opposed to "Home Rule", which would have left them a permanent minority. They were willing to carry their opposition to the point of civil war, to intrigue with the German government and to foment mutiny in the British army.

Their determined opposition, together with the increasing cost of holding down the South at a time when Ireland as a whole was less and less a source of income to British capitalism, produced partition. To make the Northern Irish statelet economically viable a substantial Catholic population had to be incorporated. So from the beginning Northern Ireland was a police state based on repression, gerrymandering and discrimination.

Today, when it is shaken to its foundations, we must be guided by the words of James Connolly:

> The Irish question is a social question. The whole age-long fight of the Irish people against their oppressors resolves itself, in the last analysis, into a fight for the means of life, the sources of production in Ireland...
>
> In this movement the North and South will again clasp hands, again will it be demonstrated, as in '98, that the pressure of a common exploitation can make enthusiastic rebels out of a Protestant working class, earnest champions of civil and religious liberty out of Catholics, and out of both a united Social Democracy.[2]

Notes

1   V I Lenin, "The Discussion On Self-Determination Summed Up" (1916) in *Collected Works*, Volume 22 (Moscow: Progress, 1974), pp320-360.

2   James Connolly, *Labour in Irish History* (1910) Chapter 16, www.marxists.org/archive/connolly/1910/lih/chap16.htm. At the time, "social democracy" referred to revolutionary socialism.

BOB CROW, deputy general secretary of the rail workers' union, the RMT, will be speaking in a forum with JULIE WATERSON on *The unions under Labour*. She will also look at the politics of workplace militancy in *Revolutionary syndicalism and revolutionary socialism*.

US socialist SHARON SMITH will be speaking on *New feminism: a critique*, part of our course on Debates in women's history. Other meetings in this series include SHEILA MCGREGOR addressing the question *Have women always been oppressed?* and JUDITH ORR looking at *Did the left forget women in the 1960s?* An additional meeting on Russian revolutionary *Alexandra Kollontai* will be introduced by CHANIE ROSENBERG.

Sheila McGregor

DUNCAN HALLAS has been a revolutionary socialist since the 1930s, and his meetings on history and Marxist theory in previous years have proved extremely popular. This year he will be introducing all four meetings in a new course on *What Marx really said*, which will look at *Human Nature, History and class struggle*, *The economics of capitalism*, and *Revolution*.

Sharon Smith (top), Julie Waterson (middle) and Chanie Rosenberg

Highlights

Programme for Marxism Festival, 1998. Speakers included Bob Crow, Julie Waterson, Sharon Smith, Sheila McGregor, Judith Orr, Chanie Rosenberg and Duncan Hallas.

The Nature of Revolution
Duncan Hallas

(July 1998)[1]

Revolution in the sense that we're using the word, is—I'm quoting Marx—a more or less rapid transformation of the political, and/or social and economic system. Now, we ought to add, it needs to take place in a fairly short time on this definition, relevant to the things I'm going to talk about. People talk about the Neolithic revolution, the discovery of agriculture, etc. Well, yes it was a revolution in the sense that the method by which you sustained life, the mode of production, was transformed. Fine. But it took several centuries. It was a relatively slow process. We're talking about revolutions in terms of things that happen relatively rapidly.

At this Marxism there are five talks on twentieth century social revolutions, and another five on the Russian revolution alone. Revolutions are not that uncommon. I mean living in Britain you might think, "My god, 1640, that's back to the Ark." No, no, on a world scale, the revolutions in the twentieth century are comparatively common. The South African instance is a very important recent example. Because it was a revolution—make no mistake about it. The destruction of the apartheid system meant a fundamental transformation in the political superstructure of society. It wasn't a *social* revolution, though—a matter which I'll come to in a moment. What matters to us really is the distinction between bourgeois and proletarian revolutions. That's what really matters to us today.

Are there any common factors that we can generalise about revolutions? This applies to both kinds, political and social. Well, Lenin wrote, there were three conditions. The first was, the old ruling class cannot go on in the old way. In other words, revolutions, or at least the immediate crack-up of the old order, starts at the top. It starts because of a crisis in the ruling class itself. Secondly, the mass of the population won't go on in the old way. That is to say, there is a radicalisation, which occurs quite quickly, quite rapidly. And thirdly, that there is a coherent and adequate leadership of the oppressed classes.

Three conditions. But wait a minute, we have to go back to Marx. You see, that's absolutely right politically, but as Marx said, changes in the economic foundations of society, the entire immense superstructure, political, ideological and so on, is more or less rapidly transformed. Again back to South Africa. You see, why didn't P W Botha [Prime Minister from 1978-1984] go on in the good old tradition of Hendrik Verwoerd [Prime Minister from 1958-1966] and D F Malan [Prime Minister from 1948-1954], and so on, and hold the thing?

Answer: Because the economic conditions, which were fundamental to the regime, or any regime, were changing. The comparatively rapid industrialisation, the development of factory industry, and so on, meant that the old bonds, again, in Marxist terms, turned into fetters: they got in the way of capital accumulation. They were a bloody nuisance to big business. Hence the ruling class itself starts to split. They attempt a series of reforms, and, in doing so, precipitate the actual revolution.

Now I've so far talked about changes in the economic structure and so on and so forth, but there is a very important component to any real revolution, that is, a revolution in ideas. Let's characterise it: first of all, there are rapid shifts in ideas. Secondly there's an expansion of the range of ideas that are considered by ordinary people, and thirdly, most important of all, people who you might say, if you were a bit contemptuous, didn't have two ideas to rub together in their pocket, suddenly take up aspects of fundamental social changes. I'll give you a couple of examples.

The great French Revolution—that's the 1789-96 one, didn't happen in Britain—nevertheless it had a profound effect on both its artisans—I won't call them workers because most of them weren't wage workers—and intellectuals. The poet Wordsworth wrote: "Bliss was it in that dawn to be alive, But to be young was very heaven!" Now Wordsworth was not a revolutionary. Far from it. In later life he became a popular establishment voice, he was conservative, and even reactionary. Nevertheless, the impact of the event transformed consciousness, or sections of consciousness and so on, in every case.

Do you remember the three women—I'm not going so far back this time—the three Portuguese women who wrote what we could describe as a feminist pamphlet, booklet [during the 1974-76 Portuguese Revolution]. I referred to the Catholic Church in Ireland and its stultifying effect, particularly on the position of women, in a previous discussion. But actually I should have ignored Ireland—I should have taken Portugal. Because though the Irish church 20 years ago was still half in the Middle Ages, it was positively progressive compared to the Portuguese hierarchy. This pamphlet's essential contents were: (1) Women ought to have equal rights with men. Revolutionary idea! It was a revolutionary idea in Portugal in the early 70s; (2) Contraception ought to be legal; (3) There ought to be a system of child benefits.

This sort of thing, written in London, Paris, Berlin, or wherever, would have created no sensation whatever. Such ideas were commonplace. Some of the objectives had been achieved, or partly achieved. But in Portugal it had a sensational success.

The print run sold out in a very short time. There were many, many editions produced, some pirated. Why? Because the actual conditions in the opening stages of the Portuguese revolution were such that people who had previously accepted, even if they didn't like, the ideas of the old order, thought, "My God, something different is possible. Anything is possible."

There's a story—I don't know if it's true or not—that one or two of the more energetic of these middle class ladies who produced this subversive work spent a little time going round in northern Portugal talking to illiterate or barely literate peasant women and they were gathering round listening. In other words, the ideological transformations are integral to any real revolution and they are of fundamental importance.

Mind you, there's the other side of the coin. If the revolution is aborted, or partially aborted, people slide back. The new ideas are marginalised. The old ideas revive in various forms. The process of the general ideology of the population shifts, changes with revolutionary ups and downs. It shifts and changes without revolutions, but in revolutionary situations it shifts and changes at enormous speed.

Second generalisation. This again applies to both political and social revolutions. Phase 1, everyone's united, except the reactionaries of course. We're all united around a certain set of demands. Different classes are united. The springtime. But after the initial phases, within a comparatively short time, you get a rapid differentiation amongst the very people who supported the revolution in the first instance. "Ah you've gone far enough, that's enough. Let's keep what we've got now." Or "we've got to go further to preserve what we have."

This reflects, of course, a class differentiation. Broadly speaking, there's never been a revolution, certainly not a proletarian revolution, or a political one either for that matter, in which the mass of the petit bourgeoisie, sections of the middle classes, did not initially support it.

In 1789, once the Bastille had been stormed, everyone is for the revolution, except the aristocracy. And even some of them, as a matter of fact. Very shortly after, however, the revolutionaries divide—and this is a simplification—you get divisions between the [more moderate] Girondists and [more radical] Jacobins and they conflict with one another. And in the third phase, the conflict becomes open, often becomes violent, often is decided by force.

In Portugal of course, everyone was against the old regime (except the reactionaries, the secret police, and so on). But within weeks, not months, we have a clear division between those that wanted to go forward and those supported by the CIA, the Social Democratic Party—financially and otherwise—who wanted to stop, who wanted to stabilise the situation, who thought it was getting out of hand, because workers were occupying the factories, not just passively occupying, but operating the factories. And finally of course, this conflict was resolved by force—not in our favour.

Now, let's go back to Lenin's three conditions. The first two are fairly simple. It's important to remember the first one: There's never been a revolution without a crisis in the ruling class itself and that is usually the precipitating factor. That the mass of the population rapidly changes its ideas, that's fairly simple. But the third thing—again, let's look at South Africa.

The ruling class was in crisis. The mass of the population was increasingly difficult to hold down in spite of the really massive coercive apparatus of police, soldiers, secret police, and so on and so forth, that was there.

What wasn't there though was the leadership. Not that there wasn't a leadership. There was—the African National Congress (ANC). And the ANC's objective was not a workers' revolution, but rather a stabilisation of the capitalist system to fit the changed conditions. And no question at all, they successfully did that. I'm not saying it's going to go on forever, but for a period anyway.

When we talk about leadership, in modern terms anyway (we can forget about Cromwell and Robespierre and so on), we're talking about parties. Leadership must require a political organisation or party. Why? There are three reasons. One is the question of ideas. I said ideas shift rapidly, that people are transformed during any revolutionary process. But ideas don't fall from the sky. There must be people arguing them, propagandising for them in advance. That's simple enough.

But then tactics. We know from experience, unfortunately, though under certain circumstances purely spontaneous movements can have considerable effect. Nevertheless they are ephemeral. They don't last very long, unless there is some kind of leadership.

Look at Poland in 1981, Solidarity. The ideas of Solidarity, suppressed by the regime, nevertheless didn't come from nowhere. Lech Walesa and all the rest of them had a set of ideas, which you can loosely call "social Catholicism." And those ideas, were the ideas that spread rapidly once the regime started to crack and continued to spread after the initial repression under Wojciech Jaruzelski. Consequently the outcome, the ultimate outcome—all the preconditions, the first two preconditions of revolution, were there—it stopped. It was aborted at the political stage.

Finally, there is the question of numbers. We, sitting in this room, with the most correct ideas in the world in our heads—we supposedly have them—and with a mastery of tactics and so on, nevertheless, cannot make a revolution in Britain, even if the conditions are right. There aren't enough of us. A party that is to have any serious effect does require numbers. Now that's a complicated question. It doesn't mean that at all stages it has to have numbers, but come the crisis, without numbers, no, you are marginalised.

What sort of party? First of all, the workers' party, the revolutionary party, cannot be a passive reflection of the ideas current in the working class. That sounds pretty obvious, doesn't it? It won't do to go around to your local pub, if it's in a working class area and reflect the ideas that you hear discussed over the bar. That's not our function. No. In that sense, the party, throughout most of its life, is not representative. It is not true that the party represents the class. Actually, that's another passive concept and it means in reality that it doesn't lead. It's a question of a conscious striving to achieve leadership in all those situations where it is possible—and not simply a propagandist one, but an interventionist one.

The Russian Marxist Plekhanov coined a useful distinction between "propaganda" and "agitation". (Plekhanov is a bad man in the Leninist tradition—the later Leninist tradition I mean. Lenin thought he was good.) He said, the distinction is this: Propaganda means many ideas are put across to a few people. Agitation means that a few ideas are put across to many people (or as many as you can reach, anyway). Both are necessary. But it is a question not only of winning this or that cause, but also of building the organisation itself.

A couple of years ago when National Union of Mineworkers leader Arthur Scargill was starting up the Socialist Labour Party, there was a meeting called in Hackney, not indeed by Scargill's own people—I don't think he had any people, though no doubt he had a lot of sympathisers—but by a combination of sects. One called itself the Provisional Central Committee of the Communist Party of Great Britain. "Provisional," you see, of a party which doesn't exist—we're talking here of only a dozen or so people.

What's lacking is interaction with the working class, of the members of the Provisional Committee, with the working class. They lack the intermediate thing, they lack the party.

But the party itself needs leadership, and this is a more contentious thing—I hope we get some criticism on it. Why is this so? Well, different people, different layers of people in the party at any given time, have different experiences, different levels of knowledge (not that knowledge is always necessary for militancy), and different experiences (and experience can be a bad guide as well as a good one). Above all, there has to be a continual interaction between the party members and the class they are aspiring to lead.

Inside the organisation there has to be a constant interaction, which quite often leads to friction, between the people who happen to be on the leading committees of the party at any given time and the membership. But even that won't do because there are members and members. We have a layer of members—quite a significant layer in numbers, some call themselves sympathisers—who are enthusiastic about this or that, will now and again do something, now and again engage in activity, but they're not really interested in dialectical materialism, or you name it.

These members are essential. Under conditions where a party grows rapidly, they will be a majority. No question about it. You deceive yourself if you think otherwise. There has to be an intermediate layer, a "cadre". It is a term of military origin. It referred originally to non-commissioned officers in the French Army. A cadre, meaning, not super theoreticians, or people who are experts on economics or whatever, but people who were seriously committed to building the organisation and who have this dual relationship: a relationship with workers outside the organisation, and an interactive relationship with the current leadership. Now that's the hardest thing of all to achieve. I don't want to sound rude—I spent a quarter of a century as one of them—but if the Central Committee of the SWP were to drop dead tomorrow, we would be able to replace it—not at random, but precisely because we do have a cadre in the sense I'm talking about.

Let me illustrate that with a few examples. In April 1917, Lenin arrives at the Finland Station and makes a speech that horrifies the dignitaries—not Tsarist anymore of course, but various shades of alleged socialists, including a number of Bolshevik leaders—and he in effect tears up the party programme and says, "We must work toward taking power." Now this was completely contrary to the Bolshevik doctrine as it had been up to that time: the democratic dictatorship of the proletariat and peasantry. Sorry about these jargon phrases. What it means is fighting to achieve a democratic republic in place of the Tsar. Why? Because the economic development, the transformation of the productive forces, which is totally inadequate for socialism in Russia, will be accelerated [under a bourgeois republic]; meanwhile, we are in opposition, trying to build a working class movement.

Therefore, talk about taking power now? The man must have lost his marbles! No! That was the position. Lenin was in a small minority in April, but in the course of a very fierce, sharp, internal conflict that immediately followed, he was able to win over decisive sections of the cadre—people who had never been on a Central Committee, people who weren't even on District Committees in many cases—actually were won to him. And so in a comparatively short time he was able to achieve a majority. The magnitude of the change is enormous. The interesting thing is, without the Bolshevik cadre—not just the membership as a whole—this could not have been achieved.

Contrast that experience with Rosa Luxemburg's. In January 1919, a newly formed German Communist Party—growing quite fast, but tiny in relation to the Social Democrats—have a conference and decide enthusiastically they must take power now by means of an insurrection in Berlin. She argued that this was nonsense, that this was impossible, patiently explaining that you have to win a significant proportion of the delegates to the then-existing workers' councils. At the moment, she argued, we haven't got any worth talking about. We've got to get a majority in the workers' councils before you can think of attempting to seize power, exactly as the Bolsheviks had to work between February and October to win a majority in the Russian workers' councils.

They wouldn't listen. They were enthusiastic. They had seen the Kaiser flee to Holland; they had seen the generals put away their uniforms and pretend "we're not really them, you know." All these changes occur very rapidly in a revolutionary situation and, well, it's been done once, we can do it again by an act of will.

Well, they tried. The result was a catastrophe. The insurrection was defeated. Some people supported it—I don't mean to say they were without support. But it was defeated by the forces of reaction who were then under the direction of the Social Democratic Party, who had a great majority in the workers' councils, and who denounced the German Communist party as "putschist," "Blanquist," and who received the support, passively, but received the support, from a great majority of the working class.

Now what was the decisive difference? The lack of a cadre. Rosa Luxemburg was preaching in the wilderness. There were not a sufficient number, there were only a handful as a matter of fact, of people who had gone through the lengthy process of learning, developing, and had some sense of tactics, of what is possible, what's necessarily possible. The party had only existed a few months. So cadres can't be improvised. Central Committees normally can be improvised. At least if you've got a Lenin or a Luxemburg around, or perhaps even a Tony Cliff. Cadres can't be improvised.

There are a few other things that I really should talk about, but instead I will summarise. First of all, a revolutionary party cannot make a revolution until the conditions are ripe. Marx used the analogy of midwifery. He described the revolutionary force as the midwife of the new society struggling to be born. Striking analogy. Trouble is, if the foetus isn't viable, the best committee of midwives can't possibly produce the infant. The conditions must be ripe.

Secondly, of course, who decides? It's not difficult in Britain to judge that we're not ripe for revolution at this minute; but in changing circumstances, you have got to change all the time your emphasis, your orientation. To judge successfully requires experience. It requires that all members of the party, although they do it in different degrees, through their activity, learning from workers, as well as trying to teach them, acquire the knack. What did Lenin call it? He didn't use the work knack. I don't think he knew English slang. But anyway, he had an impassioned passage about this: cadre can't be improvised.

It does depend on a considerable degree of experience—both working with people outside the party, and participating in the direction of the party, at the same time so that the leadership itself, which typically is not working on the buses [i.e. organising in workplaces] or what have you, does not directly therefore relate to workers in their workplaces, has to be all the time under the pressure, under the influence if you like, as well as influencing, the people who are.

And finally, unless the party is substantial... I've touched on this before—you need numbers. The process of getting numbers is a very uneven one. For the first fifteen years—more than fifteen, eighteen years—the founders of our organisation, and the few people who joined them, never exceeded 100 people. Tremendous events took place during these years, tremendous struggles in Britain. Nevertheless, we had in 1950 or 1951 some thirty-odd members and come 1967 we might have gone up to—I doubt it, personally—but nevertheless, we were claiming about one hundred. And then in the course of nine months, we were over a thousand, and it was real. That's an explosive growth rate. Suppose we'd gone on growing at that rate. We'd be a mass party now! Marvellous! But of course, not marvellous, because changing conditions meant, inevitably, that the rate of expansion slowed, and not only that, actually in the 1970s, in the first half of the 1970s, the rate of expansion was negative—i.e., on balance we were losing members.

In connection with that of course, is the question of the need we talked about before, to change your tactical orientation. We changed it fairly rapidly. The ANL [Anti-Nazi League], we would not have considered such an operation in 1970. Wouldn't have considered it. "Come on, the central thing's the industrial struggle"—and it was at the time, it was marvellous. Then the industrial struggle goes down, and fascist organisations are growing—it was the National Front at that time. Therefore, we needed a fundamental shift in orientation, which we managed to achieve without too much trouble. The trouble came later. When the fascists were no longer the main problem, the difficulty was to convince some enthusiastic comrades that we have to shift the emphasis again. To take advantage of situations where rapid growth is possible, we need the largest possible number of members in the here and now.

This is our task. This is basically what we have to do in Britain, and other socialists have to do internationally. There are certainly going to be many struggles, many shifts in the tactical line. I don't know what they are, actually nobody knows what they are because you don't know what the situation, the exact situation, is going to be in, let us say, 2000. There will be many struggles, and a good deal of learning, because we don't know everything. There are problems we haven't even thought of yet. I can't think what they are, but I'm sure they're there.

So we come to the question of the world situation today. Crisis in capitalism, wars internationally, upheavals of all kinds, basic instability which is reflected in the sphere of ideas. Large numbers of people are no longer confident that, actually, in Britain, as somebody put it, "My children will be better off than I am." They believed that in the 1960s, and to some extent the 1970s and with some justification. Large numbers of people don't believe it now. In these circumstances, yes, it's on the cards. I'm not putting a time scale on it—you can't. But yes, it's on the cards.

The final question therefore is, "But are we up to it?" Can we actually build the necessary coherent, flexible revolutionary party? Well, by our very existence we affirm that we believe we can.

Notes

1   A talk given by Duncan at the Marxism Festival on 7 July 1998. The talk had the simple title of "Revolution" and was one of the four talks he delivered at the event in a series titled "What Marx Really Said". The other three talks in the series were "Human Nature", "History and Class Struggle" and "The Economics of Capitalism". 1998 was three years after Duncan had retired from the SWP due to ill health but his series of Marxism talks showed him to be still possessed of all of his intellectual powers and his ability to hold, educate, and inspire an audience.

A recording of the talk is available here: www.marxists.org/archive/hallas/audio/1998/revolution.mp3 Transcribed by Karen Domínguez Burke for *International Socialist Review*, 77 (May 2011). A small amount of editing has been done for a non-American audience.

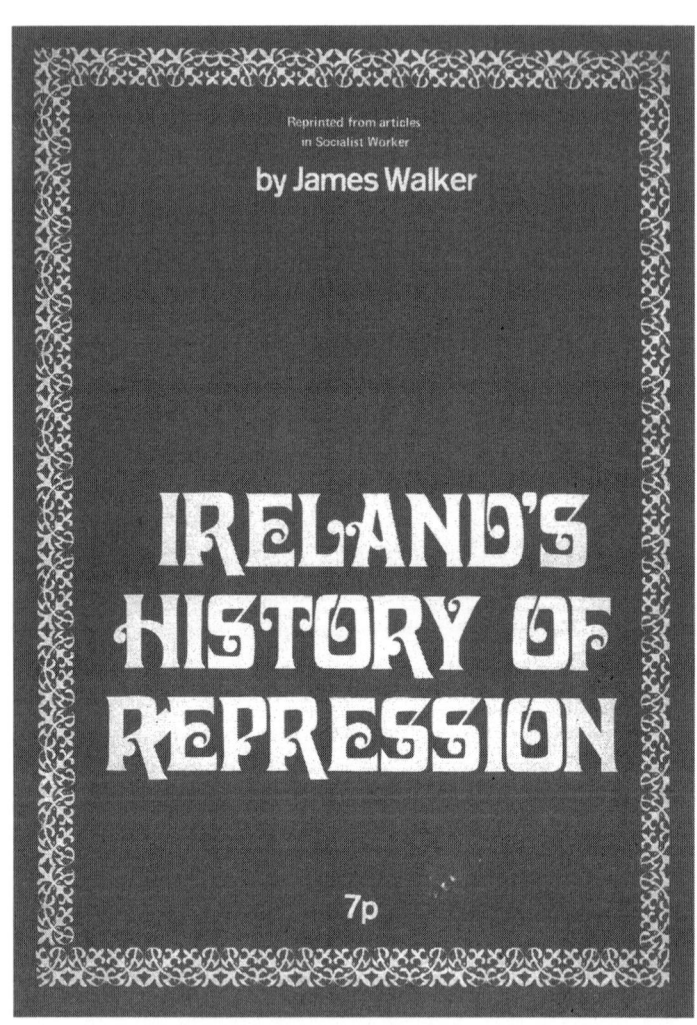

Reprinted from articles
in Socialist Worker

by James Walker

IRELAND'S HISTORY OF REPRESSION

7p

Front cover of a pamphlet containing articles on Ireland written by Duncan Hallas (under the pseudonym James Walker) in 1971.

Duncan Hallas on Darwin, Women and Human Nature
Sheila McGregor

Duncan was a brilliant speaker in both content, style and delivery. He held audiences spellbound, conveying complex ideas clearly, always interspersed with great humour. He wrote little about the origins of class society and the oppression of women but his talks on these and related subjects always drew big crowds.[1] There have been considerable developments in our knowledge about the evolution of our species and early settlements that Duncan would have kept abreast of if he were speaking today. Fundamental to his talks were two things: the state of knowledge up to the 1980s and 1990s, but above all his mastery of historical materialism. Fortunately, there are recordings of talks he gave on "Marx and Pre-history",[2] "Women in Pre-history"[3] and "The State"[4] as well as on "Human Nature"[5] that provide a record of the knowledge and insight he brought to bear on questions that remain as relevant today as they were 30 years ago, namely: How did we evolve? Have women always been oppressed? If not, how did women's oppression arise and how can it be overcome? And surely, human nature never changes? His talks wove in the development of ideas and how certain ones come to predominate in one period rather than another.

Duncan challenged his listeners to open their imaginations and think differently. Explaining the central impact of Charles Darwin and the publication of *On the Origin of Species*[6] in 1859 on 19th century thought meant reimagining a world dominated by the explanations found in the first five books of the Jewish Bible "appropriated by the Christians". According to the Church of England the world had only existed for about 4,000 years, a profoundly conservative outlook of an unchanging world in which "what is, is what has been, and what will be, is what has been". Duncan was at pains to point out that he was concentrating on the world views of Western and Central Europe up to 1860, not because of any Eurocentric viewpoint, but because that was where capitalism was born.

Darwin's empirical documentation of the evolution of species shattered this world view. *On the Origin of Species* was "an epoch-making book". It pointed to a long prehistory of the earth and change as crucial to development. No longer was it tenable to accept the view of the flood, Noah's ark and the animals embarking two by two. Within three decades, Darwin's ideas had been accepted by all serious intellectuals; evolution was an idea whose time had come. Ideas about evolution had been floating around for some time but in the conservative reaction to the French Revolution in the early 1790s, such ideas had not broken through. As illustration, Duncan pointed to a publication in 1781 by a certain Lord Monboddo that had similar ideas but which "sank without trace".[7]

By the mid-19th century, things had changed. The bourgeoisie was confident, capitalism was expanding, and "great progress" was being made, permitting a more scientific view of the past to flourish. The first 5,000 copies of *On the Origin of Species* sold out in 24 hours. Duncan mentions two other publications of note: one on archaeology by John Lubbock, 1st Baron of Avery, a Liberal banker and parliamentarian, who

 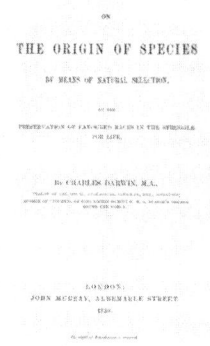

Front cover and title page of the 1859 first edition of Darwin's
On the Origin of Species.

coined the terms Palaeolithic (Old Stone Age) and Neolithic (New Stone Age)[8] and one by Karl Marx, *A Contribution to a Critique of Political Economy*, also published in 1859, in which Marx formulated the oft quoted principles of Historical Materialism.[9] Scientific research into humanity's past was under way, a subject of profound interest to both Marx and Engels. They had traced the transition from feudalism to capitalism in *The Communist Manifesto*[10] and *The German Ideology*[11] but not the development of earlier societies. Furthermore, the question of the family was of enormous ideological importance: the idea that family structures might be unchanging, regardless of the development of the means of material production, for Marx and Engels, was fundamentally wrong.

Duncan refers to a number of people whose writings played an important role in undermining the view that the institution of the family and relations between the sexes had remained unaltered through time.[12] Several of these figure in Marx's *Ethnographical Notebooks* published in 1972, including those of John Budd Phear, 13th Chief Justice of Sri Lanka (known as Ceylon at the time), Henry Maine and Lewis Henry Morgan.[13] *Mother Right,*[14] published in 1861 by Johann Jakob

Bachofen, a Swiss professor of Roman Law, influenced both Engels and Lewis Henry Morgan, whose seminal work was *Ancient Society*.[15] In the 1970s, feminists were also influenced by Bachofen. Duncan describes Bachofen as "a Swiss classicist, Hegelian and feminist who sought to show, by way of classical study, that Greek and Roman descent had been through the female line". Moreover, Duncan argued, Bachofen proved this "beyond cavil" but was ignored by bourgeois anthropologists, who avoided the evidence that the origins of "civilisation" (i.e. societies with writing and written records) were in the Middle East. Furthermore, Bachofen pointed to matriarchal societies, in other words societies ruled by women. This was a fact of utmost importance in challenging the pervasive idea that contemporary European structures of the family were natural and normal. Lewis Henry Morgan was a Presbyterian, lawyer, politician and member of the Republican Party—a very different kind of party from the Republican Party we know today. Morgan became part of Iroquois society[16] in New York State, a society with a different mode of production from his own, i.e. a non-capitalist society. He learned the language and went through the appropriate initiation ceremony to become accepted. To his astonishment, he encountered a society without a standing army, police force, written laws and without any visible means of coercion other than community pressure. There was no kind of class structure and the status of women was extraordinarily high.

In essence, Duncan explained, Morgan argued that the past was profoundly different from the present and that human society had gone through a series of stages in which accepted notions about women, legitimacy and property, for example, did not exist. They evolved. Morgan started with a hypothesis that man[17] was a social animal and lived in hordes dominated by promiscuous sexual relations. At some stage sexual relationships became shaped by notions of identity and incest, albeit with a very different idea of incest from today. Morgan argued that there were three universal stages of development that he attempted to correlate with techniques of production:

"Savagery" (an unhappy term as Duncan points out) or what we refer to as hunter-gatherer society today; "Barbarism" (another unhappy term) today known as Cultivators or Horticulturists. Neither of these stages involved a class structure. Then followed "Civilisation" (another misleading term) based on agriculture, i.e. domesticated animals and domestically cultivated plants, with writing, written records and the like. Change came over long periods of time and as Morgan says in *Ancient Society*: "It will be my object to present some evidence of human progress... and through successive ethnical periods, as it is revealed by inventions and discoveries, and by the growth of the ideas of government, of the family, and of property".[18]

One of Morgan's crucial insights was into the workings of the clan system he observed amongst the Iroquois. He sent out questionnaires around the world to discover whether such systems could be observed elsewhere. On that basis, he argued, and Duncan accepted the proposition, albeit unproven as he says, that societies based on a clan structure were in existence for 99 percent of our time on Earth, with all known pre-class societies based universally on a sexual division of labour.[19]

Morgan describes how, amongst the Iroquois, who were cultivators, the land was held in common for the clan by the women, who played a key role in producing food, i.e. in social production. Key decisions were taken by the women elders. They lived in long houses so there was very little individual privacy. Everyone was a member of a clan and marriage was based on exogamy, since a marriage partner had to come from a different clan. This meant the incest taboo applied to those classified as relatives in your own clan, and not to biological relationships. In a matrilineal society, such as the Iroquois, where land rights went through the women, the man was accepted into the clan of his wife "as a tolerated guest". Conversely, if there was a relationship breakdown, the husband would be sent back to live with his mother's clan; or as Duncan put it, quoting Ruth Benedict:[20] "Don't keep washing on the doorstep." Casual sexual relationships weren't considered important.

The crucial point for Duncan was that the high status of women Morgan encountered was linked to women's central role in social production and to a classificatory system in clan-based societies without property relations. This, Duncan argued, was because the clan was a collective where the status of the individual was not significant; every individual was part of a unit that she or he was born or adopted into.[21] Each individual was part of a classification system based on their generation, so a mother would be a mother alongside all other women of the same generation; likewise for sisters and brothers. It was not about actual biological relationships. Although individual families existed, the primary relationships and solidarity were to the men or women of your generation in your clan. In addition, Duncan stresses, the idea of a social group identity predominated. Individual rights were severely restricted and social obligations were enforced rigorously.

Without any means of coercion through a state, such societies depended on people upholding their social obligations—the only sanctions available were ridicule or death. Morgan thought the Iroquois were incredibly democratic because decisions were taken by the whole adult population. In reality, decisions were consensual and the most elderly women exercised the final say.[22] Duncan was at pains to stress that such societies should not be idealised. They were not necessarily peaceful, they could be highly militaristic and the rituals painful, so there was a high tolerance of inflicted pain.

Morgan's descriptions of the Iroquois may well have been accurate because he spoke their language, lived amongst them and had been accepted into a clan in his twenties. Nevertheless, there were flaws in his methods that Duncan draws attention to: Morgan made the assumption, as did others at the time, wrongly as Duncan argues, that there were universal stages of development and "uniform causes would give rise to uniform results".[23] Morgan also made the assumption, again wrongly, that the Iroquois were "living fossils" of a previous stage of development—he relied on the use of a living language to extrapolate to a past over a million years before.[24]

Despite these shortcomings, Duncan argues Morgan's work had two importance aspects: examining how society subsisted in a physical sense, i.e. tool use, materials and the like; and how reproduction of the society occurred. Duncan emphasised the key features of a classificatory clan-based system and women's central role in social production that are crucial to understanding the roots of the high status of women in the kind of society observed by Morgan. These are key to understanding how women's position can be transformed today.

Engels adopted Morgan's detailed scheme of social evolution and the technological reasons for change when he wrote *The Origin of the Family, Private Property and the State*,[25] a key text for the socialist movement, in 1884.[26] In addition, Engels "restates the general historical materialist position and in particular that the state did not exist for most of the time in the past and will not exist in the communist future, and is not inevitable; ditto the family, ditto the status of women and so on and so forth".[27]

Morgan's work was treated with respect,[28] until a sea change occurred about the time of the First World War with the rise of bourgeois anthropology and its establishment as an academic discipline. By then, such ideas had become unacceptable, particularly, Duncan argues, the ideas about the family. Anthropology became disconnected from a historical approach and the approach became, "that what exists now has no necessary connection with the past, what exists now is unique and has to be considered in its own terms". So the past was irrelevant and there could be no predictions about the future.

This was the era of structuralism, functionalism and configurationism, with the linguistic approach of Lévi-Strauss in France, cultural relativism with Franz Boas in the US and the functionalism of Malinowski in England. They had some valid criticisms, such as that anthropologists needed to speak the language of the societies they were studying and investigate thoroughly how societies functioned.[29] But, Duncan argues, there was a reaction against the idea that women could have played an equal role

*First German edition (1884) and first English language edition (1902)
of Engels's* The Origin of the Family, Private Property and the State.

to men in previous societies. The most reactionary elements argued, without any evidence at all, that women had always been inferior, whereas the likes of Malinowski and Lévi-Strauss put the more sophisticated argument that whatever might have been in the past, whether or not it was inevitable that women would end up with inferior status, they now had an inferior status and that was unlikely to change in the future. So, "the functionalists, the structuralists and the configurationists were socially acceptable to the bourgeoisie and therefore they filled the chairs, they taught the students, therefore we have bourgeois anthropology with a number of variants, French, British, American, all of which were fundamentally ideological".[30]

Archaeology is somewhat different, Duncan argues, because by the very nature of the discipline, dealing with material artefacts, archaeologists are pushed into a materialist understanding and use of systematic materialist science "even if idealists in their heads".[31] This is born out in the labelling of different stages in our evolution according to the main materials used for tools as in the Palaeolithic (Old Stone Age), Mesolithic (Middle Stone Age) and Neolithic (New Stone Age) and Bronze Age. The late Neil Faulkner, archaeologist, writes about archaeologist Gordon Childe:

Childe, as both academic and activist, was heavily influenced by Marxism. The compelling interpretive sweep of his grand narratives of prehistory and antiquity are rooted in his materialist approach. That is what has made *Man Makes Himself* (1936) and *What Happened in History* (1942), Childe's two popular syntheses that between them chart the history of Europe and the Near East from the Old Stone Age to the fall of the Roman Empire, probably the most widely read archaeology books ever written.[32]

It was not possible to rely on Morgan's generalisations in the way Engels had done in his classic *The Origin of the Family, Private Property and the State*.[33] Duncan says, "We have to ask ourselves, what do we actually know, as opposed to various kinds of speculation and long chains of speculation, what do we actually know, one about the evolution of human society in the past, two about the specific question about kinship society and the status of women and three about the origins of civilisation?" The first thing, Duncan insists, is that, "The bulk of the detail will not do",[34] because of the short time scale of the language data Morgan relies on, when we are going back up to 1 million years to look at the history of cultural toolmakers. (This was the term Duncan used to describe our evolution as social beings when individuals made tools according to standard patterns; that in turn implied the development of language and abstract thought.)

Morgan's whole method has to be discarded. Nevertheless, it is possible to say, Duncan continues, that there was a universal first stage of hunter-gatherer society from the very beginnings of human society until 12,000 years ago at the earliest, and that Ferguson,[35] Morgan and Engels were right about that. And as a matter of probability, they were also right that those societies that did survive that stage were kinship societies. Although "there is no direct evidence one way or another", Duncan's question of how non-class societies would otherwise hold together is pertinent.

The third point Duncan makes is about when the high status of women occurred in our prehistory. He contends, quite robustly, that the status of women is not necessarily high in hunter-gatherer societies, mentioning evidence about aboriginal societies in Australia. In contrast, in the Middle East, where agriculture first developed and was the site of the origins of civilisation, he argues, there was a stage when the status of women was high. Furthermore, Duncan proposes, "That tremendous revolution, the most important thing that happened since our species developed, the development of agriculture, must have been the work of women".[36]

Duncan deduces this from the fact that in all known hunter-gatherer societies there was a sexual division of labour: women gathered plants and hunted small game because they were encumbered with children, whilst men were often away for long periods of time involved in hunting larger game. So he concludes the development of the techniques for the transition to agriculture must have been the work of women.[37] Equally, he argues, it is safe to assume that the kinship systems in the Middle East were similar to those of the Iroquois. And since the contribution women made to production of food in early agricultural societies was more significant than that of men, the status of women was high.

Agriculture permits the development of a surplus of food to daily requirements. This sets in train a long process from about 10,000 BC to 3,000 BC that slowly undermined the old clan system and collective ownership of land. Private property and class divisions emerge slowly, triggering the need for a state. Women ceased to be central to production and were pushed into dependence on individual men in the family. This process bears out Engels's overall analysis of the rise of the family, private property and the state, validating his judgement that this spelled the "world historic defeat of the female sex".

Duncan's dating of the period of women's high status in prehistory would be contested today. Chris Harman, a leading member of the International Socialists, contemporary with

Duncan from the late 1960s, and many others like myself, would argue that hunter-gatherer societies were egalitarian on the same grounds Duncan gives for women's later high status, namely the central contribution of women to production. Such societies depended heavily on the regular contribution of women for provisioning of food.

Marxist anthropologist Eleanor Leacock refutes many of the arguments advanced about the inferior status of women amongst some hunter-gatherer bands still in existence in the 20th century in two main ways: the impact of contact with colonialists that undermines women's central role; and the inability of earlier male anthropologists to document the role of women because of their own prejudices. I would argue that Duncan applied his own method inconsistently. It's not clear whether he was familiar with Leacock's work in particular and dismissed it or had not read her work. Since he only refers to misconceptions by feminists in the 1970s about matriarchal societies and female dominance, perhaps it is the latter. Either way, I would argue, he was inconsistent about women's status amongst hunter-gatherers.[38]

Duncan concludes with the matter of women's liberation. Since the high status of women was linked to their central role in social production, it follows that women once more have to become central to social production and childcare has to be collectivised. Developments in capitalist society provide pointers in this direction with the return of women to the workforce and the availability of contraception for women to control their fertility. But, Duncan argues, even though women made up 43 percent of the workforce, they were not central to production (this is no longer true today)[39] and still bore the responsibility individually for childcare (this is still true today). So he concluded (rightly), women's liberation was fundamentally bound up with a socialist revolution that would ensure women were central to social production, decision making and the work of reproduction in the family collectivised.

The rise of the state

In a later talk at Marxism in 1993[40] discussing the nature of the state, Duncan starts with a bourgeois legal definition of the state as "a body that has a monopoly of legal force in a defined territory". He then gives a Marxist definition of the essential components of the state, namely "soldiers, policemen and their appendices", to which, Duncan points out, must be added the appearance of a bureaucratic hierarchy. He then elucidates the growth of the first states in the Middle East and North Africa approximately 5,000 years ago in a period that saw "a big expansion in human population, a truly massive expansion of population, the most rapid ever"[41] by people practising agriculture and producing a significant social surplus in a way that hunter-gatherers and horticulturalists could not.

Some of these agricultural societies developed in areas such as river valleys where the land was fertilised annually through natural flooding; this made the land much richer. This enabled much greater production of food. However, there were problems such as devastating floods. This led to the digging of irrigation channels by unknown innovators. But building an irrigation system requires a much larger degree of social coordination with the use of primitive tools, some animals and back breaking labour. The larger the scale the more coordination it requires. So, people necessary for directing the labour needed to be fed, since they were no longer direct producers. This in turn set off a process whereby someone has to decide on the allocation of the surplus to the direct producers and those directing the labour. Gradually, the direct producers lost control over the allocation of the surplus to people who perform a necessary function but are no longer direct producers. This leads to a fundamental change: the emergence of a separate layer and then a class of non-producers. Once you have a class structure, however simple, you have class struggle over control over the surplus. Since the whole structure was quite fragile, the non-producers needed some means of coercion or bodies of armed men. Such bodies are themselves no longer direct producers. Their sole purpose is to serve the controllers of the surplus. Coordination has given way to coercion. And at the end of the process, a bureaucracy emerges.

Since Duncan's talks, archaeologists have made a range of fascinating discoveries, particularly in the Middle East and southern Anatolia, of sites of sedentary hunter-gatherer societies lasting hundreds of years, where a slow transition to horticultural and then full-blown agriculture has been traced. One such example is at Abu Hureyra in Syria, which was inhabited from 13,000-8,000 years ago and has been written up in *Village on the Euphrates: From Foraging to Farming at Abu Hureyra* by archaeologists A M T Moore, G C Hillman and A J Legge.[42] Another fascinating site is at Çatalhöyük in southern Anatolia, with a neolithic settlement that flourished from 7,500 BC to 6,400 BC that shows no differentiation in terms of wealth. The excavation has been written up by lead archaeologist Ian Hodder in *The Leopard's Tail*.[43] Çatalhöyük forms the basis of a fascinating talk, "Çayönü and Çatalhöyük: Revolution and Egalitarianism in Neolithic Turkey", by Ron Margulies. He explains how this site bears out Engels's main theses about egalitarian structures in pre-class societies that show no evidence of any kind of state formation. And in the same talk he discusses an exciting discovery at another site, Çayönü,[44] that illustrates the point Duncan makes about the rise of class society leading to class struggle over any surplus being produced. The work of these archaeologists illustrates a further point made by Duncan, that working with material artefacts and scientific methods limits the more ideological tendencies of anthropologists, even if not entirely. Current debates about Stone Age temples in Anatolia and about symbolism at Çatalhöyük indicate that archaeologists are not immune to more idealist speculation.[45]

Huge strides have been made in our understanding of human evolution. A great deal more evidence, both material in terms of additional fossils, and scientific with genetic tools, has accumulated about our evolution from the family of the apes. Louise Humphrey and Chris Stringer wrote in 2018, "Over the last 150 years, since the Neanderthals were recognised as a separate species from *Homo sapiens*, scientists have named more than 20 hominim species. At least half of these species are based on fossils unearthed in the last 30 years, and the pace of new discoveries shows no sign of slowing down in the 21st century".[46] The earliest hominins go back 6 million years; the first human around 1.25 million years and modern *Homo sapiens* about 300,000 years.

Humphrey and Stringer confirm our origins from Africa: "It is generally acknowledged from genetic data that the main dispersal of *Homo sapiens* took place only 60,000 years ago," although there is also some evidence that "early modern humans could have extended across southern Asia at least 80,000 years ago".[47] Genetic evidence shows now that there was interbreeding between modern humans and Neanderthals, "and that humans originating out of Africa carry around 2 percent of Neanderthal-derived DNA in their genomes, from interbreeding events that are believed to have happened 40,000-60,000 years ago".[48] Interestingly, as we learn more about our evolution, Engels's main proposition in his pamphlet *The Role of Labour in the Transition from Ape to Man*, that toolmaking drove the evolutionary process, remains valid. This is not something Duncan dealt with in his talks but it underpins his presentations. It is worth quoting Engels's summary in full because it shows the impact of Darwin's ideas as well as Marx and Engels's materialist approach:

> Thus, the hand is not only the organ of labour, *it is also the product of labour*. Only by labour, by adaptation to ever new operations, through the inheritance of muscles, ligaments, and over longer periods of time, bones that had undergone special development and the ever-renewed employment of this inherited finesse in new, more and more complicated operations, have given the human hand the high degree of perfection required to conjure into being the pictures

of a Raphael, the statues of a Thorvaldsen, the music of a Paganini.

But the hand did not exist alone, it was only one member of an integral, highly complex organism. And what benefited the hand, benefited also the whole body it served; and this in two ways.

In the first place, the body benefited from the law of correlation of growth, as Darwin called it. This law states that the specialised forms of separate parts of an organic being are always bound up with certain forms of other parts that apparently have no connection with them... The gradually increasing perfection of the human hand, and the commensurate adaptation of the feet for erect gait, have undoubtedly, by virtue of such correlation, reacted on other parts of the organism...

Much more important is the direct, demonstrable influence of the development of the hand on the rest of the organism. It has already been noted that our simian ancestors were gregarious; it is obviously impossible to seek the derivation of man, the most social of all animals, from non-gregarious immediate ancestors. Mastery over nature began with the development of the hand, with labour, and widened man's horizon at every new advance. He was continually discovering new, hitherto unknown properties in natural objects. On the other hand, the development of labour necessarily helped to bring the members of society closer together by increasing cases of mutual support and joint activity, and by making clear the advantage of this joint activity to each individual. In short, men in the making arrived at the point where *they had something to say* to each other. Necessity created the organ; the undeveloped larynx of the ape was slowly but surely transformed by modulation to produce constantly more developed modulation, and the organs of the mouth gradually learned to pronounce one articulate sound after another.[49]

Human nature

In his talk on "Human Nature" at Marxism 1998,[50] Duncan makes a series of important points about us as social animals and how we change. He starts by defining human nature as follows: "It can't mean anything other than our average expectations of human behaviour".[51] He makes what might seem a fairly obvious point: our behaviour is not just determined by our genes, "We can't fly with wings like birds, but we can fly." Nevertheless, the view that human nature is unchanging was, and still is, deeply rooted, so Duncan counters with an obvious example: we change, not like ants purely because of evolution but because of society. We grow up in society and as societies change, our behaviour changes, so our nature changes over time. We have to take the long view. But taking the long view means: "You can't go back to nature. I know people try living in communes commonly funded by Daddy in Wales. But you can't change mentally".[52]

Duncan illustrates this fundamental point by citing a programme made by the BBC in 1978 called "Living in the Past".[53] It was an experiment. A group of people were given the task of living like Iron Age peasants from 1,000 years ago. They were given the same tools and had to build their own encampment and live like that for a year. Their behaviour was observed throughout. But Duncan pointed out that they weren't able to live in the same way. They bred pigs but couldn't bring themselves to cut their throats or wring hens' necks. And apparently, one individual was caught sneaking off to the pub. The individuals couldn't change their mental outlook and behaviour to that of Iron Age peasants. He made the same argument about meeting *Homo sapiens* coming out of Africa 60,000 years ago. Their behaviour would be very different from ours.

Such arguments about unchanging human nature were particularly relevant when Duncan was delivering his talk that year. He cites another programme, "Why Men Don't Iron" on Channel 4, about developments in genetics. "Essentially, the answer they give is because of the male genetic inclination to competitiveness—I don't know why they shouldn't compete in ironing—but nevertheless it's inherent".[54] In fact, Duncan argues, there was a revival of reductionist ideas about our behaviour being essentially shaped by our genes as a reaction to the Black and Women's movements of the 1960s and 1970s. These movements challenged the old 19th century ideas about white male ruling class superiority. From absurd arguments that the size of the brain determined intelligence—so elephants should be the most intelligent mammals on the planet—to more modern arguments from the likes of Oxford professor Richard Dawkins in *The Blind Watchmaker*[55] that, quoting Duncan, "we are robotic vehicles, blindly programmed, to do certain things and not others, then we have to say that it's his genes that made him say this. Come on. If you're a robot vehicle designed to preserve and perpetuate your genes, that must apply to him as much as to anyone else, unless he's unique amongst the human race."

So Duncan's insistence on Marx's pithy summary "It is not the consciousness of men that determines their being but their being that determines their consciousness" is as pertinent now as it was when Duncan used it to sum up his talk on human nature. The way we behave is shaped by the societies we grow up in and will change as we make them anew. So the seeds of a changing, non-sexist, anti-racist nature are sown in the struggle to bring about a world without sexism and racism. And that means socialist revolution.

Notes

1 John Rudge has found three articles in a series in *Socialist Worker* in 1977, "Facts of Family Life" (April 9th); "Wives and Property" (April 16th); "When Women had Power", (April 23rd.)

2 Duncan Hallas, "Marx and Pre-history" (July 1983), *Marxists' Internet Archive,* www.marxists.org/archive/hallas/audioindex.htm

3 Duncan Hallas, "Women in Pre-history" (July 1988,) *Marxists' Internet Archive,* www.marxists.org/archive/hallas/audioindex.htm

4 Duncan Hallas, "The State" (July 1993), *Marxists' Internet Archive,* www.marxists.org/archive/hallas/audioindex.htm

5 Duncan Hallas, "Human Nature" (1998), https://soundcloud.com/socialist-workers-party/human-nature

6 Charles Darwin, *On the Origin of Species by Means of Natural Selection (London: John Murray, 1859).*

7 Lord Monboddo, a Scottish Judge and father of Historical Linguistics, knew Darwin's father Erasmus and some argue that this influenced the development of Charles Darwin's ideas. Monboddo does not appear to have published in 1781, but he did publish on linguistics, *Of the Origin and Progress of Language,* 6 volumes. (Edinburgh and London: J Balfour and T Cadell. 1773–1792). Information taken from Wikipedia, https://en.wikipedia.org/wiki/James_Burnett,_Lord_Monboddo

8 See *The Britannica,* www.britannica.com/biography/John-Lubbock-1st-Baron-Avebury.

9 Karl Marx, *A Contribution to the Critique of Political Economy,* 1859, www.marxists.org/archive/marx/works/download/Marx_Contribution_to_the_Critique_of_Political_Economy.pdf

10 Karl Marx & Friedrich Engels, *The Communist Manifesto,* 1848, www.marxists.org/archive/marx/works/1848/communist-manifesto/

11 Karl Marx & Friedrich Engels, *The German Ideology,* 1845, www.marxists.org/archive/marx/works/1845/german-ideology/

12 He refers to Sir James Emerson Tennent, a Scottish lawyer, who published a work in 1859, *Ceylon, An Account of the Island,* which outlined how a kinship system worked. (Ceylon has been known as Sri Lanka since independence). Tennent was in fact born and educated in Ireland, became the MP for Belfast and was appointed Colonial Secretary of Ceylon. His observations form the basis for the book published in 1859 that Duncan was probably referring to.

13 Karl Marx, *The Ethnological Notebooks,* 1972, www.marxists.org/archive/marx/works/1881/ethnographical-notebooks/notebooks.pdf. These contain the often lengthy excerpts Marx made of accounts of contemporary observers that demonstrated that the institution of the family and relations between the sexes had indeed varied in different societies. These included John Dudd Phear, the 13th Chief Justice of Ceylon (now Sri Lanka), the lawyer Henry Maine, who worked initially for the East India Company and then for the British government. He described the Indian society he knew where relationships were based on kinship systems. Marx also made long excerpts from Lewis Henry Morgan's *Ancient Society, 1877,* www.marxists.org/reference/archive/morgan-lewis/ancient-society/index.htm

14 Johann Jakob Bachofen, *Mutterrecht* (Stuttgart: Verlag von Krais und Hoffmann, 1861). It was first published in English in 1967 under the title *Myth, Religion and Mother Right.*

15 Lewis Henry Morgan, *Ancient Society,* 1877, www.marxists.org/reference/archive/morgan-lewis/ancient-society/index.htm

16 Native Americans.

17 The use of the term "man" would no longer be acceptable today.

18 Lewis Henry Morgan, *Ancient Society,* Chapter 1, www.marxists.org/

reference/archive/morgan-lewis/ ancient-society/ch01.htm

19 There is a debate today about how hard and fast this sexual division of labour was in hunter-gatherer societies.

20 Ruth Benedict was an anthropologist from the Boas school. I haven't been able to find the quotation.

21 There was no difference between the two once the relevant rituals had been gone through for adoption into a clan.

22 Duncan Hallas, *Marx and Prehistory*, 1983, www.marxists.org/archive/ hallas/audio/1983/marx-and-pre-history-hallas-duncan.mp3

23 "It may be remarked finally that the experience of mankind has run in nearly uniform channels; that human necessities in similar conditions have been substantially the same". Lewis H Morgan, *Ancient Society*, Ch 1. www. marxists.org/reference/archive/ morgan-lewis/ancient-society/ch01. htm

24 For more extensive discussion of the problems of methodology that extrapolates from the present to the past, see Chris Harman, "Engels and the Origins of Human Society", *International Socialism* 2:65 (Winter, 1994), www.marxists.org/archive/ harman/1994/xx/engels.htm

25 Friedrich Engels, *The Origin of the family, private property and the state*, 1884, www.marxists.org/archive/ marx/works/1884/origin-family/ index.htm. He drew on Marx's notes as well as his own readings of Bachofen, Lewis Henry Morgan as well as his knowledge of Greek and Roman myths and German history to analyse the roots of women's oppression in relation to the rise of class society and the state. V I Lenin used this text in his influential work *The State and Revolution*, 1917, www.marxists.org/ archive/lenin/works/1917/staterev/ For a comprehensive appreciation of Engels's work see Chris Harman, "Engels and the Origins of Human Society", *International Socialism,* 2:65 (Winter 1994), www.marxists.org/ archive/harma n/1994/xx/engels.htm. Harman does not accept Morgan's initial stage of promiscuity that is

taken over by Engels and uses the most up to date research of his day.

26 Engels's analysis has been contested by two important Marxist feminist writers and activists, namely Raya Dunayevskaya and Lise Vogel. For a critique of their positions, see Sheila McGregor, "Engels on the family, women, class and gender", *Human Geography,* 14: 2 (March 2021) https://journals.sagepub.com/doi/ abs/10.1177/19427786211000047

27 Taken from the recording of Duncan Hallas on "Women in Prehistory— Part 2" (1988) www.marxists.org/ archive/hallas/audio/1988/women-in-pre-history.mp3

28 Duncan cites the entry in his copy of the *Encyclopaedia Britannica* where you can still find an entry today.

29 The Boas school led to valuable studies by the likes of Ruth Benedict and Margaret Mead which highlighted, amongst other things, the different roles of men and women in different societies and how behaviour was learned and changed from society to society. See Charles King, *The Reinvention of Humanity* (London: Penguin, 2020).

30 Duncan Hallas, "Women in Prehistory—Part 2" (1988), www. marxists.org/archive/hallas/ audio/1988/women-in-pre-history. mp3

31 Duncan Hallas, "Women in Prehistory—Part 2" (1988), www. marxists.org/archive/hallas/ audio/1988/women-in-pre-history. mp3

32 Neil Faulkner, "Gordon Childe and Marxist archaeology", *International Socialism,* 2:116 (Autumn 2007), http://isj.org.uk/gordon-childe-and-marxist-archaeology. Duncan recommended Childe's book *Man Makes Himself*, 1939. Faulkner recommends Chris Harman's *A People's History of the World* (London: Bookmark, 1999), as a corrective to errors in Childe's work. www. marxists.org/archive/harman/1999/ history/index.htm. See also Judy McVey, "Vere Gordon Childe and prehistory: a way of thinking and much more", *International Socialism*,

2:169 (Spring 2021) http://isj.org.
uk/v-gordon-childe-prehistory/

33   Duncan refers to Marx as having
collaborated with Engels on this. This,
it seems to me, is an overstatement.
We know that Engels relied on Marx's
Ethnological Notebooks, to write his
work shortly after Marx died.

34   Duncan Hallas, "Marx and
Prehistory", (1983) www.marxists.org/
archive/hallas/audio/1983/marx-and-
pre-history-hallas-duncan.mp3

35   I am assuming Duncan is referring to
Adam Ferguson (1723-1816), a Scottish
Enlightenment philosopher and
historian, who is sometimes known as
the father of sociology.

36   Duncan Hallas, "Marx and Prehistory"
(1983), www.marxists.org/archive/
hallas/audio/1983/marx-and-pre-
history-hallas-duncan.mp3

37   Duncan Hallas, "Marx and Prehistory"
(1983), www.marxists.org/archive/
hallas/audio/1983/marx-and-pre-
history-hallas-duncan.mp3

38   Chris Harman, "Engels and
the Origins of Human Society",
International Socialism, 2:65 (Winter
1994), www.marxists.org/archive/
harman/1994/xx/engels.htm. See
also Eleanor Leacock, *Myths of Male
Dominance* (Hoboken, NJ: Blackwell,
1981).

39   Duncan may well have been right
about that when he was speaking but
this is no longer true today because
women are both permanent workers
and central to the social production
process.

40   Duncan Hallas, "The State" (1993),
www.marxists.org/archive/hallas/
audio/1993/thestate.mp3

41   Duncan Hallas, "The State" (1993),
www.marxists.org/archive/hallas/
audio/1993/thestate.mp3

42   A MT Moore, G C Hillman, & A J Legge,
Village on the Euphrates (Oxford:
Oxford University Press, 2000).

43   Ian Hodder, *The Leopard's Tail*
(London: Thames & Hudson, 2006).

44   Ron Margulies, "Çayönü and
Çatalhöyük: Revolution &
egalitarianism in neolithic Turkey",
talk at Marxism 2015, www.youtube.
com/watch?v=HFiexLi7uHU

45   For a discussion about some of

these issues see Sheila McGregor,
2021, "Engels on women, the
family, class and gender", *Human
Geography,* 14: 2 (March 2021)
https://journals.sagepub.com/doi/
abs/10.1177/19427786211000047

46   Louise Humphrey & Chris Stringer,
Our Human Story (London: Natural
History Museum, 2018), p7.

47   Louise Humphrey & Chris Stringer,
Our Human Story (London: Natural
History Museum, 2018), pp 139-140.

48   Louise Humphrey & Chris Stringer,
Our Human Story (London: Natural
History Museum, 2018), p146.

49   Friedrich Engels, *The Part Played
by Labour in the Transition from Ape
to Man,* 1876, www.marxists.org/
archive/marx/works/1876/part-
played-labour/index.htm

50   Duncan Hallas, "Human Nature"
(1998) https://soundcloud.com/
socialist-workers-party/human-
nature

51   Duncan Hallas, "Human Nature"
(1998) https://soundcloud.com/
socialist-workers-party/human-
nature

52   Duncan Hallas, "Human Nature"
(1998) https://soundcloud.com/
socialist-workers-party/human-
nature

53   Living in the Past, www.youtube.
com/watch?v=99f9MqlohkY

54   Duncan Hallas, "Human Nature"
(1998) https://soundcloud.com/
socialist-workers-party/human-
nature.

55   Richard Dawkins, *The Blind
Watchmaker* (London: Longman
Scientific and Technical, 1986).
Steven Rose, *Lifelines* (Oxford: Oxford
University Press, 1997) is a book that
demolishes this version of genetic
determinism. Rose also spoke at
Marxism in 1998.

Darwin's Revolution
Duncan Hallas

(*Socialist Worker*, 8 March 1980)

First a true tale. A comrade who spent last year in the United States, and who was for a while in the coalfields of West Virginia, told me this.

A left-wing socialist miner said to him: "Round here everyone hates Blue Diamond (the coal company) but you can't get them to accept the idea of evolution."

"You mean revolution," said our comrade. "Hell, no," was the answer. "Revolution's easy. I mean evolution."

The local miners, who are so militant that they take shotguns on the picket lines, are also hard-shell Southern Baptists or supporters of even more fundamentalist sects.

They are the exception that proves the rule. Darwin's theory of evolution was first published, under the dry title of *On The Origin of Species by Means of Natural Selection*, in 1859. It had a revolutionary effect.

Why? There is nothing in it about capitalism or socialism, about feudalism, slavery or freedom.

Darwin's message was, in his own words, "that species are not immutable." That is to say all the enormous number of different kinds of plants and animals (including man) alive today are "the lineal descendants of some few beings which lived long before the first bed of the Cambrian system was developed" (i.e. more than 550 million years ago).

Moreover, "we may safely infer that not one living species will transmit its unaltered likeness to a distant futurity" (i.e. every kind of living thing is either doomed to extinction or will be drastically changed over time).

This profoundly revolutionary idea can be summed up as: nothing can stay as it is, everything changes. Marx wrote that Darwin's work "serves me as a natural-scientific basis for the class struggle in history."

There is a story that he intended to dedicate *Capital* to Darwin. Apparently, it is untrue, but the fact that it was widely believed amongst Marxists of the second generation gives some idea of the tremendous impact Darwin's thought made in its own time.

It stirred up the most violent controversy and it is instructive to look at the nature of that controversy. Darwin's opponents were not really interested in whether or not insects had evolved from worms or birds and mammals from reptiles.

They had a gut reaction against the whole notion of perpetual change because they understood, consciously or not, its social implications.

They saw that it undermined all the accepted dogmas: that "God created man in his own image," that there was an unchanging "moral law" and an "original sin," that "God gave each his station and ordered his estate."

In fact, evolution made "God the creator" redundant. For though it was not until 1871 that Darwin, a timid man, was persuaded to publish *The Descent of Man and Selection in Relation to Sex*, his conservative opponents had long before seen that, as they rather accurately put it, he was implying that "men are descended from monkeys".

Of course, Darwin was not the first to grasp the idea of the evolution of life. He *was* the first to expound it with a wealth of detailed evidence and a mechanism to explain it.

And he was lucky in his timing. 1859 was also the year in which Marx published his explanation of the materialist conception of history. Change was in the air, so to say, and the old orthodoxies were worm eaten.

As a matter of fact it had looked as though the static world outlook based on the creation myth was on the way out by the middle of the 18th century. Disbelief in Christianity was widespread amongst the upper classes in Europe.

Then came the French Revolution and the upper classes everywhere were quickly convinced of the political value of Christian orthodoxy—for keeping the masses down.

Religious revival became the order of the day. In Britain, the Blasphemy Act made it a crime to deny the truth of Christianity.

After Darwin this state of affairs was much harder to maintain—although effort was made for a long time.

Darwin was no socialist. Indeed his ideas could be (and were) used to defend capitalism "red in tooth and claw" as merely an aspect of an inevitable competitive struggle for existence.

But overall the effect of the theory of evolution was highly subversive. Marx was not wrong when he wrote of "the death-blow it dealt to all supernaturalist views of the world".

Before the Class Struggle
Duncan Hallas

(*Socialist Worker*, 15 March 1980)

A reader of this column last week asked what Darwin, or for that matter anyone from the 19th century, has to do with socialism today.

That was, I think, a mistaken objection.

One of the unique features of Marxism is that it is not simply a set of slogans or policies. It is also a world outlook, an analysis of the whole development of human society from its beginnings to its future possibilities; an analysis which Marx and Engels claimed was scientific.

A scientific theory must be capable of accommodating new data, new discoveries—perhaps becoming modified in the process. So it was with Marxism in the lifetime of its founders. Marx and Engels had worked out the basic ideas of what we call historical materialism by the middle of the 1840s.

They did not then know about the immensely long history of mankind *before* the development of class societies, still less about the evolution of the human species.

Nobody did at that time. But once some evidence about these things began to appear, and especially after Darwin had published *On the Origin of Species*, they eagerly seized on it and integrated it into their analysis.

This did involve some modification, some amplification of the basic ideas. At the heart of historical materialism is the idea of the class struggle.

"The history of all hitherto existing societies is the history of class struggles," Marx and Engels wrote in the *Communist Manifesto* (1848). The class struggle is the motor, the driving force of change.

But, the *Manifesto* argued, it would not go on forever. Capitalism would be followed by classless society, socialism. The class struggle would die with capitalism.

What about human societies *before* classes developed? This is not a trivial question and it has obvious implications for the socialist future.

It is not trivial because it is now known that human societies—if we call "human" those groups of creatures who make tools and learn from past experience—have existed for getting on for two million years and perhaps longer.

Human societies divided into *classes* did not come into existence much more than five or six thousand years ago.

All these dates are very approximate. New discoveries and new methods of dating modify from decade to decade.

What is significant for us is this. For 99 percent or so of the time human societies have been evolving class society was unknown.

That is an immensely important fact because it deals a death blow to the idea that classes, social inequality, exploitation, greed, alienation and all the rest of the features of societies which we are familiar with today are due to some unchangeable "human nature."

Manifestly they are not.

Even if we were to accept the idea that there is such a thing as "human nature"—and Marxists do not accept it—then we

327

would have to say that human nature, 99 percent of the time, demands *classless* society.

That problem remains: what is the motor of change where the class struggle does not exist?

Engels wrote in 1876 a brilliant little article—"The Part Played by Labour in the Transition from Ape to Man".

It is a most profound explanation of the distant past and, at the same time, a vision—and not a utopian vision—of the future. Everyone should read it.

Its central thesis is summed up in the opening paragraph:

> Labour is the source of all wealth, the political economists assert. And it really is the source—next to nature, which supplies it with the material that it converts into wealth.
>
> But it is even infinitely more than this. It is the prime basic condition for all human existence, and this to such an extent that, in a sense, we have to say that labour erected man himself.

For anyone who takes this seriously, even half seriously, all sorts of problems in the present, and in the future, force themselves forward. Good. They need to be discussed.

One thing is clear. If you get to grips with these issues, the petty, parochial, nationalistic ideas of the reformist left are just trifling. The Marxist perspective is a world historical perspective.

Anything less than that is simply irrelevant.

Selected Bibliography of the Works of Duncan Hallas
John Rudge

Duncan's written output over half a century was enormous so this bibliography is not intended to cover his entire output. We have instead attempted to list items that are both important and representative of his work as an activist, organiser, interpreter, populariser, polemicist and original thinker.

Many of Duncan's writings have been reproduced multiple times. For practical purposes we have not generally listed these items more than once. He also wrote many unsigned editorials and articles. These are not included unless there is specific evidence that he was the author. Likewise, many have been translated into languages other than English—these are not included.

It should be noted that Duncan often used one of two pseudonyms, Fred Hall or James Walker. In the earliest years of his political activity he was always known as Don Hallas.

Many of the writings listed here are on the Duncan Hallas section of the Marxist Internet Archive: *www.marxists.org/archive/hallas/index.htm*

Thanks are due to Ian Birchall for his assistance in producing this bibliography.

Books, Articles, Introductions and Pamphlets

Books
--

Trotsky's Marxism (London: Pluto Press, 1979) 122pp.

The Comintern (London: Bookmarks, 1985) 184pp.

Articles in Books
--

Towards a Revolutionary Socialist Party in Tony Cliff, et al, *Party and Class* (London: Pluto Press, 1971) pp9-25. This article also appeared as *The Way Forward* in *World Crisis: Essays in Revolutionary Socialism,* (London: Hutchinson & Co Ltd, 1971).

How Can We Move On? (pp1-10) in *The Socialist Register* (London: Merlin Press, 1977). Taking up the issues from Ralph Miliband's article *Moving On* in *Socialist Register (1976).*

Contribution from the Floor (pp62-64) in *The Crisis and the Future of the Left: The Debate of the Decade* (London: Pluto Press, 1980). Tony Benn and Labour governments.

Introductions
--

Introduction to *The Fourth International, Stalinism and the Origins of the International Socialists* (London: Pluto Press, 1971) pp3-13.

Introduction to Tony Cliff, *Neither Washington Nor Moscow: Essays on Revolutionary Socialism* (London: Bookmarks, 1982) pp5-10.

Introduction to Leon Trotsky, *The Lessons of October* (London: Bookmarks, 1987) pp1-8.

Introduction to V I Lenin, *'Left-wing' Communism, an Infantile Disorder* (London: Bookmarks, 1993).

Pamphlets
--

Trotsky (London: Socialist Worker, 1970) 15pp. (Second printing 1975). First appeared in *Socialist Worker,* 183 (22 August 1970).

The Meaning of Marxism (London: Pluto Press for the International Socialists, 1971) 45pp. (Second printing 1975). First appeared as series of 18 weekly articles in *Socialist Worker* between 24 October 1970 and 27 February 1971. "Why we need a theory"; "The battle for markets"; "The workers' vital role"; "Who produces the wealth?"; "The system's driving force"; "What causes the crisis?"; "The march of the giants"; "The white man's burden"; "Modern imperialism"; "Arms: key to post-war recovery"; "The end of post-war stability"; "Ideas: how the ruling class keeps its grip"; "Greedy workers"; "Public interest: dust in workers' eyes"; "European revolution defeated"; "The rise of Stalin's dictatorship"; "Stalin's zigzags"; "The only way forward: an international strategy".

Ireland's History of Repression (by James Walker). International Socialists, London, 1971. 11pp. Series of six articles reprinted from *Socialist Worker* September-October 1971. "The struggle begins in England's oldest colony"; "Catholic and Protestant unity that England had to smash"; "Murderous brutality prepares for the Great Hunger"; "Home Rule is agreed—but Tories prepare for armed revolt in Ulster"; "The guns are buried—and so are hopes of 1916"; "The North: Tories fan the flames of intolerance".

The Labour Party: Myth and Reality (2 editions). (London: Socialist Workers Party, 1981) 32pp.

The Labour Party: Myth and Reality (Third edition), (London: Socialist Workers Party, 1985) 39pp.

Why Import Controls Won't Save Jobs (with Nigel Harris), (London: Socialist Workers Party, 1981) 16pp.

The Fourth International (London: Bookmarks, 1988) 16pp Reprint of *Against the Stream* and *Fourth International in Decline* from International Socialism Nos.53 and 60 respectively. This pamphlet has a new introduction by Duncan Hallas.

Socialist Review Series 1
--

Problems of Rearmament Vol. 1, **2** (January 1951) pp1-5. Problems and challenges for workers.

The Significance of Nationalisation, Vol. 1, 4 (May 1951) pp22-29. Role of the state in modern capitalism.

The Permanent Crisis, Vol. 2, **2** (June–July 1952) pp9-11. The way out is a fighting socialist policy.

Socialist Review Group, IS and SWP Internal Documents

Socialist Review Group
--

Bill Donnelly, Ted Morris & Don Hallas, **To All Members** (28 February 1951) 2pp. Protesting against the decision to oppose joint youth work and a joint youth publication with the Grant-Deane tendency.

The Stalinist Parties, (July 1951) 9pp. Reproduced in *The Fourth International, Stalinism and the Origins of the International Socialists,* London (1971) pp65-75. It was originally written in response to Ellis Hillman's document *The Nature of the Stalinist Parties.*

A Programme for Action (6 July 1952) 4pp. Proposes a move from cadre-building to action around a programme and a perspective. Has first outlines of what was later to become the organisation's programme.

International Socialists

--

The Organisation of the IS Group, *Document for the 1969 Autumn Conference*, 5pp. Gives the current state of the organisation.

IS Teachers: Some Notes on Comrade Hodgson's Critique, *Internal Bulletin* (November 1969) pp15-16. Response to criticism of aspects of *Teachers' Rank and File.*

State and Revolution—Lenin, *Education Sub Committee Introductory Note* (undated-1969) 3pp. Introduction to Lenin's famous pamphlet.

How the Revolution was Lost—Chris Harman, *Education Sub Committee Introductory Note* (undated-1969): 3pp. A supplement to Harman's pamphlet taking forward two areas not covered.

An Autopsy—Some Comments and Corrections, *Internal Bulletin* (undated-early 1970) pp1-3. A Critique of Tony Polan's pamphlet on the Socialist Labour League.

IS and the Labour Party, "Draft Statement for July National Committee" (16 June 1971) 3pp. 14 point draft paper—see September 1971 entry below for published version.

On Regional Organisation, *Internal Bulletin* (August 1971) 2pp. Contribution to a dispute in Scotland.

The Common Market: Eight Questions to Some Critics, *Internal Bulletin* (August 1971) 1pp. Contribution to the debate on the Common Market aimed at the Trotskyist Tendency.

A Slanderous Attack on IS, *Internal Bulletin* (September 1971) 3pp. Strong riposte to the document Platform of the Trotskyist Faction of IS.

IS and the Labour Party, *Internal Bulletin* (September 1971) 3pp. Important 17-point paper that was adopted as a discussion document for the Group.

IS and the Trotskyist Tendency, *IS Bulletin—Special Supplement, Discussion Material for 4 December Conference* (October 1971) 7pp. Expanded version of Background Notes that were prepared for the IS National Committee by Hallas.

Left Unity, *IS Bulletin, Documents for Easter Conference 1972* (January 1972) 5pp. No author stated but written by Hallas and adopted at the January National Committee.

Theory and Practice, *Internal Bulletin* (February 1972) 3pp. Polemic on Marxist revolutionary organisation. For centralism, against spontaneism.

Hints on Chairmanship, *Internal Bulletin* (March 1972) 5pp. Reproduced (with cartoons) in *SW Training Series 1) Practical Notes.*

Marxism and Terrorism (with Jim Higgins), *Internal Bulletin* (March 1972) 3pp. IS Executive Committee disagreed on an *SW* editorial on Ireland. This is the majority view.

Less than Candid, *Internal Bulletin* (March 1972) 3pp. Background information on the 1971 book *The Fourth International, Stalinism and the Origins of the International Socialists.*

From Hints on Chairmanship, *1972.*

Editor's Notes, *Internal Bulletin* (May 1972) 1pp. On quantity produced and cost of the Internal Bulletin.

Towards a New Draft Programme, *IS Bulletin* (August 1972) 3pp. What a Draft IS Programme should be and how we get to it.

In Defence of Politics, *IS Bulletin* (August 1972) 2pp. The current Permanent Arms Economy controversy in IS explained in plain English.

Education Report, *IS Bulletin* (August 1972) 1pp.

Concluding Episode? *IS Bulletin* (September 1972) pp19-20. More on the Permanent Arms Economy in response to criticism from Kevin Whitston and David Yaffe.

The New IS Journal, *IS Bulletin* (November 1972) p30. The switch of the IS Journal to monthly publication explained by the editor.

The United Front Tactic and the Communist Party, *IS Bulletin* (May/June 1973) pp6-8. Written at the request of the National Committee to promote discussion.

New Members, Democracy and the Right Faction, *IS Bulletin* (May/June 1973) pp17-19. Explanation of the expulsion of members of the Right Faction from the IS Political Secretary.

Socialist Worker: Perspectives and Organisation (with Jim Higgins, John Palmer, and Roger Protz), *IS Internal Bulletin* (April 1974) pp18-24. The current dispute is about political perspectives—signed by Hallas and 12 others.

Reforming the Regime (with Chris Davison), *IS Internal Bulletin* (undated but May 1974) pp19-20. How the dispute in the organisation over *Socialist Worker* was badly handled.

IS Organisational Problems and Conference, *IS Bulletin* (April 1975) pp12-14. The present political situation means we need to look at our organisation now.

A Reply to the Platform, *Pre-Conference Discussion Documents* (April 1975) pp37-39. Reply to the *Platform of the IS Opposition*.

What is the IS Journal for?, *IS Bulletin* (May 1976) pp21-22 Attempt to answer the question in the title plus puts party literature in a wider context.

Training and Integrating New Members, *IS Bulletin* (November 1976) pp12-13. Part of a circular issued to IS branches and districts. Hallas was Training Secretary.

Socialist Workers Party
--

The Devolution Referenda (with Tony Cliff), *SWP Bulletin 1*, (February 1977) pp5-6. The correct political attitude to take on any referendum on Scottish devolution—abstain.

Why we are the Socialist Workers Party, *SWP Bulletin 1* (February 1977) pp9-10. Why we changed the organisation to the SWP from 1 January 1977.

Training Report, *SWP Bulletin 1* (February 1977) pp12-13.

Local Elections (Duncan Hallas for Central Committee), *SWP Bulletin 2* (March 1977) p19. Instruction that branches should not stand candidates in local elections without prior agreement between the District and the Central Committee.

Electoral Blocs and Joint Slates, *SWP Bulletin 3* (May 1977) pp13-15. Why we do not form electoral pacts with other organisations of the revolutionary left.

Election Strategy—Central Committee, *SWP Bulletin Pre-Conference Issue 2* (May 1978) p11-13. We made a miscalculation when we decided to stand candidates. This document is issued in the name of the CC but is a reworking of an April 1978 document by Hallas "*Elections—We Have to Think Again*".

Leading Committees and Party Democracy, *SWP Bulletin Pre-Conference Issue 3* (May 1978) p3. A review of the how and why of some leading committees.

Reply to Linda Quinn and Others, *SWP Bulletin 4* (1981) pp26-27. Contribution to the debate on the future of Women's Voice groups.

Rank and File Teacher
--

Salaries: What Can We Do? 1 (April 1968) pp2-6. A look at the situation in the run up to the 1968 NUT Conference.

Review of *The Teachers' Union. Aspects of Policy and Organisation of the NUT 1950-66* by Walter Roy, 3 (September 1968) pp12-14.

Piety and Practice (Letter from Fred Hall), (4 January 1969) p4. Headteachers are still mostly autocrats—no matter what the Minister of Education says.

Abolition of the Primary/Secondary Differential? (by Fred Hall), 5 (April 1969) p14. The impact of the abolition of the differential—headteachers do better.

Short's Smokescreen (Letter from Fred Hall), 7 (September 1969) p15. Professional status is a smokescreen to obscure the need for militant action.

Review of *Militant Teacher Issue 1*, 8 (December 1969) pp20-21.

The Three Per Cent and the Ninety-Seven Per Cent (Letter from Fred Hall), 10 (Summer 1970) p11. For R&F control of the NUT (not headteacher control).

Union Salary Policy, 11 (Autumn 1970) pp5-7. An in-depth look at salaries.

The Union Shop (Letter from Fred Hall), 12 (November/December 1970) p11. Don't allow yourself to be frightened into resisting progressive demands. Support a union shop.

We Do Not Sell Our Souls (Letter from Duncan Hallas), 15 (Summer 1971) p12. Solidarity against scapegoating.

Socialist Worker
--

Teachers Demand Strike Action (15 February 1969) p4. NUT is holding a special conference on acceptance or rejection of the employers' final pay offer.

Why The Workers Must Organise For Power (19 April 1969) p2. On Lenin's *State and Revolution.*

Workers' power—the only alternative to the Labour/Tory run-around, (8 May 1969) pp2 & 3. Why a Labour government does what it does.

Teachers to Stop Work as Salaries Campaign Hots Up, (3 July 1969) p4. By Duncan Hallas, President, Wandsworth Teachers Association. Half day stoppage in London.

Britain's Oldest Colony: A history of famine, brutality...and heroism (21 August 1969) pp2-3. The tradition of struggle in Ireland.

Pay Revolt Hits Schools, (20 November 1969). By Duncan Hallas, President, Wandsworth Teachers Association. Appears in the book *In the Heat of the Struggle: 25 Years of Socialist Worker* (London: Bookmarks, 1993).

Sell-out Danger as NUT Meets Castle (22 January 1970) p6. Sell-out in the offing.

Teacher's Strike: Leaders Duck Clash with Government (12 February 1970) p6. Limited action called by NUT Executive cannot win.

Workers have the power to smash the system...before the system destroys us all (13 June 1970) p4. Parliamentary action and the Labour Party cannot give us peace, freedom, or security.

How 'Law and Order' Aids the Rich and Powerful (19 June 1971) p6. From a series titled *Ideas in Society.*

Velvet Glove for Right, Knuckleduster for Left (26 June 1971) p6. *Ideas in Society*. The use of sedition laws against the left.

Democratic Rights Don't Add up to Real Democracy (3 July 1971) p6. *Ideas in Society*. Limits of democracy under capitalism.

MPs: Keeping Aloof from the 'Swinish multitude' (10 July 1971) p6. *Ideas in Society.* Parliament v Soviets.

Left Cannot Stand on Sidelines (17 July 1971) pp4-5. Why we Oppose the Common Market.

Violence: It Depends Who's Clenching the Fist (24 July 1971) p6. *Ideas in Society.* Bourgeois hypocrisy about violence.

One Man's Freedom is Another's Slavery (31 July 1971) p6. *Ideas in Society.* The Free World is not freedom.

Letter from Duncan Hallas, National Secretary of IS (7 August 1971) p3. Making it clear that IS is against not for abstaining on the Common Market question.

Workers' Control Cannot be Divorced from Politics (28 August 1971) p6. *Ideas in Society.* Workers' control in its historical context.

Poison of racialism used to divide workers (4 September 1971) p6. *Ideas in Society.* Racial differences are old—they are the visible facts on which racialist myths are built.

Book Review *The Decline of Working Class Politics* by Barry Hindess (13 November 1971) p9.

Communists Face Sharp Drop in Numbers (as Fred Hall), (13 November 1971) p10. On the CPGB in advance of their Party Congress.

Would the Real Lenin Stand Up (book review by Fred Hall), (9 September 1972) p9. *Lenin in his Own Words* by Ernst Fischer.

That Over Used Word—Revolution (28 October 1972) p10. New series *Out of Your Mind: Duncan Hallas on socialist ideas and capitalist myths.* What Marxists mean by "revolution".

It Could Never Happen Here! (4 November 1972) p10. *Out of Your Mind.* Workers' power cannot happen by piecemeal legislation.

The Sham that they Call Parliament (11 November 1972) p10. *Out of Your Mind.* Parliament is largely a sham to deceive the public.

Organised Violence that is the State (18 November 1972) p10. *Out of Your Mind.* The modern state.

How the Army Stopped Home Rule (25 November 1972) p10. *Out of Your Mind.* The military would act to protect the state.

Parliament No Through Road (2 December 1972) p10. *Out of Your Mind.* The CPGB believes in the parliamentary road to socialism.

The Real Meaning of Democracy (9 December 1972) p10 *Out of Your Mind.* Western Democracy is a form of class rule.

Well, What About Russia Then? (16 December 1972) p10 *Out of Your Mind.* Not a workers' state but a dictatorship.

How the Revolution Led to Stalin (23 December 1972) p8. *Out of Your Mind.* Stalin was not first among equals. He was a powerful and despotic ruler.

Europe: Tories are in—what must left do now...? (6 January 1973) p6. Britain is now a part of the Common Market. Special analysis by Duncan Hallas.

Stalin, the 'Beloved' Dictator (6 January 1973) p8. *Out of Your Mind.* The road to the great purges.

Swindle! Soaring Meat Prices Expose the Tory 'Freeze', (13 January 1973) p1. Main front page headline article. Article gave rise to letters in SW issues of 27 January and 3 February.

Stalin Takes a Bloodbath (13 January 1973) p10. *Out of Your Mind.* The purges.

The 'Freedom' Stalin Built (20 January 1973) p10. *Out of Your Mind.* What sort of society emerged from the years of Stalin's terror?

Charade that is Russian 'equality'. (27 January 1973) p10. *Out of Your Mind.* Russian bureaucracy.

Men of Property against the King (8 September 1973) pp6-7. *New Series The Great Revolutions. Part 1.* Two-part history of English Civil War (Part 1).

Civil War, then Compromise (15 September 1973) pp6-7. *The Great Revolutions 2.* Two-part history of English Civil War (Part 2).

Why Chilean Left Dug its Own Grave (by Fred Hall) (29 September 1973) p6. Those who half make revolutions only dig their own graves.

Revolt by 'Colonials' that Launched the USA (29 September 1973) pp9-10. *The Great Revolutions 3.* US Independence.

'Terrible Ones' Take up Arms (6 October 1973) pp6-7. *The Great Revolutions 4.* Two-part history of the French Revolution (Part 1).

Equality—but Only for a Few (13 October 1973) pp6-7. *The Great Revolutions 5.* Two-part history of the French Revolution (Part 2).

The Turning Point (27 October 1973) pp6-7. *The Great Revolutions 6.* 1848 revolutions across Europe.

1871: The First Workers' State (10 November 1973) p7. *The Great Revolutions 7.* The Paris Commune.

Dress Rehearsal for October (24 November 1973) p7. *The Great Revolutions 8.* Russia in 1905.

Russia on the Brink... (1 December 1973) p7. *The Great Revolutions 9.* Two-part history of Russian Revolution (Part 1).

Red October (8 December 1973) p 7. *The Great Revolutions 10.* Two-part history of Russian Revolution (Part 2).

Unequal before birth? (4 May 1974) p6. 'Natural' inequality and socialism.

It's the Butty System (11 May 1974) p6. Family and origins of women's oppression.

The Socialism of Fools (18 May 1974) p6. The origins of racism.

The Growth Fraud (1 June 1974) p6. *Talking About Socialism* series. Arguing that economic growth is the means to greater equality is false.

Rich and Poor (8 June 1974) p6. *Talking About Socialism.* Capitalism produces inequality both within and between countries.

Profits of Doom (15 June 1974) p6. *Talking About Socialism.* Root causes of state of the world are not technical, they are political.

It's a Dirty Business (22 June 1974) p6. *Talking About Socialism.* The attack on technology, as such, is reactionary.

In a Class of Our Own (29 June 1974) p6. *Talking About Socialism.* Socialism and state ownership.

The Bosses' State (6 July 1974) p6. *Talking About Socialism.* The modern state is an essentially capitalist machine.

What we Mean by Socialism (27 July 1974) p6. *Talking About Socialism.* The state according to Marx, Engels and Lenin.

Under New Management—But the Workers Still Lose (10 August 1974) p8. Norton Villiers Triumph co-operative.

All Those in Favour of Cutting Wages, Please Show (14 September 1974) p12. Duncan Hallas reports from the TUC.

But the Council Has No Money to Pay for It (10 May 1975) p4. *Questions on the Crisis.* There is no fixed-size pot, it depends which side pushes hardest.

But Aren't Redundancies Inevitable? (17 May 1975) p4. *Questions on the Crisis.* The crisis is their crisis.

Benn: Why All the Hysteria? (24 May 1975) p6. *Questions on the Crisis.* Has Benn really changed?

Nationalisation: Is it a Job Saver? (7 June 1975) p6. *Questions on the Crisis.* Demand for nationalisation under workers' control.

Are Import Controls in the Interests of Workers? (14 June 1975) p6. *Questions on the Crisis.* National and sectional interests are necessarily anti-socialist.

Pay Cuts = More Jobs? Don't be Daft! (28 June 1975) p6. *Questions on the Crisis.* The aim of the wages versus unemployment argument is to disarm workers.

Will Healy's £6 Limit on Wages Stop Prices Rising? (19 July 1975) p5. *Questions on the Crisis.* Inflation is now built into modern capitalism.

Why the £6 Limit Means More Unemployment (26 July 1975) p9. *Questions on the Crisis.* Fighting the Wage Freeze.

Talking About Socialism Series 1974-1976.

The 'Democracy' that is Class Rule (27 September 1975) p6. *Talking About Socialism.* Bourgeois and proletarian democracy.

Labour—As Low as They Can Go (4 October 1975) p1. Front page headline article. LP Conference endorses right wing, anti-working class policies.

Terror and Hypocrisy (11 October 1975) p6. *Talking About Socialism.* Marxist attitude to individual terrorism.

And This is the News? (18 October 1975) p6. *Talking About Socialism.* TV News.

Marxism and Morality (1 November 1975) p6. *Talking About Socialism.* The basis of socialist morality.

In a Class of Our Own (22 November 1975) p6. *Talking About Socialism.* Definition of working class—productive/non-productive workers.

The Tragedy of Spain, 1936 (6 December 1975) p6. *Talking About Socialism.* The role of the Communist Party in Spain.

But What About Wages? (13 December 1975) p6. *Talking About Socialism.* What happened to wages in Russia.

After 1917: Why Stalinism? (20 December 1976) p6. *Talking About Socialism.* Stalinism was the product of the reaction.

If we all got together... (3 January 1976) p4. *Talking About Socialism.* Left unity through unity in action.

The insanity of unemployment... (10 January 1976) p6. *Talking About Socialism.* How capitalism causes unemployment.

What About Russia? (14 February 1976) p6. *Talking About Socialism.* Those who say if that is socialism we want none of it are quite right.

The Workers' State (21 February 1976) p6. *Talking About Socialism.* Two linked articles on the workers' state (Part 1).

Socialism? Where? (28 February 1976) p6. *Talking About Socialism.* Two linked articles on the workers' state (Part 2).

The 'Sinking' £ (20 March 1976) p4. *Talking About Socialism.* The mystification of money in capitalist society.

11th Commandment (3 April 1976) 6. *Talking About Socialism.* Role of religion in society and education.

It's Human Nature (10 April 1976) p6. *Talking About Socialism.* Two-part article on Robert Owen (Part 1).

The Great Pioneers (17 April 1976) p6. *Talking About Socialism.* Two-part article on Robert Owen (Part 2).

Whose Revolution? (24 April 1976) p6. *Talking About Socialism.* Babeuf as pioneer of revolutionary socialism.

The Great Conspiracy (8 May 1976) p6. *Talking About Socialism.* Heroism and limits of Blanqui.

Let's Talk it Over (5 June 1976) p6. *Talking About Socialism.* The CP and IS.

How to Stop the Front (24 July 1976) p6. *Talking About Socialism.* Case for using physical action against Nazis.

The Secret Ballot (31 July 1976) p6. Tactics in union elections.

Death of a Prostitute (14 August 1976) p6. Richard Carlile and the struggle for a free press.

Will the Rich Give in? (21 August 1976) p6. *Talking About Socialism.* Marx, Engels and the debate about peaceful transition.

Why Chile was Lost (28 August 1976) p6. Chilean coup and limits of reformism.

Why a SW Candidate? (4 September 1976) p6. *Talking About Socialism.* Justification for revolutionary electoral strategy.

We won't win but... (11 September 1976) p6. More on socialist electoral strategy.

Great Men—and Slaves (25 September 1976) p6. Role of the individual in history.

Why Stalinism? (2 October 1976) p6. Argument against historical inevitability.

The Lies of Callaghan, Bankers' Man (unsigned article) (9 October 1976) p8. The lies concerning the IMF bailout and our answers.

Profit and socialism? (27 November 1976) p6. The alternative to production for profit.

Technology is Neutral (4 December 1976) p6. Against anti-technology trend on the left.

Who is Non-productive? (8 January 1977) p6. Is there any such thing as a "non-productive" worker?

The Value of Labour (15 January 1977) p6. What determines a worker's value in society?

Facts of Family Life (9 April 1977) p6. Lewis H Morgan and the Iroquois Indians.

Wives and Property (16 April 1977) p6. Engels on the subjugation of women.

When Women had Power (23 April 1977) p6. The growth of private property, the break up of the clan system, and the subjugation of women went together.

Killers or Heroes? (11 June 1977) p4. Terrorism—bourgeois hypocrisy and Marxist analysis.

Jesus Christ Super-red? (23 December 1978) pp4-5. Jesus as revolutionary in historical context.

Here and Now (13 January 1979) p4. Two-part article on transitional demands (Part 1).

Transitional demands and socialism (20 January 1979) p6. Two-part article on transitional demands (Part 2).

Labour Left v Right—Again (4 August 1979). Does the left v right argument in Labour matter? Appears in the book *In the Heat of the Struggle: 25 Years of Socialist Worker*, Bookmarks, London, 1993.

Breaking the Links (23 February 1980) p10. Industrial militancy and the struggle for socialism.

Darwin's Revolution (8 March 1980) p10. Significance of Darwin.

Before the Class Struggle (15 March 1980) p10. Human society before class.

When the Time is Right (22 March 1980) p10. When to raise the general strike slogan.

What is Sectarianism? (29 March 1980) p10. Definition of term.

THEIR Market, THEIR Forces (17 May 1980) p10. The myth of the market.

Socialism in the Eighties (31 May 1980) p10. Strengths and weaknesses of syndicalism.

International Socialism Series 1
--

Teachers, 36 (April/May 1969) pp13–14. Why the pay offer was accepted. The need for Rank and File.

Building the Leadership, 40 (October/November 1969) pp25-32. The Socialist Labour League—where it came from and why it is a dead end.

Paying the Piper (book review), 42 (February/March 1970) p37. *Economics and Economic Policy in Britain, 1946-1966* by T.W. Hutchinson.

Western Capitalism: The Latest Phase (extended book review), 44 (July/August 1970) pp36-38. Review of Kidron's *Western Capitalism Since the War.*

Stalinism in Britain (book review), 46 (February/March 1971) pp33-34. Review of Robert Black's book of the same name.

Lenin (book review—by Fred Hall), 47 (April/May 1971) pp29-30. Review of *Lenin* by Georg Lukacs.

Gramsci (book review), 47 (April/May 1971) p31. Review of A. Pozzolini's book.

The Socialist Register 1971 (book review by James Walker), 50 (January/March 1972) p41.

The Thought of Karl Marx: An Introduction (book review by Fred Hall), 51 (April/June 1972) p31. Review of David McLellan's book.

Guides to Action (book review by Fred Hall), 52 (July/ September 1972) p42. Review of Richard Hyman's *Marxism and the Sociology of Trade Unionism* and one other book.

The Decline of Reformism (unsigned editorial), 53 (October/ December 1972) pp1-4. In the face of the decline IS are best equipped to challenge the CP.

Against the Stream: The Origins of the Fourth International, 53 (October/December 1972) pp30-39. Republished in 1988 in the pamphlet *The Fourth International.*

Socialist Economics (book review), 53 (October/December 1972) pp40-41. Review of book edited by Alex Nove and D.M. Nuti.

Revolution in Perspective/Modern Revolutions (review by Fred Hall), 53 (October/December 1972) p41. Review of two books by Mary Charlsworth/Peter Lowe and John Dunn.

Do We Support Reformist Demands?, 54 (January 1973) pp18-19. Maximum, transitional demands etc.

Seedtime and Harvest (book review), 54 (January 1973) pp25-26. Review of Reg Groves book written for the centenary of the agricultural workers' union.

The Election Bogey, (Unsigned article from Notes of the Month), 56 (March 1973) pp1-3. Local organisation rooted in the workplace can deliver the solidarity required.

What is 'Economism'?, 56 (March 1973) pp18-19. Economic and political struggle.

White Eagle, Red Star/At War with the Bolsheviks (book review by Fred Hall), 56 (March 1973) p25. Review of books by Norman Davies and Robert Jackson.

Reforming the Labour Party?, 58 (May 1973) pp23-24. Based on Miliband—critique of CP strategy.

Notes of the Month, 60 (July 1973) p1-3. On Business partners; Phase Three prospects and Resolutions and Reality.

Fourth International in Decline: From Trotskyism to Pabloism 1944-1953, 60 (July 1973) pp17-23. Republished in 1988 in the pamphlet *The Fourth International.*

Introduction, Special Double Issue, 61 (June 1973) pp1-3 Introduction to a special issue of International Socialism containing five republished articles which shaped the political outlook of the IS on: Imperialism since World War Two; Permanent Revolution in the era of anti-colonial struggles; modern capitalism and the Permanent Arms Economy; an analysis of Maoism in the Crisis in China; and recent changes in the British Labour Movement.

The First Shop Stewards' Movement, 65 (December 1973) pp19-26. Narrative account of stewards in WWI, based on Hinton book.

Revolutionaries (book review), 65 (December 1973) pp19-26. Review of book by E.J. Hobsbawm.

Founding of the Communist International, 66 (February 1974) pp17-21. First of a series of four on the early years of the Communist International.

The Comintern: Mass Parties and the International, 68 (April 1974) pp19-24. Second of a series of four on the early years of the Communist International.

The Comintern: Workers and Peasant, 69 (May 1974) pp13-14. Third of a series of four on the early years of the Communist International.

The Socialist Register 1973 (book review), 69 (May 1974) p29.

Socialism Now (book review), 69 (May 1974) pp29-30. Review of book by Anthony Crosland.

White Collar Workers, 72 (October 1974) pp14-22. White collar workers, their TU's, rank and file organisation and IS.

Economic Prospects (unsigned editorial from Notes of the Month), 73 (December 1974) pp3-4. The current position and prospects for 1975.

The Class Struggle in Eastern Europe (book review), 73 (December 1974) pp26-28. Extended review of Chris Harman's *Bureaucracy and Revolution in Eastern Europe.*

The Communist International and the United Front, 74 (January 1975) pp12-15. Fourth and final part of a series on the early years of the Communist International.

A Note of Qualification (by the editor), 75 (February 1975) pp20-21. Issue taken with aspects of Peter Sedgwick's article *The Return of Bukharin.*

Centrist Currents, 75 (February 1975) p28. Review article on *The Socialist Register 1974.*

Letter to Readers (by the editor), 76 (March 1975) p2. On contents of the journal.

Building the Revolutionary Party, 79 (June 1975) pp17-22. Considerations on Leninism based on Cliff's first volume.

Letter to Readers, 80 (July/August 1975) p2. On contents of the journal.

Notes of the Month, 83 (November 1975) p3-6. On the Right Wing Ascendent; The collapse of the "lefts" and The Revolutionary Left.

Unsigned Editorial, 85 (January 1976) p3. The lessons to draw from the defeat at Chrysler.

On the United Front Tactic. Some Preliminary Notes, 85 (January 1976) p8. What the United Front is and is not.

In Chou's Lifetime—Some Dates, 86 (February 1976) pp16-17. Key dates in the life of Chinese communist leader Chou En-Lai who had just died.

Communism and Stalinism: On John Gollan's "Social Democracy Some Problems", 87 (March/April 1976) pp25-29. John Gollan's article appeared in the *Marxism Today* issue of January 1976.

The Communist Party and the General Strike, 88 (May 1976) pp16-24. Narrative account with political analysis. Reprinted in 1981 and 1986 pamphlet *Days of Hope.*

All Power to the Soviets, 89, June 1976) pp7-11. Part 1 of a review of the second volume of Cliff's *Lenin.*

All Power to the Soviets, 90 (July/August 1976) pp16-21. Part 2 of a review of the second volume of Cliff's *Lenin.*

Karl Marx: Man and Fighter (book review), 90 (July/August 1976) p28. Review of Boris Nicolaievsky and Otto Maenchen-Helfen.

The Soviet Union—State Capitalist or Socialist? (co-authored with Peter Binns), 91 (September 1976) pp16-27. The answer to the CP pamphlet of the same name that they had published as a critique of IS.

On Trotskyism (book review), 91 (September 1976) p32. Review of Kostas Mavrakis.

Some Prospects for 1977, 94 (January 1977) pp3-4. Prospects are good for the Rank and File Movement and the SWP.

The CP, the SWP and the rank and file movement, 95 (February 1977) pp10-14. Different strategies of the CP and SWP in the fight against the Social Contract.

The Stalin Phenomenon (book review), 98 (May 1977) pp28-29. Review of Jean Ellenstein.

Trotskyism Re-assessed, 100 (July 1977) pp14-19. What is living and what is dead in Trotsky's thought.

International Socialism Series 2
--

Trade Unionists and Revolution: A Response to Richard Hyman, 8 (Spring 1980) pp80-84. On Richard Hyman's article *British Trade Unionism: Post-War Trends and Future Prospects.*

Eastern European Class Societies (letter), 9 (Summer 1980) pp128-130. Extended comments on *New Theories of Eastern European Class Societies* by Peter Binns and Mike Haynes.

Revolutionaries and the Labour Party, 16 (Spring 1982) pp1-35. Attitudes of revolutionaries to the Labour Party, particularly entrism.

Three Responses to Chris Harman's account of Base and Superstructure, Comments from Duncan Hallas, 34 (Winter 1987) pp125-127. Harman's article appeared in journal number 32.

Trotsky's Heritage—On the Fiftieth Anniversary of the Foundation of the Fourth International, 40 (Autumn 1988) pp53-64. Examination of this key episode in the revolutionary tradition.

Socialist Review Series 2
--

For Inexperienced Militant (book review), 3 (June 1978) pp31-32. From *Class Society to Communism: An Introduction to Marxism* by Ernest Mandel.

The Numbers Game (as Fred Hall), 4 (July/August 1978) pp8-9. The arms race.

Natural Laws Rule, OK (letter), 5 (September 1978) p17. Is there a real distinction between science and ideology?

Clearer View of 1979, 7 (November 1978) pp. 5-6. The political outlook ahead.

The Making of a Myth, 9 (February 1979) pp35-36. Response to Martin Shaw's article *The Making of a Party.*

Where Do We Go from Here? 4 (April/May 1980) pp9-11. Interview with Hallas after the steel strike.

The return of the workers' bomb, 11, (December/January 1980) pp31-32. Socialist and nuclear weapons.

A Focus for Anger?, 1 (January/February 1981) pp3-5. Interview with Hallas in the run up to special Labour Party Conference.

The Relevance of a Revolutionary (book review), 2 (February/March 1982) p32. Review of John Molyneux's *Leon Trotsky's Theory of Revolution.*

Socialism and War, 5 (May/June) pp5-7. Basics of revolutionary internationalism starting from Falklands [included in *Socialist Review* compilation of 1998].

Is the Class Contracting?, 10 (November/December 1982) pp25-27. Critique of Hobsbawm's abandonment of the working class.

Tell It as It Is, 11 (December 1982/January 1983) p12. Obituary for E H Carr.

Essentially Amorphous (book review), 51 (2 February 1983) pp32-33. Review of *Socialist Register 1982.*

Marx, Engels and the Vote, 55 (5 June 1988) pp20-21. On Marxism, parliamentarism and electoralism.

Class Struggle, But No Party! (book review), 59 (December 1983) pp. 33-34. Review of *Politics in Britain* and *World Review 1984.*

Ideas Without Action (book review), 61 (January 1984) p32. *Socialist Arguments* edited by David Coates and Gordon Johnston.

The Federation (book review), 61 (January 1984) p33. *History of the General Federation of Trade Unions* by Alice Prochaska.

In the Beginning..., 62 (February 1984) pp12-14. TU bureaucracy from 1890s to 1926.

Agitation and Propaganda, 68 (September 1984) p10. *What Do We Mean By...?* Series. Distinction explained—basic revolutionary tasks.

Confusion Reigns (book review), 68 (September 1984) p27. Review of John Callaghan's *British Trotskyism.*

A Serious Study (letter), 69 (October 1984) p31. Clarifying a printing error in the review of Callaghan's book.

Fighting Anti-Communism (book review), 74 (March 1985) p30. Review of *The Socialist Register 1984.*

Zero Rating (book review), 74 (March 1985) p32. *Marxism and Historical Writing* by Paul Hirst.

Sectarianism, 75 (April 1985) pp24-25. *What Do We Mean By...?* Series. Basic definition

Armed Without an Army (book review), 79 (September 1985) p32. *The Swiss Army* by John McPhee.

Down The Line (book review), 80 (October 1985) pp28-29. Noreen Branson's *The History of the CPGB 1927-1941.*

Marx's Road to Marxism, 81 (November 1985) pp17-19. The development of Marx's thought. Based on a talk at Marxism 1985.

Cult Comes a Cropper, 82 (December 1985) p25. The implosion of the Workers Revolutionary Party.

Marx and Politics, 83 (January 1986) pp17-19. Development of Marx's politics and response to issues of the day. Marxism talk.

Pioneers of the Tradition (book review), 85 (March 1986) pp31-32. Bornstein and Richardson's *Against the Stream. A History of the Trotskyist Movement in Britain.*

Reality, Not the Myth (book review), 86 (April 1986) p30. Cliff and Gluckstein's *Marxism and the Trade Union Struggle: The General Strike of 1926.*

The American working class, 88 (June 1986) pp17-19. US working class up to 1940. From a talk at Skegness. [included in *Socialist Review* compilation of 1998]

Mad Dog Days (letter), 90 (September 1986) p34. On the fiftieth anniversary of the first of the three big Moscow Trials.

The Sad Fate of British Trotskyism (book review), 91 (October 1986) p21. Narrative account of WWII and after based on Bornstein-Richardson book.

Saving the System (book review), 92 (November 1986) p29. Ian Birchall's *Bailing out the System: Reformist Socialism in Western Europe 1944-1985.*

The Ruskin Debate: Their College or Ours?, 93 (December 1986) p21. The background to working class education—and why we support Ruskin against the right.

Wars Within Wars (book review), 96 (March 1987) pp30-31 Ernest Mandel's *The Meaning of the Second World War.*

The Proud Tradition (book review), 98, May 1987) p30 Stuart MacIntyre's *A Proletarian Science: Marxism in Britain 1917-1934.*

Can Labour Win?, 100 (July/August 1987) pp6-7. Have reformist politics got any future in Britain and is the Labour Party finished?

Absent Friends (book review), 100 (July/August 1987) pp29-30. *Black Athena: The Afro-Asiatic Roots of Classical Civilisation* by Martin Bernal.

October 1917, 102 (October 1987) pp14-18. Excellent narrative account of the October Revolution from speech at Marxism 87.

The Bourgeois Revolution, 105 (January 1988) pp17-20. Bourgeois revolution in England, France, Germany, Russia, Japan. From Marxism 87.

Unworthy Opponents (book review), 107 (March 1988) p28. *Making History* by Alex Callinicos.

The Decisive Settlement, 113 (October 1988) pp17-20. The Glorious Revolution England 1688.

First Stirrings (contribution to a debate), 121 (June 1989) p21 Part of the discussion on a speech by Cliff at a national SWP meeting.

Selected Memories (book review), 124 (October 1989) pp. 29-30. *Out of Apathy* an edited book on the original New Left 1957-1962.

Partial Vision (book review), 127 (January 1990) pp29-30. *Divided Societies: Class Struggle in Contemporary Capitalism* by Ralph Miliband.

Night Class Struggle (book review), 130 (April 1990) pp30-31. *The Search for Enlightenment: The Working Class and Adult Education in the Twentieth Century.*

Hard Labour, 132 (June 1990) pp17-19. Experience of 1974-79 Labour Government. Talk from the Skegness Easter Rally.

The Flame of Internationalism, 133 (July/August 1990) pp17-18. On the 50th anniversary of his murder Trotsky's consistent internationalism.

The Road to Ruin (book review), 156 (September 1992) p29 *The Good Old Cause: British Communism 1920-1991* by Willie Thompson.

Schooled in the Struggle (book review), 161 (February 1993) p29. *Keeping my Head* by Harry Wicks.

My Favourite Books, 163 (April 1993) p25.

The Shyster Lawyer (book review), 167 (September 1993) pp29-30. John Callaghan's *Rajani Palme Dutt: A Study in British Stalinism.*

The Making of a Working Class Historian, 168 (October 1993) pp20-22. Obituary for Edward Thompson.

Running a Temperature (book review), 172 (February 1994) pp30-31. *The Sharp End: The Fighting Man in World War Two* by John Ellis.

The Fight for Revolution. 176, (June 1994) pp12-13. Reform or revolution.

Rum, Sodomy and the Lash (book review), 176, (June 1994) p31. *Between the Devil and the Deep Blue Sea* by Marcus Rediker.

A Soldier's Story, 186 (May 1995) pp11-13. Interview on Duncan's experiences in and after WWII.

He Sensed Before Anyone Else the Need for Change, 241 (May 2000) p14. One of three tributes to Tony Cliff who died in April.

Miscellaneous
--

By Way of Introduction, *Edinburgh University Student's Handbook 1960-1961*, p2. Duncan Hallas was the Editor and this is his introduction.

The Legacy of Karl Marx, *Socialist Worker* (US), (March 1983). A brief introduction to Marxism given to comrades in the USA.

How Our Rulers Keep Their Grip, *Socialist Worker* (US), 248, (24 May 1996) p7. Ideology—and why it is not all powerful.

Swimming Against the Tide, *Revolutionary History,* Volume 8, Number 2, (2002) pp208-212. Interview by Ian Birchall on Duncan Hallas in Egypt with the British Army.

The Nature of Revolution, *International Socialist Review* (US) Number 77, (May 2011). Transcript of talk given at Marxism 1998.

Audio Recordings

Marxist Internet Archive Audio Archive
--

Marx and Pre-History, Marxism Festival 1983. *www.marxists. org/archive/hallas/audio/1983/marx-and-pre-history-hallas-duncan.mp3*

Decline of the Comintern, Marxism 1984. *www.marxists.org/ archive/hallas/audio/1984/decline-of-the-comintern.mp3*

The French Revolution and the Formation of Marx's Thought (incomplete), Marxism 1984. *www.marxists.org/ archive/hallas/audio/1984/french-revolution-and-the-formation-of-marxs-thought.mp3*

The Russian Revolution February 1917 (Part 2), Marxism 1987. *www.marxists.org/archive/hallas/audio/1987/ february1917.mp3*

The Russian Revolution 1917: Dual Power, Marxism 1987. *www.marxists.org/archive/hallas/audio/1987/dual-power-1917-hallas-duncan.mp3*

The Russian Revolution: October 1917, Marxism 1987. *www.marxists.org/archive/hallas/audio/1987/october-1917-hallasa-duncan.mp3*

Lenin and the Politics of Internationalism (Part 2), Marxism 1987. *www.marxists.org/archive/hallas/audio/1987/lenin-and-politics-of-internationalism-hallas-duncan.mp3*

Women in Pre-History (Part 2), Marxism 1988. *www.marxists. org/archive/hallas/audio/1988/women-in-pre-history.mp3*

1688 and all that, Marxism 1988. *www.marxists.org/archive/ hallas/audio/1988/1688-and-all-that.mp3*

Marxism and the National Question, Marxism 1988. *www. marxists.org/archive/hallas/audio/1988/marxism-and-the-national-question.mp3*

Marxism and the Trade Union Bureaucracy (Part 2), Marxism 1988. *www.marxists.org/archive/hallas/audio/1988/ marxism-and-the-tu-bureaucracy.mp3*

Trotskyism Before the War, Marxism 1988. *www.marxists. org/archive/hallas/audio/1988/trotskyism-before-the-war. mp3*

The Origins of the Socialist Review Group (Part 2), Marxism 1988. *www.marxists.org/archive/hallas/audio/1988/ origins-of-the-socialist-review-group.mp3*

The French Revolution (Part 2), Marxism 1989. *www. marxists.org/archive/hallas/audio/1989/the-french-revolution-1789.mp3*

Understanding Reformism, Marxism 1991. *www.marxists. org/archive/hallas/audio/1991/understanding-reformism. mp3*

Marxist Economics, Marxism 1993. *www.marxists.org/ archive/hallas/audio/1993/marxist-economics.mp3*

The Market and the Plan (Part 2), Marxism 1993. *www. marxists.org/archive/hallas/audio/1993/market-and-plan.mp3*

The State, Marxism 1993. *www.marxists.org/archive/hallas/ audio/1993/thestate.mp3*

Revolution, Marxism 1998. *www.marxists.org/archive/hallas/ audio/1998/revolution.mp3*

Bookmarks Bookshop Audio Archive
--

Base and Superstructure, Debate: Duncan Hallas with Chris Harman, Alex Callinicos and Colin Barker, Marxism 1987. *https://soundcloud.com/user-738785452/debate-base-and-superstructure-with-harman-halls-callinicos-and-barker*

Was World War II an Imperialist War?
Marxism 1989. *soundcloud.com/user-738785452/was-ww2-and-imperialist-war-duncan-hallas*

Historical Materialism, Marxism 1990. *soundcloud.com/user-738785452/historical-materialism?in=user-738785452/sets/marxist-theory*

SWP Website Audio Archive
--

Human Nature, Marxism 1998. *soundcloud.com/socialist-workers-party/human-nature*

Class Struggle, Marxism 1998. *soundcloud.com/socialist-workers-party/class-struggle*

Ashok Pursani Youtube Channel
--

Is There a Parliamentary Road to Socialism? Debate: Duncan Hallas and Eric Heffer. Marxism 1987. *www.youtube.com/watch?v=wWtVEDq8SfI&ab_channel=ashokpursani*

Class Struggle, The Bureaucracy and the Rank and File, Marxism 1989. *www.youtube.com/watch?v=ro1OZJQY7gg&ab_channel=ashokpursani*

Origins of the Family, Debate: Duncan Hallas and Lionel Sims. Marxism 1990. *www.youtube.com/watch?v=i9360qdh9eE&list=PLypVI9bn4-gG1uVOVM6CkK5O8CN6KMeNh&index=5*

Which Way Forward for the Left? Debate: Duncan Hallas and Jeremy Corbyn MP. Marxism 1993. *www.youtube.com/watch?v=2DXRpPyGNEE*

Bookmarks Publications Archive at Warwick Modern Records Centre

--

James Connolly, Skegness Rally 1981. *MSS.348/7/5/20. mrc-catalogue.warwick.ac.uk/records/BOO/7/5/20*

Spain 1936, Debate: Duncan Hallas and Monty Johnstone. Marxism 1986. *MSS.348/7/5/19. mrc-catalogue.warwick.ac.uk/ records/BOO/7/5/19*